TO
SERVE
THE
☆DEVIL☆

TO SERVE

THE DEVIL

VOLUME I:
NATIVES AND SLAVES

by Paul Jacobs
and Saul Landau

with Eve Pell

VINTAGE BOOKS
A Division of Random House
New York

Acknowledgment is gratefully extended to the following for permission to reprint from their works:

Guardian, independent radical newsweekly: "Dialogue Between Julius Lester and Kathleen Cleaver."

The New York Times: "Devil's Lake Sioux," by Homer Bigart, March 13, 1966. Copyright © 1966 by The New York Times Company.

The Talisman Press: From *The California Outlaw, Tiburcio Vasquez,* 1960.

Russell & Russell, New York: From *Black Reconstruction in America,* by W. E. B. Du Bois, 1935.

Random House, Inc.: "Farewell Address" from *Eldridge Cleaver: Post Prison Writing and Speeches,* edited by Robert Scheer. Copyright © 1967, 1968, 1969 by Eldridge Cleaver.

Thunder and Lightning Publishing Company, a division of Floyd B. McKissick Enterprises, Inc.: From *Negroes with Guns,* by Robert F. Williams.

International Publishers Co., Inc.: "Address of Alabama Colored Convention, 1967," in *Reconstruction,* by James S. Allen.

Humanities Press, Inc.: From *One Continual Cry: David Walker's Appeal to the Colored Citizens of the World,* by Herbert Aptheker.

Harper & Row Publishers, Inc.: From "Which One Are You?," by Clyde Warrior in *The New Indians,* by Stan Steiner, 1968.

El Grito: A Journal of Contemporary Mexican-American Thought, published by Quinto Sol Publications, Inc., P.O. Box 9275, Berkeley, California: "Brown Power," by John J. Martinez.

Clarkson N. Potter, Inc.: From *Journal of Christopher Columbus,* translated by Cecil Jane. Copyright © 1960 by Clarkson N. Potter, Inc.

Catholic University of America Press: "I. N. Clifton et al v. Abdon Salazar Puente," in *Mexican Ethnic Leadership in San Antonio, Texas,* by Sister Frances Jerome Woods.

Frank Cass & Company Ltd. and Humanities Press, Inc.: From *Apropos of Africa,* edited by A. C. Cromwell Hill and Martin Kilson.

Carnegie Institution of Washington: From "Voyage to the Coast of Africa, 1797," by Joseph Hawkins in *Documents Illustrative of the History of the Slave of America,* by Elizabeth Donnan.

Simon & Schuster, Inc.: From *Long Old Road,* by Horace R. Cayton. Copyright © 1963, 1964 by Horace R. Cayton.

VINTAGE BOOKS EDITION, February 1971

Library of Congress Catalog Card Number: 76–85616
Standard Book Number: 394–71459–8

Manufactured in the United States of America by H. Wolff Book Mfg. Co., New York

To Dr. W. E. B. Du Bois, a man who not only participated in the life of his own time, but studied the past in order to understand the future

ACKNOWLEDGMENTS

We acknowledge, gratefully, the help we received in writing this book. Joan Bowman and Karen Shillington assisted us in the early stages of research. Barbara Madison was our copyeditor and Jane Clark Seitz assumed the difficult task of general editor. We thank both of them. Donna Dowsky worked on the final steps of the manuscript. We thank especially Frances Strauss, who sometimes criticized, sometimes goaded, but always encouraged us. The Center for the Study of Democratic Institutions subsidized much of the research for the book.

"The nature of men is identical; what divides them is their customs."

Confucius, 551–478 B.C.

"Tribe follows tribe, and nation follows nation, like the waves of the sea. It is the order of nature, and regret is useless. Your time of decay may be distant, but it will surely come, for even the white man whose God walked and talked with him as friend with friend, cannot be exempt from the common destiny. We may be brothers after all. We will see."

Chief Sealth, 1855

CONTENTS

The Blacks   86

Black Documents

Contents

The Chicanos

INTRODUCTION

". . . in those days, the public both in the South and the whole of the West, together with a considerable portion of the public elsewhere, was hoodwinked by such methods as were used and actually supposed our acquisition of the new territory to be a God-fearing act, the result of the aggression and of the sinful impotence of our Spanish neighbors, together with our own justifiable energy and our devotion to the cause of freedom. It is to be hoped that this lesson, showing us as it does how much of conscience and even of personal sincerity can co-exist with a minimum of effective morality in international undertakings, will some day be once more remembered; so that when our nation is another time about to serve the devil, it will do so with more frankness and will deceive itself less by half-conscious cant. For the rest, our mission in the cause of liberty is to be accomplished through a steadfast devotion to the cause of our own inner life, and not by going abroad as missionaries, as conquerors or as marauders, among weaker peoples."

Josiah Royce,
*California, a Study
of American Character, 1886.*

THE UNKNOWN HISTORY

In the year A.D. 73, a group of Jewish zealots in the cliff fortress of Masada were besieged by the Romans for months. Finally they realized they could no longer hold out against the superior forces of the enemy. They faced a choice of being captured alive and forced into slavery or dying as free people.

They chose to die. And the account of their unique suicide pact has become one of the classic documents of history. The description of their deliberations and the manner in which they carried out their death pact was written by Flavius Josephus, the apostate Jew who was a recorder of the Roman conquests. Josephus used two women who had hidden themselves rather than die as his sources for the story. If they had not remained alive, and if Josephus had not been with the Romans at that time, the incredible story of Masada would probably have gone untold.

Documentary material such as Josephus' account provides historians with some sense of the past and its connections to the present and future. But because some societies have no written language nor a tradition of maintaining a written history, the outsider's knowledge of them is limited.

American history certainly does not suffer from shortage of written documents. In fact, anyone undertaking the task of relating the past to the present may be overwhelmed by the amount of material available, some of it dating back to the first day a white man ever set foot on this continent.

In the usual presentation of American history through documents, a special kind of selectivity has prevailed: only those documents that have interpreted American history as a gradual unfolding of progress and democracy have been used. As a result, few Americans know that such ideas as "Black Power" and self-determination, which today are considered new, have historical antecedents. Today's ghetto and *barrio* politics were *not* born with "Black Power" or *La Raza,* but date back to the formation of the first segregated—or self-segregated—communities in America. The ancestors of Malcolm X and Eldridge Cleaver are Nat Turner and Toussaint L'Ouverture. Reies Tijerina, in New Mexico, comes from a long line of Hispano-Indian leaders who organized resistance against the Anglos.

From the start, nonwhite people in this country have had to make decisions forced upon them by the white Europeans' insatiable need to increase their land holdings: should they, the natives, give up the earth on which they have lived and the civilizations associated with it, and accommodate to the conquerors; should they resist, at the cost of physical annihilation; or should they try to remain as a separate community? The Word plus the Gun forced each nonwhite group to examine its collective sense of self-preservation and explore all the options open to it.

One such option—a racial state—made familiar in the 1960s by the black separatists, is an integral part of early American Indian history, although it is rarely discussed in that context. For example, the earliest published Indian treaty signed by the newly formed United States was with the Delaware Indian tribe in September, 1778. It gave an opportunity to the Delawares and "any other tribes who have been friends to the interests of the United States to join the present confederation, and to form a state, whereof the Delaware nation shall be the head and have a representative in Congress. . . ." Not until early in the twentieth century, and the dissolution of the Cherokee nation, did Indians formally give up the notion of exercising "Red Power" by forming a separate Indian state with its own representative in Congress.

As far back as 1812, Tecumseh, the Shawnee leader, and Pushmataha, the Choctaw orator, debated fiercely at a Choctaw and Chickasaw council over the issue of how best to deal with the white man. "Are we not being stripped, day by day, of the little that remains of our ancient liberty?" Tecumseh asked the council. "Do they not even now kick and strike us as they do their blackfaces? How long will it be before they tie us to a post and whip us and make us work for them in corn fields as they do them? Shall we wait for that moment or shall we die fighting before submitting to such ignominy?"

Pushmataha opposed Tecumseh's plea for armed resistance and implored the tribes to accept the white man's good intentions. He urged them "to submit their grievances, whatever they may be, to the Congress of the United States according to the articles of the treaty existing between us and the American people. . . ."

Such bitter debates among the Indians were paralleled by similar disputes among the Spanish-speaking people. Should we let the white man come in and take our land, they asked, or should we take up arms to fight for our land and our culture? But the records of those quarrels remain buried, untranslated, in the columns of old newspapers and in *corridos,* or folk ballads.

Only recently have some young *chicanos,* the militant Mexican-Americans, rediscovered their folk heroes in reviving the tradition of *La Raza.* They have discovered that men like Juan Cortina, Gregorio Cortez, Joaquin Murieta, and Tiburcio Vasquez were not bandits, as they are described in most American history books, if they are described at all. They were champions of *La Raza,* who fought with pistols against the white conquerors, and killed any of their own who accepted the role of a conquered people.

A stanza of a Texas *corrido* begins: "Long live our country, although suffering setback . . . the mother country is home, that loves son and daughter, for Mexico has fame, military discipline."

But no folk ballad tells the story of how some of the proud Polynesian people who lived in the Hawaiian Islands tried to resist the white political and cultural invasion of their shores. "The Hawaiian people will be trodden underfoot by the foreigners," said the people of Lahaina on the island of Maui in 1845. "The laws of those governments will not do for us. These are good laws for them, our laws are for us and are good laws for us which we have made for ourselves. We are not slaves to serve them. When they talk in their clever way we know what is right and what is wrong. . . ."

It did no good for the Hawaiians to know what was right and what was wrong. Their country was taken over by the *haoles* (whites), in the course of only a few decades. The *haoles* did it with guns and religion. And the native Hawaiians began the slow descent to what they are today—a pitifully small remnant of their race, occupying the lowest rungs on the social and economic ladder of the Islands.

Few *haoles* know that the Chinese in Hawaii, like the Japanese, argued among themselves about whether to accommodate to the white man's brutal treatment or engage in active resistance to it. Resistance included helping Chinese workers to escape from the slave conditions under which they lived on the white-owned plantations. At one point, in the late nineteenth century, hundreds of Chinese gathered at a mass meeting in Honolulu to

solemnly protest against the injustices, degradation and insult threatened to be imposed upon us and our race. . . . While we ask for nothing more than equality with other residents of equally good behavior, we shall be satisfied with and shall support and respect nothing that accords to our race a lesser degree of consideration and justice than residents of other nationalities enjoy.

The white community's response to this protest was made clear by a leading Island newspaper. The Chinese, it said,

assume an attitude plainly defiant and closely bordering on the dominant and dictatorial. From the weak and lowly field hand of the time of 1851 and the wage scale of $3 a month, they have, by an unparalleled and alarming evolution, reached the station of an assertive element in the policy of the nation.

Shortly after that arrogant statement was published, the Chinese Hawaiians organized a protective group and purchased rifles to defend themselves and their homes from the whites.

The Japanese immigrant community in Hawaii was torn apart by similar conflicts. Some Japanese, at the turn of the century, sought to resist the brutalities of white plantation owners by organizing for better conditions. These organizers were jailed for their efforts; they were also attacked from within the Japanese community by accommodationists who believed that "certain things" existed in the Japanese that caused them to be "disliked by American people."

In the years before World War II, the argument within the Japanese community in Hawaii had its counterpart on the mainland. Many Nisei, or second-generation Japanese-Americans, who lived there insisted that the only way to demonstrate their Americanism was to become more American than whites; others insisted on retaining ties with Japan; a third group resisted being treated as second-class citizens.

Pearl Harbor, however, decided the fate of the American Japanese. *All* Japanese, citizens and aliens, no matter what their attitudes, were taken to relocation camps—"for the sake of internal quiet," said President Franklin Roosevelt. But the debates went on in the camps. They were now accompanied by violence. The "Blood Brothers," a group of Nisei determined to fight against the treatment they were receiving, physically and verbally attacked those who were willing to accommodate to relocation. The "Blood Brothers" called such Japanese *inu* (dogs). When the Nisei were asked to sign a loyalty oath to the United States, nearly 50 percent of them refused to do so out of resentment at the treatment they had received. After the war, some 8,000 of them emigrated to Japan. Ten years later, one congressman admitted that he had been wrong in his attitude toward the Japanese-Americans. But, while making that concession, he retained the concept of color as a gauge of loyalty. "The Japanese-Americans," he said, "were just as loyal as those whose skin was white."

The direct relationship between skin color and loyalty to America, voiced so openly by that congressman, is an important element in the American character.

Some historians have now begun to examine American

racism as a product of capitalism and imperialism. The colonizers came to the New World believing that colored people were inferior, and used that ideology to justify the enslavement of blacks, the killing of Indians and Mexicans and the importation of Oriental labor for work considered unfit for whites. The identification of colored skin with evil, with the devil, with inferiority, infused the entire culture of the Anglo-Saxons during the first centuries of colonization.

In each case, the racism coincided with economic need for slave labor and for land. At the same time, racist attitudes were institutionalized as laws, religion, and everyday practice. Each school child learned, along with the principles of republicanism and democracy, about the inferiority of colored people. Ministers explained to their flocks that slavery was God's will.

Racist law and racist behavior became an integral part of American culture, as much a part of it as democracy. Racist attitudes not only made whites feel superior by virtue of their skin color, it also made all colored, colonized people feel inferior because of their skin color. Writings on American history are filled with racist axioms. It is sometimes conceded that the colored peoples have suffered injustices. But their attempts to resist, their politics and debates, were not considered important enough to merit inclusion.

Thus the history that has been and is being written, by its nature, is a racist history, which excludes minorities and women from its pages. And so written American history, along with American culture, law, religion and philosophy, has skewed the attitudes of the American people. To blacks, Indians, Mexicans, and Orientals, George Washington was not the father of the country, but a slaveholder and a racist —as was Jefferson. If the great heroes of the history books were judged by the character of their behavior to the colored peoples, Jackson would be called a bitter racist; Lincoln's belief that blacks were innately inferior would be decried; and Woodrow Wilson would be criticized for writing history that apologized for slavery and favored segregation. But these men remain heroes for most Americans, white and colored, because for more than three centuries the values, the criteria for judging good and bad, superior and inferior, what is worthy of record and what is not, have not taken racism into account.

The history and struggles of the colored peoples, the losers, have rarely been recorded. Only now are they becoming subjects deemed worthy of investigation. The documents on the colonized peoples' resistance, and their anguish, are an indictment not only of America's past but of all those writers who have excluded the colored peoples' struggle for freedom from their work. Too much of American history has been a celebration of a past that merits severe criticism. But the celebration of America was brought to an end for many people in the 1960s. The task of rewriting American history, with a new perspective on racism as well as democracy and progress, is just beginning.

Nonwhites have permanent alien status in the white society of America. The documents in this book demonstrate the nonwhites' belief that they are never completely trusted by most whites, and that they are always considered inferior no matter how superior they may be either within their own community or even in the larger world outside it.

TO SERVE THE DEVIL

"We shall be as a city upon a hill," John Winthrop told the Puritan settlers in 1630. Winthrop assured the men and women who had risked the Atlantic crossing that they had been sent from the Old World to the New at the Lord's bidding, to build a Zion in the Wilderness, a place from where the light could shine. The Puritans were convinced that only in the New World, unspoiled by centuries of European warfare and sin, could they build a new society.

It would be fit for the return of Christ, a society so pious that He would reward His children by ushering in the Kingdom of the Millennium.

But as pious as the Puritans were, they could not ignore the vast wealth of the new continent that lay before them. So they incorporated these riches into their theology, made the great wealth a central part of their religious mission. The need to expand the frontier, so essential to the early economy of the North and the South, came to be interpreted as the Lord's will. The massacre of Indians and the profits from the slave trade were also justified in the name of the Lord's will. Developing American Protestantism combined the teachings of the Church of England, Calvin, and John Locke with the values of British mercantilism. It damned the Indians, reduced the blacks to soulless animals, and made a virtue of expanding capitalism.

The men in the New World kept pushing onward. They expressed but a twinge of anxiety over the fact that they were abandoning the Lord's mission along the way. And a handful of moralists felt that some day there would be a terrible atonement and begged the settlers and pioneers: "stop and reflect upon what you are doing." Dr. Increase Mather, for one, gave a thundering address to the students at Harvard in 1696:

It is the Judgment of very learned Men, that, in the glorious Times promised to the Church on Earth, *America* will be *Hell.* And, although there is a Number of the Elect of *God* to be born here, I am very afraid that, in Process of Time, New England will be the wofullest place in all *America;* as some other parts of the World once famous for Religion, are now the dolefullest on Earth, perfect pictures and emblems of *Hell,* when you see this Academy fallen to the Ground, then know it is a terrible Thing, which God is about to bring upon this land.

Most of the young men at Harvard paid no heed to Mather; expansionism made his Puritan piety seem anachronistic. Eccentrics and radicals like Mather were either ignored or put in jail. If the Lord had not wished us to conquer the West, the colonists rationalized, why would He have sent us to the New World and laid before us such a challenge?

The American expansion proceeded, spurred on by economic needs and sanctioned by a pious but pragmatic religion. That religion damned adultery, but ignored the Ten Commandments when Indians were killed and their land stolen, and Negroes enslaved. (The word "Negro" has been used historically by both races until recently. Many blacks now resent the word, linking it, correctly, with centuries of white domination in culture, language, and thought. In the succeeding chapters "Negro" is used only in a historical context, so that the separation between the usage of the past and our contemporary language does not get lost in our attempt to present some of our history as it was thought of by previous generations of Americans.) The original missionary fervor remained, but it became more and more secular. By the 1760s the British had taken the place of the Devil as the enemy of progress and justice. One of the things the British did was to limit westward expansion with the Proclamation of 1763. The British refusal to support expansion became one of the most important grievances uniting the colonies against the mother country.

Each of the thirteen colonies had its own distinct culture and economy. But some of the more visionary colonists realized that conquest of the West would be impossible for thirteen separate nations. Among other factors, the lure of western land helped the colonies to submerge their differences and unite as one nation in a war for independence and the right to own and exploit the rich western lands.

The newly formed nation called on its God to justify the expansion. By the time of the heated political debates preceding the writing of the Constitution, God had been converted into an active advocate of white expansionism.

"Providence has been pleased," wrote John Jay in one of the Federalist Papers, "to give this one connected country to one united people—a people descended from the same ancestors, speaking the same language, professing the same religion, attached to the same principles

of government, very similar in their manners and customs.
. . ." Providence, then, was handily available to justify
white lust for the land and wealth owned by Indians,
Mexicans, Spaniards, Hawaiians, and Eskimos. Providence
supported the plantation owners in the use of Negro slaves,
Providence vindicated the indenturing of Orientals and the
importation of Filipinos and Puerto Ricans as cheap laborers. All these groups were nonwhites, and by nature
inferior to those whom Providence had marked as virtuous
because of the color of their skin and their ability to
conquer. Might became Divine Right, and Providence justified the acceptance of slavery in the Constitution, which
said a slave was only 3/5 of a man (for voting purposes
only).

The function of Negroes, described in the Federalist
Papers as "this unfortunate race," was to work for the white
man. The Indian, who proved to be poor slave material, got
in the white man's way, so the Puritans theologized that the
Red Man was predestined to damnation even though he
heard the revealed Word. The Mexican, although not exactly colored like Indians and Negroes, was another cultural enemy who occupied territory the white man needed.
The Hawaiians were also to be civilized by having their
lands taken from them.

Justifying the need for missionary work among the
Indians, a minister of the gospel wrote, typically, "One
thing is very certain, that the influence of the gospel will
have the tendency to make them more submissive to the
rule of the whites. . . ."[1] The same missionary spirit
moved the Christian missionaries in Hawaii in the middle
of the nineteenth century. "Christianity civilizes in the
broadest sense. Commerce, science and industry all accom-
pany her majestic march to universal dominion. Thus while
it denies the sufficiency of commerce alone to transform the

[1] "The Oregon Missions as Shown in the Walker Letters, 1839–1851,"
edited by Paul C. Phillips, in *Frontier Omnibus*, pp. 105–111. Cited by
Alvin Josephy, *The Nez Percé Indians and the Opening of the Northwest*, New Haven, 1955, pp, 222–23, footnote 31.

savages, it encourages a legitimate commerce and even courts its alliance as one of its most important instrumentalities."[2]

Yet there were always some Americans who recognized that Mephistopheles had agents in the pulpit as well as in business circles and government. These Americans resisted being recruited to serve the Devil. Their roster is a long one, and includes both famous and obscure names.

Among the first colonists were dissenters who protested against the manner in which their fellow settlers acted toward the Indians. Later, their counterparts voiced indignation at American behavior during the Mexican War and the way the United States acquired the West and Southwest. From the day the first slaves were brought to the colonies, there were some white Americans who attacked the practice and sought to abolish it. Some white Americans objected to the manner in which the lands of the Mexicans and Hawaiians were taken. And others resisted national policies based on fear of "The Yellow Peril," policies which ultimately forced thousands of Japanese-Americans into detention camps during World War II.

But moralists who called upon the nation to stop and think about its policies, who pointed to slavery and racism as a deep, internal sore that could not be healed by constantly pushing outward, were always an isolated minority; often they were castigated as traitors. Perhaps the proudest and most righteous voice of morality was John Quincy Adams. Despite the misgivings of his family, he "stepped down" to run for Congress after he had been defeated for his second term as President. He soon became hated and feared by the slavocracy for his attacks on slavery and the values that supported it. Adams described John C. Calhoun as "the high priest of Moloch," and called Daniel Webster "a heartless traitor to the cause of human freedom" because of his "traffic with slavemongers."

---

[2] Statement of Professor W. D. Alexander in an article on "Science and Missions," in 1857, in *Pilgrims of Hawaii* by Rev. and Mrs. Orramel Hinckley Gulick. Fleming H. Revell Co., 1918, p. 299.

But the more Adams pointed to the moral sickness he felt would destroy the nation, the more isolated he became. He was considered an obstacle in the path of progress, a hindrance to the dynamics of American economics. The country's economic and political leaders had built an expanding system for an ambitious people and could not afford to hear the pleas and cries of such moralists. Intellectuals had molded a pragmatic God and a convenient Clio to reassure Americans that what they were doing—no matter how bloody—was right, necessary, and even pious. The dissenters stood alone against the forces of expansion and the racism that accompanied it. Even in history books written years later, these lonely figures are portrayed as brave but overanxious prophets who did not have faith in the American system and character.

The emerging American system was based on the increase of land holdings. Land was the great stake, and the whites always won any fight for it. They won not only because they had more deadly arms, but because Indians, Mexicans, and Hawaiians did not understand the white Europeans' view of the land or the depths of their desire for it. Individual possession and use of land was not a concept people like the Indians understood. They believed in a mystical relationship between Earth and the Sun, and thought that the land was for everyone. Sitting Bull once said his people were willing "to yield to our neighbors, even our animal neighbors, the same right as ourselves to inhabit this land."

Such concepts, forged from a sense of collective identity, were unknown in the Old World, and so were foreign to most white Americans. There were exceptions, of course. The Quakers understood the meaning of what one Indian chief said to the Governor of Pennsylvania in 1796:

We love quiet; we suffer the mouse to play; when the woods are rustled by the wind, we fear not; when the leaves are disturbed in ambush, we are uneasy; when a cloud obscures our brilliant sun, our eyes feel dim; but when the rays appear, they give great heat to the body and joy to the heart. Treachery darkens the chain of friendship; but truth makes it brighter than ever. This is the peace we desire.

But the majority of the Indians were not to have the peace they desired, any more than were the Negroes, the Mexicans, the *Californios,* the Hawaiians, the Maroons, or any other group who were seen as obstacles to expansion.

"If human progress follows a law of development, if 'Time's noblest offspring is the last,' our civilization should be the noblest; for we are 'The heirs of all the ages in the foremost files of time' and not only do we occupy the latitude of power, but *our land is the last to be occupied in that latitude,*" wrote Frederick Jackson Turner in 1898. "There is no other virgin soil in the North Temperate Zone. If the consummation of human progress is not to be looked for here, if there is yet to flower a higher civilization, where is the soil that is to produce it?"

Foreign observers have found the American experience puzzling. Gunnar Myrdal, for one, has described it as a dilemma. America is the birthplace of modern democracy, yet the new nation created an institutional racism. The ideals of equality and freedom were born on the same soil where slavery and racism already existed. A frontier democracy restricted to whites was shaped in the wars against the Indians and Mexicans, for only through collective agreement and political unanimity could the white settlers protect the lands they had taken. The voting franchise was extended to all whites. By the 1830s each white man, but not woman, was entitled to one vote. Assimilation of European immigrants, combined with the westward movement, shaped new, democratic institutions on the frontiers. But these new institutions, it turned out, functioned within the context of the old racial hates that pervaded urban centers and southern slave culture. This linking together of racism and democracy made for the bigotry that has been transmitted down through every generation of Americans. Yet in the face of reality, American history has been distorted into a glorious example of freedom and democracy for all peoples. Until recently the history of the colored peoples got short shrift or was relegated to small paragraphs in obscure texts. That is beginning to change.

AMERICA THE MYTH

Today most Americans who live outside the ghettos still know so little of what is happening inside them that they are shocked when racial conflicts rip cities apart, when anti-Semitism affects an election in New Jersey, when Mexican-Americans become mountain guerrillas in New Mexico, when Indians in the Pacific Northwest go to jail rather than give up their rights to fish.

They are shocked because they live in a mythical country "discovered" by Columbus. As far as they are concerned, the Indians did not exist until a white European found them. In this mythical America, the conditions of Negroes, Indians, and Spanish-speaking Americans are assumed to be gradually but inevitably improving, as court decisions, government efforts, and education break down the barriers of discrimination and prejudice. The injustices and crimes committed by frontier Americans against the Indians are described as regrettable but necessary. The reservation system, for example, in which the government actually made wards of the Indians, is explained as a genuine effort to redress those wrongs. The wholesale theft of land from Mexico through the expedient device of the Mexican War and the degradation of Spanish-speaking people are claimed as further regrettable but necessary episodes in the country's expansion.

Modern Americans tend to feel that the dark-skinned people, some of whom lived on the land long before English was ever heard, are now becoming part of the larger society after all; a few colored people are even in Congress. Many assume that a gradual movement toward equality has been occurring. Slavery is acknowledged as a moral wrong, although some unreconstructed historians and novelists still mourn the passing of an aristocratic way of life based on slavery. Overt discrimination is also considered wrong. The grade school textbooks say so, and every recent President has put the country on record. "We shall overcome," President Johnson said in his speech proposing the new Civil Rights Bill for 1965.

In mythical America, the first stop of the white immigrants who came to the country during the period of unlimited immigration was the cities along the Eastern Seaboard. There, in the legendary America, they lived together in slum areas, maintaining their Old World cultures, eating their own kinds of foods, practicing their own religions, and still speaking the language of their homelands.

Then, goes the myth, the children and grandchildren of the immigrants become assimilated into the American mainstream. The acculturation process is accompanied by the development of tension between the first generation of immigrants and the second, which is not familiar with old ways, cannot speak the language of their parents, and rejects the old customs. The second generation is in turn succeeded by another, for whom the past is not so disturbing; they have become so sure of their American identity that they are able to find a source of pride in their foreign heritage. In the meantime, the original ghetto changes, as the descendants of the original immigrants move out. It becomes a harbor for a new wave of immigrants who prepare, in their turn, to be melted down into homogeneous Americans.

This social process has a mythical economic parallel in which the immigrant groups begin at the bottom of the work ladder, performing the most difficult, least desirable and lowest-paid jobs. In the acculturation process, they move up the economic scale, and the newer immigrant groups take their place on the lower rungs.

Like all myths, the one about America as the melting pot of the world does have some basis in fact. It is true that a great many white immigrants and descendants of white immigrants have achieved political power, financial success, and considerable social status. The walls that once separated these groups from the white Americans who preceded them have been broken down. But a great many Americans still live in enclaves, separated from each other and from the mainstream by their colors, countries of origin, ethnic backgrounds, and religions.

In Milwaukee, Wisconsin, Gary, Indiana, and other cities, the sense of Slavic identity is still so strong that the cry of "Black Power" was met with the cry of "Polish Power." Whole wards of Slavs voted against black candidates and fiercely resisted attempts to break segregated housing patterns.

On Long Island, in New York, the "Golden Ghettos" are towns where virtually no one but middle-class Jews live, isolated in their social and cultural life from the gentiles who surround them. In Los Angeles, crowds of Jews, young ones as well as those from older generations, throng Fairfax Avenue, which has become a Jewish street with Jewish restaurants, kosher meat markets, fish stores, and bookstores featuring Hebrew books and Hebrew records.

In every American city, the ghettos are almost totally black. In the *barrios,* from metropolitan New York to rural California, Spanish is the spoken language, even in the third and fourth generations. In fact, one of the demands being made by the younger Spanish-speaking groups is that the schools of the South and Far West use Spanish along with English as a teaching language.

New Little Tokyos are growing up in the cities where most of the Japanese-Americans live, while in San Francisco those Chinese-Americans who cannot afford the fantastically high rents of Chinatown move out to the edges of the city, where they clump together in what will soon be Little Chinatowns. On weekends, though, they return to the older and larger Chinatown, anxious to visit with their families, eat in familiar restaurants, do their shopping, and see their friends. Here, too, in the streets of Chinatown, the young have taken a new interest in things Chinese; they identify themselves, openly and proudly, as Asians.

What America is witnessing is a new kind of clustering together of ethnic groups. They are perhaps afraid of being isolated from the familiar and reassuring. In a country that seems to be spinning apart in a centrifugal storm of politics and social upheaval, one's own special identity becomes increasingly essential for survival.

When a black leaves New York's Harlem for Los Angeles, he goes quickly to that city's Central District, leaving behind him the potentially hostile white world for the reassurance of black faces like his own, the "soul" food he has always eaten, and customs he has been familiar with since he was born. To the Jewish stranger in a city, the synagogue or temple is much more than a place of worship; it is a place to meet other Jews with whom to visit and socialize, a place where no one need worry about what the Christians might say if they overheard the conversation.

The real life of the Chinese in San Francisco's Chinatown, the life that goes on in the homes behind the shops and restaurants, is just as unknown to the Caucasians who walk the districts' streets today as it was when the Chinese were first brought to America to supply cheap labor that was needed to expand the country's frontiers. Few Caucasians notice the irony of children in San Francisco speaking Chinese as they walk to public schools while carrying Dick and Jane readers under their arms.

What is true for the Chinese has also been true for some white groups. Only recently have Catholic priests and nuns been seen inside synagogues and Protestant churches; the Irish wake in Boston is as queer a ceremony to the New England Unitarians as is the burial rite of a tribe in New Guinea. Few "strangers" ever venture into the store-front card rooms where Italian men sit for hours. Anyone who is not an Italian from that neighborhood is a "stranger."

While more than twenty million blacks continue to live in ghettos; while Orientals, Mexicans, Filipinos, and other colored people remain in their racial enclaves; while millions of white Europeans cling to their neighborhoods and their old languages—other white Americans cling tenaciously to the idea that America is truly a great melting pot. They are not aware of the fact that in 1960 at least nineteen million Americans still had a mother tongue, a primary language other than English,[3] and that approximately half of these people were born in America, and that 15 percent of them are third generation.[4]

Society was willing to absorb only those white immigrants who assimilated most easily, accepted racism most readily. Poles in Milwaukee, Italians in New York, Jews in Los Angeles, to mention just a few examples, practice open racism toward one or more minority groups; to do otherwise would be un-American, they think, and might reveal their uneasy feelings about their true status in the United States.

The assimilated immigrant is the one who has blended into the kind of America seen in TV commercials which glorify the middle-class way of life, so attractive to the truck driver who hates niggers and curses them in Polish or Italian. To be truly assimilated is to have only memories of the Old World culture, romanticized myths about the "good old days." By the third and fourth generation there is a truly assimilated progeny whose grandfathers are as foreign a cultural type to them as a Georgia slave is to a black auto worker in Detroit. To be sure, a cultural heritage remains —food, religion, certain family behavior patterns.

But if the third-generation European immigrant tries to merge successfully into the middle class, he must join the American of the TV screen. And if he remains in the working class and continues to live in an Old World enclave, he will affirm his Americanism through racist attitudes toward blacks and newly arrived immigrants. In both cases, a blending of cultures *does* occur. In one, a bland, homogenized representative of suburban America emerges; his origins are distinguished only by a "sky" or "itz" at the end of his name. In the other, a bitter acceptance of the

[3] Joshua A. Fishman, *Language Loyalty in the United States,* The Hague, The Netherlands, 1966. p. 392.

[4] *Ibid.,* p. 42.

worst of both cultures occurs; primitive and reactionary Old World attitudes are combined with notions of white supremacy and worship of gaudy consumer goods.

Immigrants from Europe encountered white America's racism, and a new outlet was provided for the ancient hostilities which had permeated their lives in the old countries. There, Norwegians and Danes hated Swedes, northern Italians despised Sicilians, Poles persecuted Jews, Serbs killed Croatians, the Irish fought the English, the Germans made war on the French, and the French felt nothing but disdain for the Spanish.

But now, in the New World, the old hatreds and feuds were put aside as the Europeans tried to become Americans. And to become an American meant accepting the white stereotype of the black, brown, red, and yellow-skinned peoples. Religious, national, and regional prejudices of Europe were converted to the color prejudices of America. The American culture was so thoroughly suffused with racism that the immigrants found it comparatively easy to adjust to the new society. That aspect of America was familiar to them; only the objects of the hatred were different. So the newcomers quickly and passionately adopted precisely that part of the American heritage which was destined to keep democracy from ever functioning properly. Descendants of the first Virginia slaveholders have little in common with the sons and grandsons of midwestern Polish steelworkers. Virginians have accepted very few Polish Old World patterns, but second- and third-generation Poles have assimilated the racist heritage of the first Americans. Ironically, the melting pot did work—but only in one direction.

D. H. Lawrence once expressed his judgment of this country. It was harsh, but fitting.

The American landscape has never been at one with the white man. Never. And white men have probably never felt so bitter anywhere, as here in America, where the very landscape in its very beauty seems a bit devilish and grinning, opposed to us.

The desire to extirpate the Indian. And the contradictory desire to glorify him. Both are rampant still, today. . . .

But you have there the myth of the essential white America. All the other stuff, the love, the democracy . . . is a sort of by-play. The essential American soul is hard, isolated, stoic, and a killer. It has never yet melted.

TO
SERVE
THE
☆DEVIL☆

THE INDIANS

A few hundred years ago there were no white people in this country. The only inhabitants of the United States were the Indians. These Indians usually lived in small bands and wandered about from place to place. They lived mostly by hunting and fishing. They were often quarrelsome. Some of the different tribes or bands had settled homes and were partly civilized, but most of them were wandering savages who did nothing to develop this great country."
—D. L. Hennessey, "Twenty-five Lessons in Citizenship," Berkeley, 1969. This pamphlet is recommended by the U.S. Immigration and Naturalization Service to all those filing applications to become U.S. citizens in California.

"Behold, my brothers, the Spring has come; the earth has received the embraces of the sun and we shall soon see the results of that love!

"Every seed is awakened and so has all animal life. It is through this mysterious power that we too have our being

*and we therefore yield to our neighbors, even our animal
neighbors, the same right as ourselves, to inhabit this land.*

*"Yet, hear me, people, we have now to deal with another
race—small and feeble when our fathers first met them but
now great and overbearing. Strangely enough they have a
mind to till the soil and the love of possession is a disease
with them. These people have made many rules that the
rich may break but the poor may not. They take tithes from
the poor and weak to support the rich and those who rule.
They claim this mother of ours, the earth, for their own and
fence their neighbors away; they deface her with their
buildings and their refuse. That nation is like a spring
freshet that overruns its banks and destroys all who are in
its path.*

*"We cannot dwell side by side. Only seven years ago we
made a treaty by which we were assured that the buffalo
country should be left to us forever. Now they threaten to
take that away from us. My brothers, shall we submit or
shall we say to them: 'First kill me before you take possession of my Fatherland. . . .' "*

Sitting Bull at the Powder
River Council, 1877

The metal boat swung out into the river near Seattle.
Two men stood in it, an Indian in his early thirties and an
older white. The shore was crowded with Indians, standing
and watching, waiting for what they knew was going to
happen. A score of police cars were parked on the highway
above the river bank, their red lights turning lazily in the
bright sunshine. Overhead, a helicopter flew back and forth,
noisily repeating its circling pattern. A group of uniformed
men from the State Fish and Game Division walked slowly
back and forth, talking quietly among themselves, watching
the Indian fisherman and his white companion.

Suddenly the Indian threw a fish from the water into the
boat. From the shore, one of the uniformed men shouted
through an electric bullhorn to the Indian, "You're under
arrest. Come to the shore. You're under arrest."

Quietly the Indian started poling the boat back to the river's edge. "How many times have you been arrested for doing this?" asked the white man.

"This will be my thirteenth arrest," answered the Indian. "They'll take me downtown, book me for fishing illegally, let me out on bail and then I'll be tried and found guilty. The judge offers me a fine or a jail sentence and I take the jail sentence. Then, when I get out of jail, I go home to the family for a few days and come back here and get arrested all over again."

"Why do you do it?"

The Indian thought for a moment before replying, "Well, I guess it is like this. My father is the chief of our tribe and I'll be the chief someday. My wife, up there on the bank, you can see her, the woman with the eyeglasses and my kids standing next to her, she's the daughter of a chief. Our tribes made a treaty a hundred years ago with the Federal Government that we could fish in this river, but now the state says we can't. The state people they tell me I should go into Seattle and get a job or go on relief. But I'm a fisherman, like my father was and his father was. I'm not going to Seattle and get a job. I'm going to fish and I'm going to fish where I got a right to fish, right here in this river. So, I guess they'll just have to keep arresting me and I'll have to keep going to jail until I get to fish in the river the way the treaty says I'm supposed to."

On a dry, arid reservation in Arizona, 1,500 miles from the river, a gang of Indians worked on the still unfinished roof of a large building, nailing boards to the beams that hold up the structure. The sun was broiling hot, and from the roof the heat waves rose and undulated over the desert and the faraway mountains. Located near the building under construction were the reservation store, a deserted gas station, the tribal council hall, and the offices of the Bureau of Indian Affairs. Across the street from the BIA offices sat the houses of the BIA officials, neat white homes with picket fences. They stood in sharp and bitter contrast to the huts made of cactus ribs and mud in which the Indians live.

A car drove up to the council building and three white men got out and went inside. In a few minutes they came out again, accompanied by four Indians, all old, their faces seamed. Together the six men strolled over to the unfinished building and stood watching the men above as they hammered nails and wrestled planks. The men, prisoners from the reservation jail, were working out their sentences by getting credit of two days jail time for each day of work. Most of them had been sentenced for drunkenness and fighting. They looked down at the group below without curiosity.

"Who are them?" asked one heavy-set Indian, his stomach sagging over his belt. The young Indian next to him, a *Pachuco* alcoholic with four blue dots tattooed on the bridge of his nose, answered, "I dunno. Maybe from the government. Look who's with them. The old farts. It don't mean nuthin'. Gimme some nails from that keg."

After a few minutes the group of BIA officials and Indians walked back to the council hall where an argument began. The whites were opposed to the tribe's putting up the building. They were convinced that the plan to make the reservation into a tourist attraction featuring new exhibition hall and a dirt stadium would fail. When they argued that the work should be stopped, one of the Indians said to them, "I agree with you and so do the others here. We always work good with BIA, but now too many here say they want to go ahead with the building no matter what BIA says. They say if they make mistake, it's Indian mistake, not BIA's."

Angry, the BIA officials answered, "You tell them we know what's best. We know the whole idea will flop. We have lots of experience with things like this. That's our job, that's what we're here for, to help the tribe make a decision we know is right."

The Indian shrugs and says, "I'll tell them, but I don't know if they'll listen."

*   *   *

Glorified and reviled, loved and hated, succored and
abused, needed and unwanted, the American Indian has
sometimes been treated generously by the whites and more
often exploited by them. The whites have never understood
the Indians, and perceive of them only in the most contradictory terms. In fact, the historical relationship between
the Indians and the whites demonstrates the basic contradictions between American ideals and behavior, between the
ethos of democracy and equality and the policies of racism
and genocide.

White men's versions of Indian-white history have become part of a folklore generally accepted by most Americans—including the Indians. Every child who has been
taught that Columbus "discovered" America has internal-
ized these versions, just as though Indians had not existed
before the white man's arrival.

Beginning with the early dime novels about the wild
West and continuing through countless movies and television series, Indians have been portrayed in one dimen-
sion—as the bad guys.

Occasionally Indians appear on the right side, the white
side, but always as subordinate to the whites, as Tonto was
to the Lone Ranger. Sometimes the Indian killer is portrayed sympathetically—he has become a killer because an
evil white man raped his squaw sister and killed his squaw
mother. But to the typical American, the sister and the
mother always remain squaws and the men bucks, labels
still filled with as much contempt as when they were first
used by white men to express their scorn for Indians.
Furthermore, in popular versions of frontier history,.
Indians are only abused by individual whites—a gunrun-
ner, a whiskey peddler, an avaricious trader—never by
white society as a whole. Only evil white men—who always
die later—spark Indian wars against whites. And, of course,
the whites ultimately triumph because they are better-
trained fighters with justice on their side.

Until recently Indians, too, have accepted much of the

white man's version of their history. "When I was a kid, I always cheered for the white guys in the movies," says a middle-aged Indian. "And when we played cowboys and Indians, none of us wanted to be the Indians."

Stripped to its bare essentials, the standard version of Indian-American history is one in which heroic soldiers and frontiersmen, accompanied by their brave wives, resisted the ferocious raids of bloodthirsty Indians who set fire to their homes with flaming arrows, raped their women, kidnapped their children, and killed off most of the men. Yet an uneasy sense of guilt has been woven into the story, as though whites have sensed that the history they have been taught, which they pass on to their children, is not accurate or even true.

Despite the elements of guilt, white men's versions persist today as they always have. ". . . never in the entire history of the inevitable displacement of hunting tribes by advanced agriculturists in the 39,000 generations of mankind has a native people been treated with more consideration, decency and kindness," insists John Greenway, an anthropologist specializing in Indian life. "It could be argued," says Greenway in a *National Review* article, "that the only real injury the white man ever did the Indian was to take his fighting away from him. Indians did not fight to defend their land, their people or their honor . . . like the Irish, they fought for the fighting. Without war and raiding and scalping and rape and pillage and slavetaking, the Indian was as aimless as a chiropractor without a spine. There was nothing left in life for him but idleness, petty mischief and booze."[1]

Greenway's peregrinations in the conservative *National Review* do not represent so aberrant a view as appears on first reading. Felix Cohen, a prototype of the "liberal" Indian expert, took much the same position as did Prof. Greenway on how the "native people" have been treated, although he couched his views in more elegant and academic language. "There is no nation on the face of the

[1] John Greenway, "Will the Indians Get Whitey?," *National Review*, March 11, 1969, p. 224.

earth which has set for itself so high a standard of dealing with a native aboriginal people as the United States," wrote Cohen, "and no nation on earth has been more self-critical in seeking to rectify its deviation from those high standards."[2]

It cannot be accidental that such a scrupulously careful historian as Arthur Schlesinger, who received the Pulitzer Prize for his work *The Age of Jackson,* did not discuss in that book Jackson's brutal use of military force to remove Indians from their lands, his ordering of unnecessary military expeditions against them, or his encouragement of wholesale treaty violations against the Indians. In Schlesinger's analysis of the Jackson era, the only mention of Indians comes in a few short sentences explaining Jackson's refusal to support a Supreme Court decision ordering the release of missionaries arrested for working among the Cherokees. (Actually, Jackson's bitter hostility towards Indians and blacks is well known, although that knowledge cannot be gained from Schlesinger's "definitive" work.)

In stark and bitter contrast to history as written by the Greenways, Cohens and Schlesingers are such devastating accounts as the one given by a volunteer soldier from Georgia who participated in the forced removal of the Cherokees from their lands. "I fought through the Civil War and have seen men shot to pieces and slaughtered by the thousands but the Cherokee removal was the cruelest work I ever knew." When General Philip Sheridan, in 1869, tersely stated, "The only good Indians I ever saw were dead," he was voicing a commonly-held view that had been, and would continue to be, translated into government policy.

The Indian fisherman, son of a chief, whose belief in his rights forces him to alternate between fishing and a white man's prison, the indifferent Pachuco Indian, whose alcoholism and fighting propensities regularly drive him into a reservation jail, and the tribal officials who always cooper-

[2] Felix Cohen, *Handbook of Federal Indian Law*. Washington: Government Printing Office, 1942.

ate with the Bureau of Indian Affairs are all authentic
Indian types. They have counterparts wherever Indians live
in the United States, and the present differences in their
attitude toward whites existed also among their forefathers.
The problem of how to respond to the white society has
been the cause of controversy among Indians for hundreds
of years.

The white state officials who order the fisherman's arrest,
the white police who take him to jail, the white judges who
sentence him, and the white Federal officials from the
Bureau of Indian Affairs, are all authentic American types
too. Their spiritual ancestors can be found among the first
whites who came to Zion and saw it as did William Bradford in 1620: ". . . the vast and unpeopled countries of
America which are fruitfull and fitt for habitation, being
devoyd of all civil inhabitants, where there are only savage
and brutish men, which range up and down, little otherwise
than the wild beasts of the same."[3]

Although Bradford's harsh judgments, Sheridan's terse
comment on Indians, Greenway's peregrinations, and
Cohen's misreading of history represent attitudes which
dominate the American view of the Indian, other traditions
exist. Some white lawyers, for example, vigorously defend
the right of the Indian fisherman to live by the treaty his
ancestors signed, and those lawyers also have their proto-
types in American history.

William Penn's view of the Indians he knew was reflected
in his seventeenth-century writings about their language,
which he took the trouble to learn. "I know not a language
spoken in Europe that hath more words of sweetness and
greatness, in accent or emphasis, than theirs. Their language is lofty, yet narrow, like the Hebrew, in significance,
full. . . ."[4]

Benjamin Franklin was another early American who

[3] Virgil J. Vogel, *The Indian in American History*. Chicago: Integrated
Education Associates, 1968, p. 3.
[4] Steiner, *The New Indians*. New York: Harper & Row, 1968, p. 77.

tried hard to understand Indians and their strange way of life. Even though he failed, he noted many facets of their existence which he found admirable. They had, he wrote, a life in which "There is no force, there are no prisons, no officers to compel obedience or inflict punishment."[5] In 1754 Franklin cited the Iroquois Indians' League of Six Nations in putting forth his own suggestions for a confederation of the colonies: "It would be a strange thing if Six Nations of ignorant savages should be capable of forming a scheme for such an union and be able to execute it in such a manner as that it has subsisted ages and appears indissoluble; and yet that a like union should be impracticable for ten or a dozen English colonies, to whom it is more necessary and must be more advantageous, and who cannot be supposed to want an equal understanding of their interests."

At the start of the nineteenth century, Lewis and Clark, the Northwest explorers, wrote in their *Journal* of the Indians they had encountered on the Great Plains: "Those people are Durtey, Kind, pore & extravagant, possessing national pride, not beggarly. . . ."

John Collier, United States Commissioner of Indian Affairs from 1933 to 1945, saw the history of relationships between Indians and whites far differently than did Greenway:

An exploitation totally ravenous was practiced by nearly all the white invaders from the first day. Such exploitation breeds hate and scorn towards the victim and soon the exploiting white soul perceived no longer that garden of marvelous bloom, the Indian spirit in its long summer. Instead, the white man perceived diabolism, benightedness, sloth, bloodthirstiness and racial impracticality. Secular ruthlessness was supported by religious fanaticism. The destruction of the Indian civilizations came to be an end in itself, and not only a means toward quick wealth; and there was launched the most determined, centuries-long-lasting program of social and spiritual destruction that the world has ever known.[6]

[5] *Ibid.*, p. 150.
[6] John Collier, *On the Gleaming Way*. Denver: Sage Books, 1962, p. 38.

White historians have generally ignored the fact that Indians have always disputed among themselves whether they should accommodate to or resist the white world, whether to become part of the white society or retain the "Indian way of life," and even whether an Indian way of life still exists.

But however Indians have felt about such issues, their view of whites was expressed in 1787 by Pachgantachilias, a Delaware chief:

I admit that there are good white men, but they bear no proportion to the bad; the bad must be the strongest for they rule. They do what they please. They enslave those who are not of their color, although created by the same Great Spirit who created them. They would make slaves of us if they could; but as they cannot do it, they kill us. There is no faith to be placed in their words.

They are not like the Indians who are only enemies while at war, and are friends in peace. They will say to an Indian, "My friend; my brother!" They will take him by the hand and, at the same moment destroy him. And you will also be treated by them before long. Remember that this day I warned you to beware of such friends as these. I know the Long-knives. They are not to be trusted.

The warnings in that speech were echoed in the 1960s when another chief told a Pueblo tribal council:

If the Senators and Congressmen come to you and tell you what they will do for you, do not believe them. They are not your friends. They will give you crumbs. . . . If an Indian is ugly, illiterate and poor and if an Indian is well-dressed and college educated, he is your friend. The white man is not your friend; he is your friend only when he wants something from you. He will forget you. The Indian cannot forget.[7]

From the moment Columbus saw the first native Americans and named them "Indians" in the mistaken belief that he had discovered the Indies, the white man has misunder-

[7] Steiner, *op. cit.*, pp. 243–44.

stood the people who originally lived on the new continent.

Columbus described with accuracy what he saw:

They all go naked as their mothers bore them and the women also although I saw only one very young girl. . . . Some of them paint their faces, some of them their whole bodies, some only the nose. They do not bear arms or know them for I showed them swords and they took them by the blade and cut themselves through ignorance.

But he did not understand the Indians' behavior. "Anything they have," he wrote, "if it be asked for they never say no, but rather invite the person to accept it, and show so much lovingness as though they would give their hearts."[8]

Such behavior was so odd in the context of Columbus' world that he thought he had somehow stumbled upon a new Garden of Eden. Soon afterward, a picture of the Indian as the Noble Savage began to emerge, celebrated by philosophers like Montaigne and Rousseau and titillating the salons and ballrooms of Europe. "They seem to live in that golden world of which old writers speak so much," wrote Peter Martyr in the sixteenth century, "wherein men lived simply and innocently without enforcement of laws, without quarrellings, judges and libels, content only to satisfy nature, without further vexation for knowledge of things to come."

Columbus' voyage to the New World marked the expansion of the Spanish Empire. Spanish interest in the New World was not just colonization as such, but the exploitation of its riches for the benefit of the mother country and the conversion of its inhabitants to Catholicism. When Columbus landed in the Caribbean Islands, he was convinced he was in Asia, the land heralded as a storehouse of great wealth. In the pursuit of gold and in the name of glory for God and country, the Spanish explorers became conquerors, the natives victims.

After Columbus' initial "discovery" of the West Indies, he left a small party behind and returned to Spain in

---

[8] *Journal of Christopher Columbus,* translated by Cecil Jane. New York: Clarkson N. Potter Publishing Co., 1960, pp. 23–24.

triumph. He was greeted with joy, for he brought with him enough gold articles to convince the Spanish rulers that he had discovered the riches of the Indies.

Columbus went back to the West Indies with seventeen ships, manned by 1,500 men (many of them of the nobility), ferocious bloodhounds, and a well-equipped cavalry. The party he had left behind had been killed by the natives in retaliation for the abuses and injuries inflicted by the Spanish. Columbus responded by declaring war and wiping out the natives, who were totally unprepared for armed cavalry and ferocious dogs.

Gaspar Corte Real, a Portuguese explorer, landed on the shores of Labrador, part of continental America, and repaid the natives' friendly reception of his party by kidnapping more than fifty of them to sell as slaves back in Europe. (Ironically, the name "Labrador" means "place with an abundance of labor materials.")

In 1524, Giovanni da Verrazzano, an Italian in the service of the French, landed on the shores of North Carolina, where he was greeted hospitably by the natives. A short time later, he made another landing farther north and kidnapped an Indian child as a trophy of his visit. Then he sailed on to explore the Bay of New York (the new bridge across that bay is named for the kidnapper) and, not surprisingly, met with suspicion from the natives, who by that time had well-founded grounds for their distrust. In 1527, Verrazzano was hanged as a pirate.

Another European, Lucas Vasquez de Ayllon, following the pattern of Real and Verrazzano, landed in Georgia and South Carolina, and took away with him more than a hundred Indians to be sold as slaves in Haiti. By that time, not even the long distances separating the tribes were enough to keep the Indians ignorant of what they could expect from the white man. Tales of the white man's cruelty began to spread throughout the Indian world.

Since the primary thrusts of the Spanish drive for colonies and conversions had been in Central and South America, it was not until after those ancient civilizations had been completely plundered that the Spaniards began to move north in search of more gold, more forced conversions, more land to be made into huge haciendas, more natives to be pressed into labor.

The search for gold led Hernando de Soto, who had helped Pizarro conquer Peru, north to Florida. Starting out from Tampa Bay in 1539, de Soto and his party moved northward and westward through Georgia, Alabama, Mississippi, and Arkansas. For three years, everywhere they went, they raped, robbed, and killed the Indians, including even those who befriended them. Indian hospitality to whites was repaid with wholesale slaughter of men, women, and children. The Spaniards burned unsuspecting villages in which they had slept, taking the village chiefs as hostages and the village children as slaves. De Soto was, according to one historian of the period, "much given to the sport of slaying Indians."

Even Coronado, one of the most humane *conquistadores,* betrayed a truce. A Pueblo village had started a war against the Spaniards because the rape of an Indian woman by a Spanish soldier had gone unpunished. After the Indians had been told there would be no reprisals, Coronado ordered all the Indian warriors killed. His captain, Don Garcia, proceeded to carry out the orders by preparing to burn the Indian men alive. "Then," wrote Pedro de Castebada, historian of Coronado's explorations, "when the Indians saw that the Spaniards were binding them and beginning to roast them, about a hundred men who were in the tent began to struggle and defend themselves with what was there and with the stakes they could seize. Our men who were on foot attacked the tent on all sides, so that there was great confusion around it, and then the horsemen chased those who escaped. As the country was level, not a man of them remained alive."[9]

The Spaniards' mistreatment of the Indians was equaled by that of the English, who abused the Indians' friendship

9 Collier, *op. cit.,* p. 88.

from the start. In 1585, Sir Richard Grenville landed on the shores of Virginia, was treated with great cordiality by the Indians, and repaid that cordiality by burning and plundering an Indian village because one Indian had allegedly stolen one of his silver drinking cups.

The Dutch, too, behaved towards the Indians in much the same way as did other white European settlers. "Behold! The gods have come to visit us!" was the first response of the Delaware Indians to the sight of Hendrick Hudson anchoring the *Half Moon* off New York in 1609. But after 100 years of dealings with the whites, the Delawares had learned from embittering experiences that such gods were truly devils.

By the time the English settlements of Jamestown and Plymouth were established in the first decades of the seventeenth century, many Indians had good cause for fearing the whites. The white settlers and explorers did not believe that the rules of warfare, which governed the conduct of civilized enemies, extended to fighting the heathen and barbaric Indians. No justification was needed for the most brutal and punitive actions taken against the Indians, who according to John Smith of the Jamestown Colony, were a "viporous brood," despite the fact that they had saved the colony from starvation. Benjamin Trumbull, an early settler of New England, believed that "as Connecticut abounded in wild animals, so it did also with wild savage men," and Cotton Mather was convinced "that probably the devil decoyed these miserable savages hither in hopes that the gospel of the Lord Jesus Christ would never come here to destroy or disturb his absolute empire over them."[10]

The early arguments among whites about the true nature of the North American natives were disputes about whether the Indians were savages or humans. If the Indians were savages, something less than human, then the modes of permissible behavior toward them included killing them, just as wild animals might be hunted and killed without fear of public disapproval. That view was so pervasive that the

[10] Vogel, *op. cit.,* p. 3.

Colorado State Legislature once debated whether or not to offer bounties for "the destruction of Indians and Skunks." In 1872, a United States Indian Commissioner said that "with wild men as with wild beasts the question of whether in a given situation one shall fight, coax or run is a question merely of what is easiest and safest."[11]

Even those English settlers, such as the Puritans, who did not physically mistreat the Indians, were convinced that an important part of their mission in the New World was to educate the Indians in the white man's ways, and to make Christian converts of them. Few of these whites questioned the superiority of their ways over those of the Indians. It was believed that Indians were an inferior race incapable of making decisions, and that the whites must assume responsibility for directing the Indians' lives into the correct channels.

In Massachusetts, for example, the mission of spreading Puritan Christianity among Indians included the education of Indian children. By 1642 colonists reported that "Divers of the Indian children, Boyes and Girles were received into our homes, who are long since civilized, and in subjection to us, painful and handy in their business and can speak our language familiarly; divers of whom can read English and begin to understand, in their measure, the grounds of Christian religion."

This same missionary concept was embodied in the charter of Harvard University, written in 1650. One of the objectives of the university was to be "the education of the English and Indian youth of this country in Knowledge and Godliness." In the belief that educated Indians would automatically become teachers and converters of their people, money was raised in England to provide for their university training. Subsequently the building called the Indian College was constructed at Harvard in 1656 for "six hopefull Indian youthes."

These six Indians and those who followed needed tutoring before they could enter the college; they were sent to

11 *Ibid.*, p. 3.

study with two local grammar-school teachers. During the course of their studies, however, almost all of them died—of tuberculosis, fevers, or other illnesses resulting from exposure to civilized life. "By reason of the death and failing of Indian scholars"[12] the Indian College was not much used for its stated purpose, said one historian in that period. In fact, not one student was actually enrolled in the College before 1660. (One Indian, Sassamon, briefly attended Harvard before the Indian College was founded.)

Only four Indians enrolled after 1660; two died while still students; the third, the only one to ever graduate from Harvard, was Caleb Cheeshahteaumuck who died of tuberculosis the winter after his commencement; the fourth, who was praised for his "apt witt" while at Cambridge, left after a short stay.

The sparse records available today make it difficult to reconstruct the attitudes of whites toward the Indian students, but there is a letter from Charles Chauncy, president of the university, written in 1664, requesting money for a "fit salary" for those who "have to deale with such nasty salvages."[13] By 1665 the Indian College had been improved for the use of English students. The only reminder of its original purpose was its name.

Initially, however, some Indians were needed by whites engaged in either commercial or political competition. The fur trade, one of the staples of early commerce, was dependent upon Indians, and so the whites found it expedient to leave the trapper Indians undisturbed, with their culture more or less intact. In the wars the French, British, and Americans fought against each other, the Indians were used as allies by all three.

As the unlimited opportunities of the New World became apparent to the white settlers, they became more avaricious, shifting from bartering with Indians for furs to seizing control of their lands. The racism of the Europeans coin-

[12] Samuel Eliot Morison: *Harvard in the Seventeenth Century*. Cambridge, Mass.: Harvard University Press, 1936, Part I, p. 343.
[13] *Ibid.*, p. 358.

cided with their desire to expand their sovereignty over the New World and the Indians.

Thus the destruction of the Indians was written into the first chapter of successful white colonization in America. The pure ideals of Christianity were easily molded into a racist ideology that matched the economic and social needs of the expanding settlers.

When Columbus arrived in the West Indies, about one million Indians lived in the New World, in about six hundred different societies, ranging from highly sophisticated to almost aboriginal ones. Along the Northeast coast the Iroquois lived in well-built log houses, constructed formidable fortifications, were highly developed agriculturists, and were politically sophisticated enough to have established the League of Six Nations. In the Southeast there were tribes equally well adapted to their environment. The Cherokees, Creeks, Chickasaws, Seminoles, and other smaller tribes, lived in settlements hidden behind palisades. These tribes lived within a complex clan system, built temples to the sun, and had, like the Iroquois, evolved a complicated network of alliances.

In the Midwest, the Great Lakes Indians lived in houses, were expert hunters, fishermen, and truck gardeners. The Southwest Indians were primarily farmers; the men did the agricultural work and developed elaborate irrigation systems that made it possible for them to grow crops in the arid deserts. Other Southwest Indian tribes lived in many-roomed buildings and functioned under a very efficient political system. In the Northwest, along the Pacific Coast from Alaska to northern California, lived the Indians who were sea-oriented and whose social structure was based on rigid class and ancestor distinctions.

The Indians of southern California were not organized along class lines; they had few social distinctions and few social graces. Their diet was crude, with acorns as the basic food, and they lived in very primitive structures and traveled on rafts, rather than in canoes.

The Great Plains Indians were hunters, rather than fishermen or farmers. In order to remain mobile and follow the game, they developed the teepee as a form of habitation that could be put up and taken down very quickly. (In popular folklore about Indians, the teepee is still regarded as the standard form for all Indian housing, although it is used only by one specific group of Indians.)

The political range of Indian societies was varied, extending from the well-developed and structured tribal alliances of some of the tribes to the primitive forms of the California Indians. While some tribes continually warred with each other, there were alliances between others. Language differences, cultural patterns, and differentiated responses to varying physical conditions created wide variations of political and social structures among the tribes.

Long before Columbus arrived on the shores of the New World, the "savages" had succeeded in growing, under controlled conditions, wild plants which they continuously improved by carefully selecting seeds, cultivating the soil and using fertilizer to keep it productive.

It was the North American Indian who taught the white man how to grow corn properly; it was the Indian of South America who first grew white potatoes. Indian crops included pumpkins and tomatoes, beans and squash, peanuts, gourds, cashew nuts, chili peppers, sweet potatoes, and a host of others, as well as tobacco which was unknown in the Old World. The only product developed independently in both the Old and New World was cotton. One of the best-known types of Egyptian cotton, the Pima strain, was developed first by the Pima Indians of the Southwest and then taken by the British to Egypt.

The white settlers probably would have starved to death in the New World had the "uncivilized" Indians not shown them how to raise their crops. It is one of the bitter ironies of history that Thanksgiving, the all-American holiday, should be celebrated by eating turkey, sweet potatoes, cranberries, and pumpkin pie, all foods the Indians introduced

to the white settlers, but which few Indians can afford to
buy today.

In all the Indian cultures, the most commonly-held attitude was a special reverence for the land. This attitude
became one important source of conflicts between the Indians and the whites (including those whites who were
initially disposed to equitable relations with the Indians).

To most Indians, the land was, as Sitting Bull described,
"this mother of ours" mystically linked to the "embraces of
the sun." And because of the "mysterious power" created
by this union, most Indians had no understanding of the
concept of land possession held by the English and the
Europeans. Land was not something that could be given
away or sold; their view was that "we therefore yield to our
neighbors, even our animal neighbors, the same right as
ourselves to inhabit this land."

Inevitably conflicts developed between the Indians and
the settlers over land, and not only because some whites
stole land from the Indians. When the colonists "bought"
the land, they assumed they were buying all the rights to it
in the traditional European sense. The Indians, however,
were not aware they were giving up their rights to fish and
hunt on the land they had ceded or sold to the settlers.

The clash of values between the Indians and the whites
over the ownership of land was characteristic of the larger
clash between the Indian and European cultures. Most
Indian societies were integrated cultures in which, for example, no separation was made between daily life and
religion. No separate time of day or day of the week existed
for praying and religion, every routine act had its mystical
connection, all of life was suffused with the embrace between the sun and the earth.

But such concepts were incomprehensible and irrelevant
to the whites in whose culture a separate day was set aside
for worship. The whites were also impatient with the Indians' mode of arriving at decisions communally after what
must have seemed, to them, interminable speeches broken
up by lengthy silences.

Indians and whites also had sharply different views about the need to work. To the whites, work was an integral part of life, for without work possessions could not be accumulated. In addition, Puritanism made work part of the religious ethos. Each man pursued his calling and the more success he enjoyed, the more proof there was that God blessed him. Indian men hunted, fished, or farmed, not to grow wealthy in the white sense, but simply to live. And when enough hunting, fishing, or farming had been done to provide for the family and the tribe, the Indians spent their time in the wilderness alone, in the council house with their peers, or in their own habitations with their families.

The refusal of the Indians to follow the white pattern of work resulted in the myth that Indians were lazy. Sitting on the ground, wrapped in his blanket, and responding to all questions with "Ugh," the "lazy injun" image became another standard part of American folklore, especially since it helped justify the atrocities committed against him.

Furthermore, the whites, settlers and conquerors alike, did not understand Indian family relationships, especially the close ties between parents and children. Because of those ties, the Indians resisted sending their children to the schools opened for them by well-meaning whites anxious to bring "civilization" to the savages. In Virginia, Indian parents were offered ten pounds in payment for each boy willing to live in a colonist's house. Very few Indian parents permitted this, especially since a certain mark of white "civilization"—corporal punishment meted out to children —was particularly repugnant to them.

Father LeJeune, a Jesuit priest in Quebec, described an incident that occurred in the early part of the seventeenth century when a group of Indians crowded so closely around a French drummer boy that he became angry and lashed out at one Indian, cutting him in the face with a drum stick. The angry Indians demanded an apology and, as was their custom, a present. The French responded by stripping the drummer boy and preparing to flog him. When the Indians saw that the boy was to be beaten, one of them threw himself over the boy, shouting, "Scourge me, if you choose, but do not strike the boy!" Father LeJeune then added the comment that the Indian unwillingness to physically punish any child "will probably occasion trouble to us in the design we have to instruct their youth."

Still another source of tension was the increasing dependence of Indians on whites. Deprived of their land by treaties and prohibited from fishing, hunting, and trapping, the Indians were forced to trade with whites for food and supplies. But the Indians were in no position to bargain as equals with the whites since they neither understood the whites' language nor their concept of profit. Also, many whites gave the Indians alcohol to make it easier to cheat and degrade them.

Sometime in 1748, at a war council, a Creek Indian warned his fellow tribesmen against alcohol in a bitter speech against the

. . . emissary of the evil principle of darkness. Tis that pernicious liquid which our pretended *white friends* artfully introduced and so plentifully pour among us. . . . tremble o ye Creeks! when I thunder in your ears this denunciation; that if this cup of perdition continues to rule among us with sway so intemperate, ye will cease to be a nation! Ye will have neither heads to direct nor hands to protect you.

While this diabolical juice undermines all powers of your body and minds, with inoffensive zeal, the warrior's enfeebled arm will draw the bow or launch the spear in the day of battle. In the day of Council, when national safety stands suspended on the lips of Sachem, he will shake his head with uncollected spirits and dribble the babblings of a second childhood.

Think not, o ye Creeks, that I presume to amuse or affright you with an imaginary picture. Is it not evident (alas, it is too fatally so) that we find the vigor of our youth abating; our numbers decreasing; our ripened manhood a premature victim to disease, to sickness, to death and our venerable Sachems a solitary number?

This warning from the Creek warrior went unheeded by many Indians, for alcohol filled a vacuum left in their lives.

Faced with the destruction of their cultures, some Indians responded by intensifying their warfare against the whites. Others succumbed to alcoholism. Of course fighting and drinking only served to reinforce the white man's stereotype of the Indians.

These value conflicts between whites and Indians were further intensified by the practice of hauling Indians accused of misdeeds into court to be tried under English procedures. These procedures were totally unintelligible to the Indians, not only because they did not understand the language in which the courts were conducted, but also because English justice and common law were foreign to them. By the same token, the settlers had little or no understanding of Indian justice.

The pattern of Indian-white relations established in the colonial era continued with further attacks and counterattacks, lies and treacheries, the signing of treaties and subsequent violations of them. As French attempts to colonize North America conflicted with those of the English, the Indian tribes became pawns in the French and Indian Wars. Later the Indians were used by both the English and the Americans in the War of 1812, and by the Americans and Spanish in the fight over the possession of Florida. By the nineteenth century, desire for land had become need as the white population expanded. The Indians began to see their territories, their "mother," shrinking.

In 1811, John Randolph, a member of the House of Representatives from Virginia, analyzed the reasons why some Indian tribes helped the British prepare for war against the United States. He pointed out to his colleagues "that for this signal calamity and disgrace the House was, in part, at least answerable. Session after session, their table had been piled up with Indian treaties for which the appropriations had been voted as a matter of course, without examination. Advantage had been taken of the spirit of the Indians, broken by the war which ended in the Treaty of Greenville. Under the ascendancy then acquired over them, they had been pent up by subsequent treaties into nooks, straightened in their quarters by a blind cupidity, seeking to extinguish their title to immense wildernesses, for which, (possessing as we do already, more land than we can sell or use) we shall not have occasion for half a century to come. It was our own thirst for territory, our own want of moderation that had driven these sons of nature to desperation of which we felt the effects. . . ."

One of the "effects" felt by the white man was the bitter ideological dispute among the Indians about whether they should accommodate and "walk in the ways of the white man," or resist him in battle.

In 1812, Tecumseh, the great Shawnee leader, pleaded with a large Choctaw and Chickasaw council to unite with other tribes in resisting the white man by saying, "Before the pale-faces came among us, we enjoyed the happiness of unbounded freedom and were acquainted with neither riches, wants, nor oppression. How is it now? Wants and oppression are our lot; for are we not controlled in everything and dare we move without asking, by your leave? Are we not being stripped, day by day of the little that remains of our ancient liberty? Do they not even now kick and strike us as they do their blackfaces? How long will it be before they will tie us to a post and whip us and make us work for them in corn fields as they do them? Shall we wait for that moment or shall we die fighting before submitting to such ignominy?"

To Tecumseh's plea for armed resistance, Pushmataha, the Choctaw orator, gave the classic accommodationist answer, asking the council "not yet to have recourse to war, but to send ambassadors to our Great Father at Washington, and lay before him our grievances, without betraying too great eagerness for war, or manifesting any tokens of pusillanimity. . . . I implore you, while healing measures are in the election of us all, not to break the treaty, nor violate your pledge or honor, but to submit our grievances, whatever they may be, to the Congress of the United States, according to the articles of the treaty existing between us and the American people. . . ."

The Choctaws and the Chickasaws heeded the advice of Pushmataha and were cheated of their lands and their rights, as were almost every other Indian tribe, whether they trusted or resisted the Americans.

Ostensibly, relationships between Indians and white Americans were fixed by the terms of 370 treaties signed by the tribes and the United States Government between 1789 and 1871. They were based on the assumption that Indian tribes were like sovereign states, or foreign powers, and that treaties with them had to be ratified by the Senate. The initial and primary purpose of the treaties was to remove the Indians from tribal lands to new western lands, supposedly set aside for their exclusive use. Often the treaties were negotiated through less than competent interpreters, so that misunderstandings were inevitable. Sometimes they were based on outright frauds perpetrated by unscrupulous white officials; occasionally they were signed by Indians under great duress. Almost always the Indians were paid less money than their land was worth. A few treaties, however, were based on principles of justice that attempted to protect Indian rights.

By 1840, the Indians had been dispossessed of or removed from nearly all the land east of the Mississippi. The treaties had reduced them to the status of conquered peoples, displaced in their own homeland. Thousands, especially women and children, died of starvation and cold as they made long journeys, often accompanied by soldiers who kept them in line. A typical description of the food served on the journey was given by an assistant surgeon-general in the Army. Into a vat were thrown "beef, beef-heads, entrails of the beeves, some beans, flour and pork. . . . It was about the consistency of very thin gruel. . . . It had a very offensive odor. It had the odor of the contents of the entrails of the beeves . . . the settleings smelled like carrion, like decomposed meat. Some of the Indians refused to eat it, saying they could not, it made them sick." In fact, thousands died of diarrhea and other stomach ailments brought on by the "carrion" they were given.[14]

Some tribes refused to leave their lands, arguing that earlier treaties acknowledged their rights to remain. So the Americans declared war. Tens of thousands of Indians were killed in the Indian wars. From 1612 to 1890, two hundred major battles and hundreds more skirmishes were fought between Indians and whites. Cruelty and treachery, truce violations and broken promises marked these wars on both sides. But contrary to popular notions, the whites behaved as reprehensibly, if not more so, than the Indians.

The final major battle of the Indian Wars was a characteristic one. It was fought on December 28, 1890, when a large force of U.S. Army soldiers surrounded an Indian encampment at Wounded Knee Creek, South Dakota, training howitzers on the camp. No one is certain exactly what triggered off this unequal fight, but whatever the cause, it became a slaughter. A government investigation reported later that ". . . In a few minutes, two hundred Indian men, women and children, with sixty soldiers were lying dead and wounded on the ground, the teepees had been torn down by the shells and some of them were . . . above the helpless wounded, and the surviving handful of Indians were flying in wild panic to the shelter of the ravine, pursued by hundreds of maddened soldiers and followed up by a raking fire from the Hotchkiss guns, which had been moved into position to sweep the ravine. There can be no question that the pursuit was simply a massacre, where fleeing women, with infants in their arms were shot down after resistance had ceased and when almost every warrior was stretched dead or dying on the ground."[15]

The public justification for such atrocities and large-scale campaigns was that Indians were treacherous and cruel savages who could never be trusted. It was wrong, said one

[14] Helen Hunt Jackson, *A Century of Dishonor.* Reprint. Minneapolis: Ross & Haines, 1964, p. 394.
[15] John Tebbel and Keith Jennison, *The American Indian Wars.* New York: Harper & Row, 1960, pp. 296–97.

historian in 1889, "to suppose that savages, whose business is to torture and slay, can always be dealt with according to the methods in use between civilized peoples. . . ."[16] Another said, "Their intractable, unchanging character leaves no alternative than their gradual extinction. . . ."[17]

These justifications are the ones we have chosen to pass on to our children, particularly via their school books. Children still read today that "Settlers had gone beyond the Appalachians. The Indians made war upon them. The President had to see that the settlers were protected."[18] And that "In order for the cattlemen and their families to live safely, the Indian tribes that ruled the plains had to be defeated."[19]

The real reasons for the wars are not explained in children's books. They were fought to extend the frontier and protect American political ideology. One vivid example was the war fought against the Seminoles of Florida under the direction of Andrew Jackson. Jackson said, "This must be done or the frontier will be much weakened by the Indian settlements and be a perpetual harbor for our slaves. These runaway slaves . . . must be removed from the Floridas or scenes of murder and confusion will exist."[20]

Some Americans, past and present, have objected to the removal policies advocated by Jackson and others. Jedidiah Morse, reporting to Secretary of War John C. Calhoun in 1820, wrote, "To remove these Indians far away from their present homes, into a wilderness among strangers, possibly hostile, to live as their new neighbors live, by hunting, a state to which they have not lately been accustomed, and which is incompatible with civilization, can hardly be

[16] John Fiske, *The Beginnings of New England.* Boston: Houghton Mifflin Co., 1889, p. 184.

[17] Francis Parkman, *The Conspiracy of Pontiac.* New York: E. P. Dutton, 1908, II, p. 101.

[18] *Story of American Freedom,* p. 130, cited in *The Indian Historian,* San Francisco, Vol. 1, Number 1.

[19] *Story of Our Country,* p. 279. *Ibid.*

[20] Joshua Giddings, *The Exiles of Florida.* Gainesville: Univ. of Florida Press, 1964, p. 71.

reconciled with the professed object of civilizing them."[21] In 1838, General Thomas Jessup, then in command of the war against the Seminoles, wrote to the Secretary of War protesting that, "In regard to the Seminoles, we have committed the error of attempting to remove them when their lands were not required for agricultural purposes; when they were not in the way of the white inhabitants and when the greater portion of their country was an unexplored wilderness of the interior of which we were as ignorant as of the interior of China. We exhibit in our present contest the first instance perhaps since the commencement of authentic history, of a nation employing an army to explore a country (for we can do little more than explore it) or attempting to remove a band of savages from one unexplored wilderness to another."[22] One modern critic has seen the wholesale acceptance of Indian dispossession as a determining influence on American character today. "Has not this perhaps led us into demanding no proper accounting from public servants so long as they feed us righteous pap . . . ? Perfect training for later financial plundering . . . the whole ethic of later corporation growth and monopoly—here in the Indian struggle is to be observed the whole American psychology of getting something for nothing, or at most for a little trickery."[23]

But men like Morse, Jessup, John Quincy Adams, John Randolph, and others did not effect major policies of the government toward the Indians. These policies were determined, basically, by the expansionist demands of the newly developing American economy, the sense of political and religious mission felt by most whites, and the search for power by what has come to be the military-industrial complex.

Military leaders viewed the Indian Wars as an oppor-

[21] Morse, "Report to the Secretary of War on Indian Affairs." New Haven: S. Converse, 1822, p. 82.

[22] Giddings, *op. cit.,* p. 183.

[23] Carleton Beals, *American Earth.* Philadelphia: J. B. Lippincott, 1939, pp. 63–64.

tunity to exterminate the Indians; civilians generally saw the white man "in loco parentis" to the Indians. In any case the Indians were doomed.

But for a while things went well for the Indians. The Cherokees, for example, gave up fighting in 1788; they also gave up their old hunting ways, and took up farming. Impressed by the ideals of the Declaration of Independence and the Constitution, they formed their own republic with a written constitution, a chief, bicameral legislature, codified laws, a system of courts, and a police force. A Cherokee named Sequoia invented a syllabary so that their language could be written, and they established a printing press and newspaper. (The Cherokees took to reading with such enthusiasm that one peddler had a runaway business peddling spectacles.) A capital city, in which the Cherokees took great pride, was built and named New Echota. With their territory guaranteed by the United States, the Cherokees were able to enjoy phenomenal advances in civilization and the refinements which civilization brought to their lives.

But it was not long before the Cherokees were forbidden to set foot in their own capital. The State of Georgia wanted the land. Then gold was discovered in 1830 and by the spring a bill for the removal of the Indians of the Southeast to the West was passed by Congress. The Cherokees, who still had faith in the word of the United States as given in its treaties, took their case to the Supreme Court, convinced that they were in the right. In a landmark decision spelling out endless future misery for Indians, the Court ruled that it had no jurisdiction in the case since the tribes were "domestic dependent nations." With this failure of the Supreme Court to hold the nation to its word, all treaties with Indians became meaningless.

One other Supreme Court decision of great importance to the Cherokees was the one which Chief Justice Marshall ruled that the State of Georgia had no right to abrogate the treaty rights of Indians and that the Indians could stay on their farms. It was rendered worthless by President Jackson who said "John Marshall has made his decision: now let him enforce it."[24] The decision was not enforced; white depredations upon Indian territory continued.

By 1832, Georgia was holding lotteries for Cherokee lands, and whites were claiming their winnings. In 1835, a fraudulent treaty was made with the government by a small group of Cherokees (500 out of 20,000) without authority to act for their nation. They agreed to the removal desired by the whites. The Cherokees, who were given until May of 1838 to move, believed that such an injustice would never be carried out. They were not prepared when the Army came to move them. That move, the infamous Trail of Tears, marked one more bitter lesson in the chicanery of the white man.

CHICANERY AND VENALITY

Chicanery and venality were also characteristic of relations between the Bureau of Indian Affairs and the Indians. Originally in the 1820s, within the War Department, the Indian Bureau was later shifted to the Interior Department. But the War Department was not satisfied with this arrangement, claiming that it had successfully dealt with the Indians for many years by keeping the peace among the tribes, moving them out of their eastern lands to the West, and when necessary, subduing them in battle. The Interior Department answered these arguments by pointing out that military force was not the proper method for civilizing the Indians and that Army personnel had often been ruthless and arbitrary in their dealings with the Indians.

In this intra-Department battle, the Indians were always the losers, for they became the victims of the bickering and quarreling of the two agencies. And if it was true, as the Interior Department charged, that Army officers had been ruthless and arbitrary, it was also true, as the War Department alleged, that the personnel appointed to the Indian Bureau by the Interior Department were inefficient, corrupt, and dishonest, and more often interested in increasing their personal fortunes at the expense of their Indian wards, than in helping them.

How the Interior Department generally conducted affairs is revealed in an excerpt from a report made in the nineteenth century by an inspector for the Indian Service:

The Indian Bureau has been made the dumping ground for the sweepings of the political party that is in power. . . . As soon as a report that is derogatory to these people goes to Washington, their friends rush to the Interior Department and say that these reports are wrong and that another trial must be given and they are kept on and on. . . . If you go to an Indian school or an agency and stay there a month and get behind the scenes into the arcanum, you will find two or three who are physically, mentally or morally incapacitated. You find good, earnest people among them but they are the exceptions. You will find people who are there only to draw their pay. You will find cliques, wrangles, quarrels going on that are a disgrace to any institution.

Conditions were especially disgraceful in the Indian schools. In 1819, Congress appropriated $10,000 for the purpose of teaching Indians "the habits and arts of civilization" by employing "capable persons of good moral character to instruct them in the mode of agriculture suited to their situation; and for teaching their children in reading, writing and arithmetic. . . ." But since no administrative machinery existed to carry out the policy, the money was divided among the missionary groups who conducted schools for the tribes.

Over the years there was a slow increase in the number of Indian schools, both government- and church-supported. But neither type had much impact on the lives of the Indians. Instruction in the federal schools, for example, was given only in English, which many Indian children did not understand. The boarding schools, which by government policy were favored over day schools, totally disrupted Indian family life. It was believed that in the paternalistic boarding schools Indian children would be removed from the bad influences of their homes and become more like the whites who provided the education.

However, the first over-all report on the status of Indian education, made in 1889, showed that many teachers in the schools were incompetent, that the schools had very bad facilities for teaching, that few of them maintained proper standards for health or sanitation, and that the supply system used by the schools had more to do with profiteering than with the needs of the students. Supply and demand did not always coincide. For example, an enormous quantity of pins was discovered at one school, while at another flatirons were a huge surplus item.

By 1869, the situation of the Indians had become so desperate that the president appointed a Board of Commissioners, ten people "eminent for their intelligence and philanthropy," to improve the administration of Indian affairs. The Board's first report recommended that the Indians be collected on small neighboring reservations within the limits of a large reservation that would eventually form a State of the Union, that the treaty system be abolished, that the Indians be made legal wards of the government, that schools and missions be established and English taught in them, that Indian courts be set up, that the promises made to the Indians in the treaties of the past be fulfilled, and that individual plots of land be given to the "civilized" and "capable" Indians.

These recommendations were partially fulfilled in 1871 when the Indians were given areas with fixed boundaries in which to live. The reservations came into being. But not even segregation in these large ghettos saved the Indians from physical assaults by whites, or from economic depredations. All of the Great Plains tribes, for example, looked to the buffalo as the primary staple of their existence. Fifty to seventy-five million buffaloes provided the Indians on the reservations with most of their food, clothing, homes, weapons, and even the fuel for their fires.

While the buffalo represented the staff of life to the

Indians, who only killed what they needed for their collective sustenance, the animals represented a large-scale profit potential for the white men, since the building of the post-Civil War railroads had opened up national markets for buffalo hides and meat. Within the space of little more than 20 years, the white hunters wiped out the buffalo, slaughtering them by the hundreds of thousands. By 1895, there were only 800 buffaloes left in the entire country.

The white man's indiscriminate killing of the Indians' basic source of life forced the Indians to be even more dependent on the white man since the government had to then provide their basic necessities of life, lest they starve to death. The Indians became hostile because of their enforced position and because of the grudging way in which assistance was given them. When General William Sherman told an interviewer in the 1890s that "Injuns must either work or starve. They have never worked. And they never will work,"[25] he was expressing a commonly held view. Obviously this did not take into account the fact that the whites had forced the Indians into the very condition which the whites then condemned.

In 1887, Congress passed the Allotment Act which marked an important shift in government administrative policy. Under the terms of the act, the President was authorized to allot lands to individual Indians who lived on reservations whenever reservation land was suitable for grazing or agriculture. Ostensibly the Allotment Act was designed to make the Indians more like white landowning Americans, by giving Indians with families 160 acres, and single ones 80 acres. These allocations doubled if the land could be used only for grazing purposes. A few men in Congress understood the real import of the act and protested in a minority, that ". . . If this were done in the name of greed, it would be bad enough; but to do it in the name of humanity, and under the cloak of an ardent desire to promote the Indian's welfare by making him like ourselves, whether he will or not, is infinitely worse."

[25] Steiner, *op. cit.*, p. 127.

The Allotment Act failed miserably in achieving its stated objectives. Sixty percent of the land given the Indians by the Allotment Act fell into the hands of the whites. The result was that the 118 reservations divided into allotments for individual Indians became red and white checkerboards as the whites leased larger and larger squares of the best lands. The land inheritance problem then became extremely complicated. When an individual Indian died, leaving his small allotment to his heirs, the original allotment was split into smaller units, which were then split again after the heirs died. As the land units grew smaller they became less productive and the poorer Indians who owned them began leasing them to whites. Eventually the whites accumulated large segments of land, each made up of many pieces. The inevitable consequence of the Allotment Act was that all too quickly nearly two-thirds of the Indians in the country were left either landless or without enough land to use productively. The Indians had become completely subjugated.

Those tribes that survived the forced removals and the genocidal wars became the victims of a kind of cultural genocide. The Indians were not permitted to teach their own language in their schools and were forbidden to practice their own religion. The reservations on which they lived were like concentration camps and their daily lives controlled by the Army or the Bureau of Indian Affairs. The administrators of the BIA lived apart from the Indians, even on the reservations, and had little interest in doing anything more than forcing the Indians to accept the white man's ways. Furthermore, the customary methods of redressing grievances in America were not even open to Indians; for instance, they lacked access to political power, including the vote. Indians were not granted the right to vote until 1924 and in New Mexico and Arizona that right was not granted until 1948. So they were forced to suffer the injustices committed against them in silence.

By 1934, when the allotment process ended, the Indians were the objects of contempt, discrimination, and persecution. They were miserably poor, in very bad health, living in the worst kinds of housing, with very little or very bad education, and almost completely demoralized. They were America's shame and America hid them from sight, except when they were put on display for tourists and when presidential candidates had their photos taken in war bonnets. The once proud tribes had sunk to an absurd level. At Baraboo, Wisconsin, a Menomene chief was once called upon to sing a "genuine Indian song" for the spectators. He sang, "When I'm calling you-oo-oo-oo. . . ."

After 1934, daily life improved slightly, but the paternal attitude of the government remained the same. By World War II, propagandists for the American war effort "discovered" the Indians again and the Indian warrior was transmuted into a true "brave" fighting for democracy. When one of the Marine heroes immortalized in the famous Iwo Jima photo turned out to be Ira Hayes of the Pima tribe in Arizona, it seemed as if the Indians might hope for a better life after the war.

But the hope was in vain. The end of the war brought little or no change in the condition of the Indians. Ira Hayes ended his life back on the reservation; he eventually drowned after falling drunk into a drainage ditch with only a few inches of water in it.

After the Republican electoral victories in 1952, another disastrous policy was foisted upon the Indians. In an effort to reduce governmental expenditures, Congress passed a resolution stating its intent to end federal supervision and support of Indian tribes "at the earliest possible time." Many Indian tribes were forced to accede to termination, as this policy was called, by governmental pressures.

Some Paiutes in Utah, for example, were promised Federal recognition of their marriages if they would agree to the removal of Federal services. (Even after the services were removed, the marriages were not recognized.)[26] In at

[26] Vine Deloria, *Custer Died for Your Sins.* Macmillan Company, Toronto, Ontario, 1969, p. 63.

least two cases, the Klamaths of Oregon and the Menominees of Wisconsin, the government refused to pay money owed to the tribes unless they would agree to termination. In order to collect, the tribes acceded. As a result of termination, the Menominees, who had previously been quite prosperous and had paid for their own tribal services out of the earnings of their lumber business, became destitute, and a considerable welfare burden on both state and federal governments.

The determination to dispossess Indians of their traditional lands and treaty rights was expressed by Dillon Myer, Commissioner of Indian Affairs (who had been in charge of Japanese internment camps during World War II) in 1952. "I realize that it will not be possible always to obtain Indian cooperation. Full understanding by the tribal membership should be attained in any event, and agreement with affected Indian groups must be attained if possible. In the absence of such agreement, however, I want our differences to be clearly defined and understood by both the Indians and ourselves. We must proceed, even though Indian cooperation may be lacking in certain cases."[27]

The Indian reaction to this policy was expressed by Vine Deloria, Jr., former Executive Director of the National Congress of Indian Affairs. "In practice, termination is used as a weapon against the Indian people in a modern war of conquest.[28] And though the pace of termination has slowed since the 1950s, the policy still is in force, continuing the erosion of Indian rights begun by the white man in 1492.

In the 1960s things were the same. A recent Commissioner of Indian Affairs, the highest ranking administrator in BIA, said of his agency's relationship to the Indians that, "It is very difficult to get away from complete paternalism. This is a relationship based upon a trustee and a ward. . . ." It is still true that the trustees become richer

[27] *Ibid.*, p. 61.
[28] *Ibid.*, p. 76.

and more affluent, while the wards grow poorer and poorer. Disease, malnutrition, and poverty still hound huge numbers of American Indians, while the Indian schools have changed only a little over the years. Unemployment is high and so is alcoholism. As for Indian professionals, the U.S. Commission on Civil Rights reported in 1961 that ". . . jobs, homes and public places are not as accessible to them as to others. Poverty and deprivation are common. Social acceptance is not the rule. In addition, Indians seem to suffer more than occasional mistreatment by the instruments of law and order both on and off the reservation. . . ." To be either a ward on a reservation or an exact copy of a middle-class American, these have been the only choices for Indians. Over the years, individual Indians have left the reservations, but many of them then return to go "under the blanket" again because of their inability or unwillingness to adjust to life outside.

But today the spirit of resistance is stirring again in the tribes, spurred on by a generation of younger Indians who have seen military duty, as well as by the increasing ethnic and color identity among the unassimilated groups of Americans. This new spirit of resistance is called "Red Power" by the young Indian militants who reject as "Uncle Tomahawks" those Indians who serve the interests of the white man. Important questions remain unanswered for the Indians, however. What and where is their "rightful place"? Is reservation life possible in America today? How will Indians fit into the increasingly technological and industrialized society? What are the sources of independent power for those Indians who are now imbued with a new spirit of resistance?

Alongside the growing number of Indians with a developing sense of insistence on their rights is an increasing number of alienated white youth who view the Indian as a superior human. They glorify and emulate Indian ways, often to the extent of embarrassing the Indians. But adulation of the Indian overlooks an important aspect of American history. The Indians had a civilization with a complicated way of life and rich language, despite the vulgar white view of them as mere savages. Yet the Indians fought among themselves and some even fought their brothers on behalf of the whites. Whether the Indian civilization was "primitive" or "advanced" was irrelevant as far as the white world was concerned: white civilization in America could not live side by side in peace with *any* other civilization, no matter what its stage of development. White civilization meant expansion and expansion meant annihilation for anyone who could not fit or be accepted into the rapidly expanding nation. The only way the Indians could have joined the American celebration was to stop being Indians.

Few whites understood the dimensions of the moral dilemma posed by the existence of Indians to a growing America. To most Americans Indians were no more than obstacles to the policymakers of expansionism and threats to the frontiersmen. The only possible solutions were extinction or removal.

In November of 1969, a band of Indians invaded Alcatraz, claimed the abandoned prison island under an old treaty, and remained there in defiance of Federal officials. With money and supplies from the mainland, they made the old buildings habitable, established a school for the children, and settled into a daily routine.

A Bureau of Caucasian Affairs was established to deal with the white caretaker and his family; white visitors, except for the press, were refused admittance. One student, who had left college to join his people, stated his reasons for doing so:

"I got reason to stay," he said. "Those people back home, they need help. Thirteen people died in the last month back there (on his tribe's reservation in Nebraska). And they died from things like colds and other diseases that people don't die from anymore. They need help bad, so I'm staying here. We're trying. Maybe if we can do something here it might change things for the people back there on the reservation."

One leader, Richard Oakes, left the island with his family after his eldest daughter was killed in a fall down a stairway. And as the months go by, others leave, disillusioned by quarrels and boredom. For a brief period the Indians of Alcatraz had become a popular cause; but gradually, once again, most Americans forgot about them. A few held out on the Rock, some found ways to get poverty program funds. For most of the assembled invaders looking toward mainland America there was no place to go. To their backs was the sea.

In May 1970 the Department of the Interior declared that Alcatraz Island would be converted into a National Park. The Indians on the island rejected the government's plan. On the following day the government cut off the electric and water supply.

Introduction to Indian Documents

The complexity and richness of Indian life, and the special quality of the Indians' relationship to the physical environment have been unknown to most Americans. The Indians had no written language until the middle of the nineteenth century and the whites, not understanding the high regard Indians had for their orators, grew impatient with what they thought was only endless "palavering."

The real feelings and attitudes of Indians, the ways in which they saw their culture threatened, have remained unknown to all but a small handful of whites. The documents in this section reveal, dramatically, how lopsided and narrow is the perception of most non-Indians about the original inhabitants of the continent.

Here, in intricately woven, closely reasoned speeches, Indians voice, often with great beauty of phrase, how they feel about the world in which they live. And here, too, are some of the great debates among the Indians over what policies they should adopt toward the people who had so intruded into their world.

(1)

Night Chant, a Navajo Poem*

The White man finds it hard to understand how an Indian can live as the Navajo do in their desert wilderness, in a harsh climate, bitterly cold at night and like a hot oven when the sun is high. The ancient Navajo "Night Chant" tells, eloquently, how the Indian sees the world in which he lives.

House made of dawn,
House made of evening light,
House made of the dark cloud . . .
Dark cloud is at the house's door,
The trail out of it is dark cloud,
The zigzag lightning stands high upon it . . .
Happily may I walk.
Happily, with abundant showers, may I walk.
Happily, with abundant plants, may I walk.
Happily, on the trail of pollen, may I walk.
Happily may I walk.
May it be beautiful before me.
May it be beautiful behind me.
May it be beautiful below me.
May it be beautiful above me.
May it be beautiful all around me.
In beauty it is finished.†

* "Navajo Poem," John Collier, *On the Gleaming Way* (Denver: Sage Books, Inc., 1962).
† Washington Matthews' translation.

(2)

Columbus' Description of the First Indians
He Encountered*

> In this excerpt from a letter of
> Christopher Columbus, he de-
> scribes his own actions toward the
> first natives he encountered and
> their attitude to him.

As soon as I arrived in the Indies, on the first island
which I found, I took some of the natives by force, in order
that they might learn and might give me information of
whatever there is in these parts. And so it was that they
soon understood us, and we them, either by speech or signs,
and they have been very serviceable. At present, those I
bring with me are still of the opinion that I come from
Heaven, for all the intercourse which they have had with
me. They were the first to announce this wherever I went,
and the others went running from house to house, and to
the neighbouring towns, with loud cries of "Come! Come!
See the men from Heaven!" So all came, men and women
alike, when their minds were set at rest concerning us, not
one, small or great, remaining behind, and they all brought
something to eat and drink, which they gave with extraordinary affection.

(3)

An Indian Chief's Criticism of
French Civilization†

> Many Indians were convinced that
> their way of life was not only equal
> to that of the whites, but even su-
> perior to it. Here, an Indian chief
> in Nova Scotia reproves the French
> for their mistaken belief in the
> greatness of French civilization.

* *Journal of Christopher Columbus,* trans. by Cecil Jane. (New York:
Clarkson N. Potter, 1960, pp. 196–97.)
† Indian Chief in Nova Scotia speaking to French, excerpt from
LeClercq, *New Relations in Gaspesia,* in *Indian Voices,* Feb., 1965.

Thou reproachest, very unappropriately, that our country is a little hell on earth in contrast with France, which thou comparest to a terrestrial paradise, insomuch that it yields thee, so thou sayest, every kind of abundance. Thou say of us also that we are most miserable and most unhappy of all men, living without religion, without manners, without honour, like the beasts in our woods and forests, lacking bread, wine, and thousands of other comforts, which thou hast in superfluity in Europe. Well, my brother, if thou doest not yet know the real feelings which our Indians have towards thy Country and towards all thy nations, it is proper I should inform thee at once.

I beg thee now to believe that, all miserable as we seem in thy eyes, we consider ourselves nevertheless much happier than thou, in this that we are very content with what we have . . . thou deceivest thyselves greatly if thou thinkest to persuade us that thy country is better than ours. For if France, as thou sayest, is a little terrestrial paradise, art thou sensible to leave it? And why abandon wives, children, relatives, and friends? Why risk thy lives and thy property every year? And why venture thyself with such risk in any season whatsoever, to the storms and tempests of the sea in order to come to a strange and barbarous country which thou considerest the poorest and least fortunate of all the world. Besides because we are wholly convinced of the contrary we scarce take the trouble to go to France because we fear with good reason, least [lest] we find little satisfaction there, seeing in our own experience that those who are natives thereof leave it every year in order to enrich themselves on our shores. We believe, further, that you are also incomparably poorer than we, and that you are only simple journeymen, valets, servants, and slaves, all masters and Grand Captains though you may appear, seeing that you glory in our rags, and in one miserable suit of beaver which can no longer be of use to us, and that you find among us the fishing for cod that you make in these parts, the wherewithall to comfort your miseries and poverty which oppress you. As to us, we find all our riches and all our conve-

niences among ourselves, without trouble, without exposing
our lives to the dangers in which you find yourselves constantly through your long voyages and whilst feeling compassion for you in the sweetness of our repose, we wonder
at the anxieties and cares which you give yourselves, night
and day, in order to load your ships. We see that all your
people live, as a rule, on cod which you catch among us.
. . . It is everlastingly nothing but cod—cod in the morning, cod at midday, cod at evening, and always cod, until
things come to pass that if you wish some good morsel it is
at our expense, and you are obliged to have recourse to the
Indians (whom you despise so much), and to beg them to
go a-hunting that you may be regaled. Now tell me this one
little thing, if thou hast any sense, which of these two is the
wisest and happiest. He who labours without ceasing and
only obtains at that with great trouble, enough to live on, or
he who rests in comfort and finds all he needs in the
pleasure of hunting and fishing? Learn now my brother
once and for all, for I must open my heart to thee. There is
no Indian that does not consider himself infinitely more
happy and powerful than the French.

(4)

Chief Flying Hawk's Account of the
Massacre at New Amsterdam*

> Chief Flying Hawk of the Dakota
> Sioux was a living book of Indian
> history. Here, he tells what hap-
> pened to the tribe that sold Man-
> hattan Island to the Dutch.

The Indians had befriended the helpless adventurers
when they came among them, and for their kindness the

---

* Chief Flying Hawk, "New Amsterdam Massacre," as told to M. I.
McCreight (Tchanta Tanka), Chief Flying Hawk's Tales (New York:
Alliance Press, 1936).

settlers attacked them one night and killed more than a hundred and twenty men, women, and children while they were asleep in their wigwams. This was about the first massacre. But it was a white-man massacre of Indians. They ran their bayonets through the stomachs of little babies and flung them out into the river. They cut off the hands of the men and cut open the women with their swords. They went among them with a torch of fire and burned their homes until no Indians were left; and these all were friendly Indians who sold the white people their island for needles, awls, and fish-hooks, and brought the furs to them. (This was in 1642 under Kieft's regime.)

The white man's account of this affair tells us that on February 25 at midnight Kieft sent Sergeant Rodolf with a party of soldiers to Pavonia and another party under Adriensen to Corlear's Hook where they rushed in upon the sleeping families and killed them all in the most hideous butchery that can be found in American annals.

An eye witness records it in these words: "I remained at the Director's (Kieft) and took a seat in the Kitchen near the fire. At midnight I heard loud shrieks and went out on the parapet of the fort to look—at the flash of guns. I heard no more of the cries of the Indians; they were butchered in their sleep. Sucklings were torn from their mothers' breasts, butchered before their mothers' eyes and their mangled limbs thrown quivering into the river or the flames. Babes were hacked to pieces while fastened to the boards; others were thrown alive into the river, and when the parents rushed in to save them the soldiers prevented them from landing." DeVries said of it: "some came running to us from the country having their hands cut off; some lost both arms and legs; and some were supporting their entrails with their hands, and mangled in other horrid ways, too horrible to be conceived."

The white man's own history refers to this massacre in the following language: "This crime has hardly a parallel in the annals of savage atrocities, directed as it was, upon a friendly village of harmless, unsuspecting Indians."

(5)
"Responses of Indians to Religious Questions"*

> On March 8, 1644, a Sagamore chief and four other members of the tribe put themselves under the protection of the Massachusetts Colony and agreed to be instructed in Christianity. The document gives the questions they were asked and their answers.

1st. Will you worship the only true God, who made heaven and earth, and not blaspheme? *Ans.* "We do desire to reverence the God of the English and to speak well of Him, because we see He doth better to the English, than other gods do to others." 2d. Will you cease from swearing falsely? *Ans.* "We know not what swearing is." 3d. Will you refrain from working on the Sabbath, especially within the bounds of Christian towns? *Ans.* "It is easy to us,—we have not much to do any day, and we can well rest on that day." 4th. Will you honor your parents and all your superiors? *Ans.* "It is our custom to do so,—for inferiors to honor superiors." 5th. Will you refrain from killing any man without just cause and just authority? *Ans.* "This is good, and we desire so to do." 6th. Will you deny yourselves fornication, adultery, incest, rape, sodomy, buggery, or bestiality? *Ans.* "Though some of our people do these things occasionally, yet we count them naught and do not allow them." 7th. Will you deny yourselves stealing? *Ans.* "We say the same to this as to the 6th question." 8th. Will you allow your children to learn to read the word of God, so that they may know God aright and worship him in his own way? *Ans.* "We will allow this as opportunity will

---

* "Responses of Indians to Religious Questions," Joseph B. Felt, *History of Ipswich, Essex and Hamilton* (Cambridge, Mass.: Charles Folsom, 1834).

permit, and, as the English live among us, we desire so to do." 9th. Will you refrain from idleness? *Ans.* "We will." After Masconnomet and the other chiefs had thus answered, they present the Court with twenty-six fathoms of wampum. The Court, in return, order them five coats, two yards each, of red cloth, and a pot full of wine.

(6)

Benjamin Franklin Explains How Indians Relate to the Gospel*

Benjamin Franklin tried, with patience and humility, to understand the Indians and their way of life. In these pages, from his writings on political economy, Franklin explains certain aspects of Indian culture which most of his contemporaries did not understand.

A Swedish minister, having assembled the chiefs of the Susquehanna Indians, made a sermon to them, acquainting them with the principal historical facts on which our religion is founded; such as the fall of our first parents by eating an apple, the coming of Christ to repair the mischief, his miracles and suffering, &c. When he had finished, an Indian orator stood up to thank him. "What you have told us," says he, "is all very good. It is indeed bad to eat apples. It is better to make them all into cider. We are much obliged by your kindness in coming so far, to tell us those things which you have heard from your mothers. In return, I will tell you some of those we have heard from ours.

"In the beginning, our fathers had only the flesh of animals to subsist on; and, if their hunting was unsuccessful, they were starving. Two of our young hunters, having killed a deer, made a fire in the woods to broil some parts of it. When they were about to satisfy their hunger, they beheld a

* *Works* of Benjamin Franklin, Vol. II, ed. Jared Sparks (Boston: Hilliard, Gray & Co., 1836).

beautiful young woman descend from the clouds, and seat herself on that hill, which you see yonder among the Blue Mountains. They said to each other, it is a spirit that perhaps has smelt our broiling venison, and wishes to eat of it; let us offer some to her. They presented her with the tongue; she was pleased with the taste of it, and said, 'Your kindness shall be rewarded; come to this place after thirteen moons, and you shall find something that will be of great benefit in nourishing you and your children to the latest generations.' They did so, and, to their surprise, found plants they had never seen before; but which, from that ancient time, have been constantly cultivated among us, to our great advantage. Where her right hand had touched the ground, they found maize; where her left hand had touched it, they found kidney-beans; and where her backside had sat on it, they found tobacco." The good missionary, disgusted with this idle tale, said, "What I delivered to you were sacred truths; but what you tell me is mere fable, fiction, and falsehood." The Indian, offended, replied, "My brother, it seems your friends have not done you justice in your education; they have not well instructed you in the rules of common civility. You saw that we, who understand and practice those rules, believed all your stories; why do you refuse to believe ours?"

When any of them come into our towns, our people are apt to crowd round them, gaze upon them, and incommode them, where they desire to be private; this they esteem great rudeness, and the effect of the want of instruction in the rules of civility and good manners. "We have," say they, "as much curiosity as you, and when you come into our towns, we wish for opportunities of looking at you; but for this purpose we hide ourselves behind bushes, where you are to pass, and never intrude ourselves into your company."

(7)

Chief Old Tassel Refuses the White Demand for More Land*

Again and again, Indians attempted to explain the principles of Indian life to the whites. But they succeeded only rarely. In this speech, made during a set of treaty negotiations in the 1780s, Chief Old Tassel, a Cherokee, tells the whites why he refuses to accept their demands for more land.

It is surprising that when we enter into treaties with our fathers the white people, their whole cry is more land. Indeed it has seemed a formality with them to demand what they know we dare not refuse. But on the principles of fairness of which we have received assurance during the conduct of this treaty I must refuse your demand.

What did you do? You marched into our towns with a superior force. Your numbers far exceeded us, and we fled to the strongholds of our woods, there to secure our women and children. Our towns left to your mercy. You killed a few scattered and defenseless individuals, spread fire and desolation wherever you pleased, and returned to your own habitations.

If you term this a conquest, you have overlooked the most essential point. You should have fortified the junction of Holston and Tennessee Rivers, and thereby conquered all the waters above. It is now too late for us to suffer from your mishap of generalship. Will you claim our lands by right of conquest? No! If you do, I will tell you that WE marched over them, even up to this very place; and some of our young warriors whom we have not had opportunity to recall are still in the woods and continue to keep your people in fear.

Much has been said of the want of what you term "civilization" among the Indians. Many proposals have been made

* Chief Old Tassel, excerpt from John P. Brown, *Old Frontiers,* (Kingsport, Tenn.: 1938) in *Indian Voices,* December, 1964.

to us to adopt your laws, your religions, your manners, and your customs. We do not see the propriety of such a reformation. We should be better pleased with beholding the good effect of these doctrines in your own practices than with hearing you talk about them, or of reading your papers to us on such subjects. You say, "Why do not the Indians till the ground and live as we do?" May we not ask with equal propriety, "Why do not the white people hunt and live as we do?"

We wish, however, to be at peace with you, and to do as we would be done by. We do not quarrel with you for the killing of an occasional buffalo or deer on our lands, but your people go much farther. They hunt to gain a livelihood. They kill all our game; but it is very criminal in our young men if they chance to kill a cow or a hog for their sustenance when they happen to be in your lands.

The Great Spirit has placed us in different situations. He has given you many advantages, but he has not created us to be your slaves. We are a separate people! He has stocked your lands with cows, ours with buffalo; yours with hogs, ours with bears; yours with sheep, ours with deer. He has given you the advantage that your animals are tame, while ours are wild and demand not only a larger space for range, but art to hunt and kill them. They are, nevertheless, as much our property as other animals are yours, and ought not to be taken from us without our consent, or for something of equal value.

(8)

The Indians Rebuff a Missionary*

> To many Indian tribes, the missionaries were a continual source of irritation. In 1805, Red Jacket, an Iroquois chief, explained to a young Christian evangelist why he was being denied permission to set up a mission in the Indian country.

* "The Indians Rebuff a Missionary," in *The American Spirit—United States History as Seen by Contemporaries,* Vol. I, ed. Thomas A. Bailey (Boston: D. C. Heath & Co., 1963 and 1968).

Brother, listen to what we say.

There was a time when our forefathers owned this great island [continent]. Their seats extended from the rising to the setting sun. The Great Spirit had made it for the use of Indians. . . .

But an evil day came upon us. Your forefathers crossed the great water and landed on this island. Their numbers were small. They found friends and not enemies. They told us they had fled from their own country for fear of wicked men, and had come here to enjoy their religion. They asked for a small seat. We took pity on them; granted their request; and they sat down amongst us. We gave them corn and meat; they gave us poison [liquor] in return.

The white people, brother, had now found our country. Tidings were carried back and more came amongst us. Yet we did not fear them. We took them to be friends. They called us brothers. We believed them and gave them a larger seat. At length their numbers had greatly increased. They wanted more land; they wanted our country. Our eyes were opened and our minds became uneasy. Wars took place. Indians were hired to fight against Indians, and many of our people were destroyed. They also brought strong liquor amongst us. It was strong and powerful and has slain thousands.

Brother, our seats were once large and yours were small. You have now become a great people, and we have scarcely a place left to spread our blankets. You have got our country, but are not satisfied. You want to force your religion upon us.

Brother, continue to listen.

You say that you are sent to instruct us how to worship the Great Spirit agreeably to his mind; and, if we do not take hold of the religion which you white people teach us, we shall be unhappy hereafter. You say that you are right and we are lost. How do we know this to be true? We understand that your religion is written in a book. If it was intended for us, as well as you, why has not the Great Spirit given to us, and not only to us, but why did he not give to our forefathers the knowledge of that book, with the means of understanding it rightly? We only know what you tell us about it. How shall we know when to believe, being so often deceived by the white people?

Brother, you say there is but one way to worship and serve the Great Spirit. If there is but one religion, why do you white people differ so much about it? Why not all agreed, as you can all read the book?

Brother, we do not understand these things. We are told that your religion was given to your forefathers, and has been handed down from father to son. We also have a religion, which was given to our forefathers and has been handed down to us, their children. We worship in that way. It teaches us to be thankful for all the favors we receive, to love each other and to be united. We never quarrel about religion.

Brother, the Great Spirit has made us all, but he has made a great difference between his white and red children. He has given us different complexions and different customs. To you he has given the arts. To these he has not opened our eyes. We know these things to be true. Since he has made so great a difference between us in other things, why may we not conclude that he has given us a different religion according to our understanding? The Great Spirit does right. He knows what is best for his children. We are satisfied.

Brother, we do not wish to destroy your religion or take it from you. We only want to enjoy our own.

Brother, you say you have not come to get our land or our money, but to enlighten our minds. I will now tell you that I have been at your meetings and saw you collect money from the meeting. I cannot tell what this money was intended for, but suppose that it was for your minister; and, if we should conform to your way of thinking, perhaps you may want some from us.

Brother, we are told that you have been preaching to the

white people in this place. These people are our neighbors. We are acquainted with them. We will wait a little while and see what effect your preaching has upon them. If we find it does them good, makes them honest, and less disposed to cheat Indians, we will then consider again of what you have said.

Brother, you have now heard our answer to your talk and this is all we have to say at present. As we are going to part, we will come and take you by the hand, and hope the Great Spirit will protect you on your journey and return you safe to your friends.

(9)

Chief Tecumseh's Plea for Resistance*

> Tecumseh, a Shawnee chief, was one of the greatest Indian leaders. He attempted to weld an alliance of many tribes to resist the whites. In this speech, made in 1812, he tried to convince a Choctaw and Chickasaw Council of the need to fight the Americans.

In view of questions of vast importance, have we met together in solemn council tonight. Nor should we here debate whether we have been wronged and injured, but by what measures we should avenge ourselves; for our merciless oppressors, having long since planned out their proceedings, are not about to make, but have and are still making attacks upon those of our race who have as yet come to no resolution. Nor are we ignorant by what steps, and by what gradual advances, the whites break in upon our neighbors. Imagining themselves to be still undis-

* Chief Tecumseh, excerpt from H. B. Cushman, *History of the Indians* (Greenville, Texas, 1899), in *Indian Voices*, September, 1964.

covered, they show themselves the less audacious because
you are insensible. The whites are already nearly a match
for us all united, and too strong for any one tribe alone to
resist; so that unless we support one another with our
collective and united forces; unless every tribe unanimously
combines to give a check to the ambition and avarice of the
whites, they will soon conquer us apart and disunited, and
we will be driven away from our native country and
scattered as autumnal leaves before the wind.

But have we not courage enough remaining to defend
our country and maintain our ancient independence? Will
we calmly suffer the white intruders and tyrants to enslave
us? Shall it be said of our race that we knew not how to
extricate ourselves from the three most to be dreaded
calamities—folly, inactivity, and cowardice? . . .

Sleep no longer, o Choctaws and Chickasaws, in false
security and delusive hopes. Our broad domains are fast
escaping from our grasp. Every year our white intruders
become more greedy, exacting, oppressive, and overbearing. Every year contentions spring up between them and
our people and when blood is shed we have to make
atonement whether right or wrong, at the cost of the lives of
our greatest chiefs, and the yielding up of large tracts of our
lands. Before the pale-faces came among us, we enjoyed the
happiness of unbounded freedom, and were acquainted
with neither riches, wants, nor oppression. How is it now?
Wants and oppressions are our lot; for are we not controlled in everything, and dare we move without asking, by
your leave? Are we not being stripped day by day of the
little that remains of our ancient liberty? Do they not even
now kick and strike us as they do their black-faces? How
long will it be before they will tie us to a post and whip us,
and make us work for them in cornfields as they do them?
Shall we wait for that moment or shall we die fighting
before submitting to such ignominy? . . . The annihilation
of our race is at hand unless we unite in one common cause
against the common foe. Think not, brave Choctaws and
Chickasaws, that you can remain passive and indifferent to

the common danger, and thus escape the common fate. Your people too, will soon be as falling leaves and scattering clouds before their blighting breath. You too will be driven away from your native land and ancient domains as leaves are driven before the wintry storms.

Have we not for years had before our eyes a sample of their designs, and are they not sufficient harbingers of their future determinations? Will we not soon be driven from our respective countries and the graves of our ancestors? Will not the bones of our dead be plowed up, and their graves be turned into fields? Shall we calmly wait until they become so numerous that we will no longer be able to resist oppression? Will we wait to be destroyed in our turn, without making an effort worthy our race? Shall we give up our homes, our country, bequeathed to us by the Great Spirit, the graves of our dead, and everything that is dear and sacred to us, without a struggle? I know you will cry with me. Never! Never! Then let us by unity of action destroy them all, which we now can do, or drive them back whence they came. War or extermination is now our only choice. Which do you choose, brave Choctaws and Chickasaws, to assist in the just cause of liberating our race from the grasp of our faithless invaders and heartless oppressors. The white usurpation in our common country must be stopped or we, its rightful owners, be forever destroyed and wiped out as a race of people. I am now at the head of many warriors backed by the strong arm of English soldiers. Choctaws and Chickasaws, you [have] too long borne with grievous usurpation inflicted by the arrogant Americans.

Be no longer their dupes. If there be one here tonight who believes that his rights will not sooner or later, be taken from him by the avaricious American pale-faces, his ignorance ought to excite pity, for he knows little of the character of our common foe. And if there be one among you mad enough to undervalue the growing power of the white race among us, let him tremble in considering the fearful woes he will bring down upon our entire race, if by his criminal indifference he assists the designs of our common enemy against our common country. Then listen to the voice of duty, of honor, of nature, and of your endangered country. Let us form one body, one heart, and defend to the last warrior our country, our homes, our liberty, and the graves of our fathers.

Choctaws and Chickasaws, you are among the few of our race who sit indolently at ease. You have indeed enjoyed the reputation of being brave, but will you be indebted for it more from report than fact? Will you let the whites encroach upon your domains even to your very door before you will assert your rights in resistance? Let no one in this council imagine that I speak more from malice against the pale-face Americans than just grounds of complaint. Complaint is just toward friends who have failed in their duty; accusation is against enemies guilty of injustice; especially when such great acts of injustice have been committed by them upon our race, of which they seem to have no manner of regard, or even to reflect. They are a people fond of innovations, quick to contrive and quick to put their schemes into effectual execution, no matter how great the wrong and injury to us; while we are content to preserve what we already have. Their designs are to enlarge their possessions by taking yours in turn; and will you, can you longer dally, o Choctaws and Chickasaws? Do you imagine that people will not continue longest in the enjoyment of peace who timely prepare to vindicate themselves, and manifest a determined resolution to do themselves right whenever they are wronged? Far otherwise. Then haste to the relief of our common cause, as by consanguinity of blood you are bound; lest the day be not far distant when you will be left singlehanded and alone to the cruel mercy of our most inveterate foe.

(10)

Pushmataha's Reply to Tecumseh*

> Tecumseh's plea for unified Indian
> resistance to the Americans was
> answered by another Indian ora-
> tor, Pushmataha, the Choctaw.
> Pushmataha's speech was a decisive
> factor in influencing the Choctaws
> and Chickasaws that they should
> not join with Tecumseh.

It was not my design in coming here to enter into a
disputation with anyone. But I appear before you, my
warriors and my people, not to throw in my plea against the
accusations of Tecumseh; but to prevent your forming rash
and dangerous resolutions upon things of highest importance, through the instigations of others. I have myself
learned by experience, and I also see many of you, o
Choctaws and Chickasaws, who have the same experience
of years that I have, the injudicious steps of engaging in an
enterprise because it is new. Nor do I stand up before you
tonight to contradict the many facts alleged against the
American people, or to raise my voice against them in useless accusations. The question before us now is not what
wrongs they have inflicted upon our race, but what measures are best for us to adopt in regard to them; and though
our race may have been unjustly treated and shamefully
wronged by them, yet I shall not for that reason alone
advise you to destroy them unless it was just and expedient
for you so to do; nor would I advise you to forgive them,
though worthy of your commiseration, unless I believe it
would be to the interest of our common goal. We should
consult more in regard to our future welfare than our
present. What people, my friends and countrymen, were so
unwise and inconsiderate as to engage in a war of their own
accord, when their own strength, and even the aid of others,

* Pushmataha's Reply, excerpt from H. B. Cushman, *History of the
Indians* (Greenville, Texas, 1899), in *Indian Voices,* December, 1964.

was judged unequal to the task? I well know, causes often
arise which force men to confront extremities, but, my
countrymen, those causes do not now exist. Reflect, therefore, I earnestly beseech you, before you act hastily in this
great matter and consider with yourselves how greatly you
will err if you injudiciously approve of and inconsiderately
act upon Tecumseh's advice. Remember the American
people are now friendly disposed toward us. . . . My
friends and fellow countrymen! you now have no just cause
to declare war against the American people, or wreak your
vengeance upon them as enemies, since they have ever
manifested feelings of friendship toward you. It is besides
inconsistent with your national glory and with your honor,
as a people, to violate your solemn treaty; and a disgrace to
the memory of your forefathers, to wage war against the
American people merely to gratify the malice of the
English.

The war, which you are now contemplating against the
Americans, is a flagrant breach of justice; yea, a fearful
blemish on your honor and also that of your fathers, and
which you will find if you will examine it carefully and
judiciously, forbodes nothing but destruction to our entire
race. It is a war against a people whose territories are now
far greater than our own, and who are far better provided
with all necessary implements of war, with men, guns,
horses, wealth, far beyond that of all our race combined,
and where is the necessity or wisdom to make war upon
such a people? Where is our hope of success, if thus weak
and unprepared we should declare it against them? Let us
not be deluded with the foolish hope that this war, if begun,
will soon be over, even if we destroy all the whites within
our territories, and lay waste their homes and fields. Far
from it. It will be but the beginning of the end that termi-
nates in the total destruction of our race. And though we
will not permit ourselves to be made slaves, or, like inexperienced warriors, shudder at the thought of war, yet I am
not so insensible and inconsistent as to advise you to
cowardly yield to the outrages of the whites, or willfully to

connive at their unjust encroachments; but only not yet to have recourse to war, but to send ambassadors to our Great Father at Washington, and lay before him our grievances, without betraying too great eagerness for war, or manifesting any tokens of pusillanimity.

Heed not, o my countrymen, the opinions of others to that extent as to involve your country in a war that destroys its peace and endangers its future safety, prosperity and happiness. Reflect, ere it be too late, on the great uncertainty of war with the American people, and consider well, ere you engage in it, what the consequences will be if you should be disappointed in your calculations and expectations. Be not deceived with illusive hopes. Hear me, o my countrymen, if you begin this war it will end in calamities to us from which we are now free and at a distance; and upon whom of us they will fall, will only be determined by the uncertain and hazardous event. Be not, I pray you, guilty of rashness, which I never as yet have known you to be; therefore, I implore you, while healing measures are in the election of us all, not to break the treaty, nor violate your pledge or honor, but to submit our grievances, whatever they may be, to the Congress of the United States, according to the articles of the treaty existing between us and the American people. If not, I here invoke the Great Spirit, who takes cognizance of oaths, to bear me witness, that I shall endeavor to avenge myself upon the authors of this war, by whatever methods you shall set me an example.

We are not a people so impertinently wise as to invalidate the preparations of our enemies by a plausible harangue, and then absolutely proceed to a contest; but we reckon the thoughts of the pale-faces to be of a similar cast with our own, and that hazardous contingencies are not to be determined by a speech. We always presume that the projects of our enemies are judiciously planned, and then we seriously prepare to defeat them. Nor do we found our success upon the hope that they will certainly blunder in their conduct, but upon the hope that we have omitted no proper steps for our own security. Such is the discipline which our fathers have handed down to us; and by adhering to it, we have reaped many advantages. Let us, my countrymen, not forget it now, nor in short space of time precipitately determine a question in which so much is involved. It is indeed the duty of the prudent, so long as they are not injured, to delight in peace. But it is the duty of the brave, when injured, to lay peace aside, and to have recourse to arms; and when successful in these, to then lay them down again in peaceful quiet; thus never to be elevated above measure by success in war, nor delighted with the sweets of peace to suffer insults. For he who, apprehensive of losing the delight, sits indolently at ease, will soon be deprived of the enjoyment of that delight which interesteth his fears; and he whose passions are inflamed by military success, elevated too high by a treacherous confidence, hears no longer the dictates of judgement.

Many of the schemes, though unadvisedly planned, through the more unreasonable conduct of an enemy, which turn out successfully; but more numerous are those which, though seemingly founded on mature counsel, draw after them a disgraceful and opposite result. This proceeds from the great inequality of spirit with which an exploit is projected, and with which it is put into actual execution. For in council we resolve, surrounded with security; into execution we faint, through the prevalence of fear. Listen to [the] voice of prudence, o, my countrymen, ere you rashly act. But do as you may, know this truth, enough for you to know, I shall join our friends, the Americans, in this war.

(11)

Logan the Mingo Chief Explains His War on Whites*

> "I have neither wife, nor child, nor sister to howl for me," Logan, a Mingo chief, said to Lord Dunsmore in 1774, as he explained why he had made war upon the white man.

* Mingo Chief Logan, *Cherokee Advocate*, Vol. I, No. 8 (Nov. 16, 1884).

My cabin since first I made one of my own has ever been open to any white man who wanted shelter. My spoils of hunting, since first I began to range these woods, have ever freely imparted to appease his hunger and clothe his nakedness. *But what have I seen? What?* But that at my return at night and laden with spoil my numerous family lie bleeding on the ground by the hands of those who had found my little hut a certain refuge from the inclement storm—who had eaten my food and covered themselves with my skins. *What have I seen? What?* But that those dear little mouths for which I had sweated the livelong day when I returned at eve to fill them had not one word to thank me for my toil.

What could I resolve upon? My blood boiled within me and my heart leapt up to my mouth. Nevertheless, I bid my tomahawk be quiet and lie at rest for that war because I thought the great men of your country sent them not to do it. Not long afterwards, some of your men invited our tribe to cross the river and bring their venison with them. They, unsuspicious of design, came as they had been invited. The white men then made them drop, killed them, and turned their knives even against the women. Was not my sister among them? Was she not scalped by the hands of that man whom she had taught how to escape his enemies when they were scenting out his track? What could I resolve upon? My blood now boiled thrice hotter than before and thrice again my heart leapt up to my mouth. No longer did I bid my tomahawk be quiet and lie at rest for that war; because I no longer thought the men of your country sent them not to do it. I sprang from my cabin to avenge their blood; which I have fully done this war by shedding yours from your coldest to your hottest sun. Thus revenged, I am now for peace and have advised most of my countrymen to be so too. Nay, what is more I have offered and still offer myself as a victim, being ready to die, if their good require it.

Think not that I am afraid to die; for I have no relations left to mourn for me. Logan's blood runs in no veins but these. I would not turn my heel to escape death; for I have neither wife, nor child, nor sister to howl for me when I am gone.

(12)

An Iroquois Tells of His Tribe's History*

In May, 1847, at a Meeting of the
New York Historical Society, a paper was given on the Ancient Trails
and Territorial Boundaries of the
Iroquois. After the paper had been
delivered, one member of the society got up to announce that an
Iroquois was present at the meeting
who should be allowed to speak.
The Indian did talk about a statement made by his white predeces-
sor on the floor: "The Iroquois had
left no monuments." The Indian
said:

The honorable gentleman has told you that the Iroquois
had left no monuments. Did he not previously prove that
land of Ganono-o or 'Empire State' as you love to call it
was once laced by our trails from Albany to Buffalo—trails
that we had trod for centuries—trails worn so deep by the
feet of the Iroquois that they became your own roads of
travel as your possessions gradually eat into those of my
people? Your roads still traverse those same lines of communication and bind one part of 'long house' to another.
The land of Ganono-o, the Empire State, then is our
monument! We shall not long occupy much room in living;
the single tree of the thousands which sheltered our forefathers—one old elm under which the representatives of the
tribes were wont to meet—will cover us all; but we would
have our bodies twined in death among its roots, on the
very soil on whence it grew! Perhaps it will last no longer
for being fertilized by their decay. . . .

I have been told that the first object of this society is to
preserve the history of this State of New York.—You, all of

* "Iroquois Speech," in *Literary World* (1847).

you know that alike in its wars and its treaties the Iroquois long before the Revolution formed a part of that history; that they were one in council with you and were taught to believe themselves one in interest. In your last war with England, your red brother—your elder brother—still came up to help you as of old on the Canada frontier! Have we, the first holders of this prosperous region, no longer a share in your history? Glad were your fathers to sit upon the threshold of the "long house," rich did they then hold themselves in getting the mere sweepings from its door.

Had our forefathers spurned you from it when the French were thundering at the opposite end to get a passage through and drive you into the sea? Whatever has been the fate of other Indians, the Iroquois might still have been a nation; and I—I instead of pleading for the privilege of lingering within your borders—I—I might have had—a country!

(13)

President Andrew Jackson's Warning Letter to the Seminoles*

When Andrew Jackson became President, he was able to carry out what he believed to be the correct policy toward Indians—removal from their own lands. In this letter, written in 1835, he tells the Seminole tribe what is in store for them if they do not obey his orders to them.

My Children—I am sorry to have heard that you have been listening to bad counsel. You know me, and you know that I would not deceive, nor advise you to do anything that was unjust or injurious. Open your ears and attend to what I shall now say to you. They are the words of a friend, and the words of truth.

* "President Andrew Jackson's Letter to the Seminoles," Henry Trumbull, *History of the Indian Wars* (Boston: George Clark, 1841).

The white people are settling around you. The game has disappeared from your country. Your people are poor and hungry. All this you have perceived for some time. . . .

My Children, I have never deceived, nor will I ever deceive any of the red people. I tell you that you must go, and that you will go. Even if you had a right to stay, how could you live where you now are? You have sold all your country. You have not a piece as large as a blanket to sit down upon. What is to support yourselves, your women, and children? The tract you have ceded will soon be surveyed and sold, and immediately afterwards will be occupied by a white population. You will soon be in a state of starvation. You will commit depredations upon the property of our citizens. You will be resisted, punished, perhaps killed. Now is it not better peaceably to remove to a fine, fertile country, occupied by your own kindred, and where you can raise all the necessaries of life, and where game is yet abundant? The annuities payable to you, and the other stipulations made in your favor, will make your situation comfortable, and will enable you to increase and improve. If, therefore, you had a right to stay where you now are, still every true friend would advise you to remove. But you have no right to stay, and you must go. I am very desirous that you should go peaceably and voluntarily. You shall be comfortably taken care of, and kindly treated on the road, and when you arrive in your new country, provisions will be issued to you for a year, so that you can have ample time to provide for your future support.

But lest some of your rash young men should forcibly oppose your arrangements for removal, I have ordered a large military force to be sent among you. I have directed the commanding officer, and likewise the agent, your friend Gen. Thompson, that every reasonable indulgence be held out to you. But I have also directed that one third of your people, as provided for in the treaty, be removed during the present season. If you listen to the voice of friendship and truth, you will go quietly and voluntarily. But should you listen to the bad birds that are always flying about you, and refuse to move, I have then directed the commanding officer to remove you by force. This will be done. I pray the Great Spirit, therefore, to incline you to do what is right.

Your Friend,
A. Jackson
Washington, February 16, 1835

(14)

Chief Sealth's Prediction*

> The eloquence of the Indians stemmed directly from the strength of their belief in the Indian ways of life. Even when they knew they were doomed, they defended their convictions as did Chief Sealth when he addressed a treaty negotiating party in 1855. It is reported that he spoke in Duwamish, because he would not use either English or the Chinook jargon.

. . . Our good father at Washington—for I presume he is now our father as well as yours, since King George has moved his boundaries further north—our great good father, I say, sends us word that if we do as he desires he will protect us. His brave warriors will be to us a bristling wall of strength, and his wonderful ships of war will fill our harbors so that our ancient enemies far to the northward—the Hydas and Tsimshians—will cease to frighten our women, children, and old men. Then in reality will he be our father and us his children.

But can that ever be? Your God is not our God! Your God loves your people and hates mine. He folds his strong and protecting arms lovingly about the pale-face and leads him by the hand as a father leads his infant son—but He has forsaken His red children—if they are really his. Our God, the Great Spirit, seems also to have forsaken us. Your

---

* Speech of Chief Sealth, in *An Uncommon Controversy*. Prepared for the American Friends Service Committee (National Congress of American Indians, Sept., 1967).

God makes your people wax strong every day. Soon they will fill the land. Our people are ebbing away like a rapidly receding tide that will never return.

The white man's God cannot love our people or He would protect them. They seem to be orphans who can look nowhere for help. How then can we be brothers? How can your God become our God and renew our prosperity and awaken us in dreams of returning greatness? If we have a common heavenly father He must be partial—for He came to his pale-face children. We never saw Him. He gave you laws but He had no words for His red children whose teeming multitudes once filled this vast continent as stars filled the firmament. No; we are two distinct races with separate origins and separate destinies. There is little in common between us.

Day and night cannot dwell together. The red man has ever fled the approach of the white man, as morning mist flees before the morning sun. However, your proposition seems fair and I think my people will accept it and will retire to the reservation you offer them. Then we will dwell apart in peace, for the words of the Great White Chief seem to be the words of nature speaking to my people out of dense darkness.

It matters little where we pass the remnant of our days. They will not be many. A few more moons; a few more winters—and not one of the descendants of the mighty hosts that once moved over this broad land or lived in happy homes, protected by the Great Spirit, will remain to mourn over the graves of a people once more powerful and hopeful than yours. But why should I mourn at the untimely fate of my people? Tribe follows tribe, and nation follows nation, like the waves of the sea. It is the order of nature, and regret is useless. Your time of decay may be distant, but it will surely come, for even the white man whose God walked and talked with him as friend with friend, cannot be exempt from the common destiny. We may be brothers after all. We will see.

And when the last red man shall have perished, and the

memory of my tribe shall have become a myth among the white men, these shores will swarm with the invisible dead of my tribe, and when your children's children think themselves alone in the field, the store, the shop, upon the highway, or in the silence of the pathless woods, they will not be alone. . . . At night when the streets of your cities and villages are silent and you think them deserted, they will throng with the returning hosts that once filled and still love this beautiful land. The white man will never be alone.

(15)

Chief Joseph's Lament Over the Forced Removal of His Tribe*

The Nez Percé (Pierced Nose) Indians were a proud tribe of the Northwest, led by Chief Joseph, an amazing man. Joseph refused to accept an order removing the tribe from their lands in Oregon and putting them into Idaho. He fought the whites over a territory of a thousand miles until he was finally caught, in 1877, near Canada. Then, what was left of the tribe was sent to the Indian Territory where they died by the score. Chief Joseph appealed to the President for help, and went to Washington to plead, successfully, for the return of his people to the Northwest. Here he tells his story.

I have heard talk and talk, but nothing is done. Good words do not last long unless they amount to something. Words do not pay for my dead people. They do not pay for my country, now overrun by white men. They do not protect my father's grave. They do not pay for my horses and cattle.

Good words do not give me back my children. Good

* "Chief Joseph's Lament," in *The American Spirit—United States History as Seen by Contemporaries,* Vol. II, ed. Thomas A. Bailey (Boston: D. C. Heath & Co., 1963 and 1968).

words will not make good the promise of your war chief, General Miles. Good words will not give my people good health and stop them from dying. Good words will not get my people a home where they can live in peace and take care of themselves.

I am tired of talk that comes to nothing. It makes my heart sick when I remember all the good words and all the broken promises. There has been too much talking by men who had no right to talk. Too many misinterpretations have been made; too many misunderstandings have come up between the white men and the Indians.

If the white man wants to live in peace with the Indian, he can live in peace. There need be no trouble. Treat all men alike. Give them the same laws. Give them all an even chance to live and grow.

All men are made by the same Great Spirit Chief. They are all brothers. The earth is the mother of all people, and all people should have equal rights upon it. You might as well expect all rivers to run backward as that any man who was born a free man should be contented penned up and denied liberty to go where he pleases. If you tie a horse to a stake, do you expect he will grow fat? If you pen an Indian up on a small spot of earth and compel him to stay there, he will not be contented nor will he grow and prosper.

I have asked some of the Great White Chiefs where they get their authority to say to the Indian that he shall stay in one place, while he sees white men going where they please. They cannot tell me.

I only ask of the government to be treated as all other men are treated. If I cannot go to my own home, let me have a home in a country where my people will not die so fast. I would like to go to Bitter Root Valley [western Montana]. There my people would be healthy; where they are now, they are dying. Three have died since I left my camp to come to Washington. When I think of our condition, my heart is heavy. I see men of my own race treated as outlaws and driven from country to country, or shot down like animals.

I know that my race must change. We cannot hold our own with the white men as we are. We only ask an even chance to live as other men live. We ask to be recognized as men. We ask that the same law shall work alike on all men. If an Indian breaks the law, punish him by the law. If a white man breaks the law, punish him also.

Let me be a free man—free to travel, free to stop, free to work, free to trade where I choose, free to choose my own teachers, free to follow the religion of my fathers, free to think and talk and act for myself—and I will obey every law or submit to the penalty. . . .

(16)

The Department of Interior Views the Indian*

> These documents illustrate, clearly, how the government viewed its "paternal" role towards Indians. Unlike some of the military, the officials of the Department of Interior were not committed to the physical destruction of the Indians; all they wanted to do was wipe them out, culturally, and impose upon them all the values of the white society.

The special attention of Indian agents is directed to the following copy of Department letter, viz:

Department of the Interior,
Washington, December 2, 1882.
Sir:

I desire to call your attention to what I regard as a great hindrance to the civilization of the Indians, viz, the continuance of old heathenish dances, such as the sun-dance, scalp-dance, &c. These dances, or feasts, as they are sometimes called, ought, in my judgment, to be discontinued, and if the Indians now supported by the Government are not

---

* Letters, from H. M. Teller, Secretary of Department of Interior, to Col. S. F. Tappan, in *Regulations of the Indian Department* (Washington, D.C.: Government Printing Office, 1884).

willing to discontinue them, the agents should be instructed to compel such discontinuance. These feasts or dances are not social gatherings for the amusement of these people, but, on the contrary, are intended and calculated to stimulate the warlike passions of the young warriors of the tribe. At such feasts the warrior recounts his deeds of daring, boasts of his inhumanity in the destruction of his enemies, and his treatment of the female captives, in language that ought to shock even a savage ear. The audience assents approvingly to his boasts of falsehood, deceit, theft, murder, and rape, and the young listener is informed that this and this only is the road to fame and renown. The result is the demoralization of the young, who are incited to emulate the wicked conduct of their elders, without a thought that in so doing they violate any law, but, on the contrary, with the conviction that in so doing they are securing for themselves an enduring and deserved fame among their people. Active measures should be taken to discourage all feasts and dances of the character I have mentioned.

The marriage relation is also one requiring the immediate attention of the agents. While the Indians remain in a state of at least semi-independence, there did not seem to be any great necessity for interference, even if such interference was practicable (which it doubtless was not). While dependent on the chase the Indian did not take many wives, and the great mass found themselves too poor to support more than one; but since the Government supports them, this objection no longer exists, and the more numerous the family the greater the number of the rations allowed. Some system of marriage should be adopted, and the Indian compelled to conform to it. The Indian should also be instructed that he is under obligations to care for and support, not only his wife, but his children, and on his failure, without proper cause, to continue as the head of such family, he ought in some manner to be punished, which should be either by confinement in the guardhouse or agency prison, or by a reduction of his rations.

The value of property as an agent of civilization ought

not to be overlooked. When an Indian acquires property, with a disposition to retain the same, free from tribal or individual interference, he has made a step forward in the road to civilization. One great obstacle to the acquirement of property by the Indian is the very general custom of destroying or distributing his property on the death of a member of his family.

It will be extremely difficult to accomplish much towards the civilization of the Indians while these adverse influences are allowed to exist.

The Government having attempted to support the Indians until such time as they shall become self-supporting, the interest of the Government as well as that of the Indians demands that every possible effort should be made to induce them to become self-supporting at as early a day as possible. I therefore suggest whether it is not practicable to formulate certain rules for the government of the Indians on the reservations that shall restrict and ultimately abolish the practices I have mentioned. I am not ignorant of the difficulties that will be encountered in this effort; yet I believe in all the tribes there will be found many Indians who will aid the Government in its efforts to abolish rites and customs so injurious to the Indians and so contrary to the civilization that they earnestly desire.

Very respectfully,
H. M. Teller
Secretary

The general policy of the Department in regard to Indian education is defined in the following letter:

Department of the Interior,
Washington, April 24, 1884.

Col. S. F. Tappan,
Genoa, Nebr.
Dear Sir:

I take this occasion to give you my idea of the proper course to be pursued in the purchase of clothing, food, &c., and the general training of the children in your school. In the first place, allow me to say, while I consider it very desirable that they should receive some instruction in book knowledge, I do not consider that the main object of their attendance at school. That education is the best which enables a person to take care of himself to the best advantage. He who can feed and clothe himself without the assistance of others is at least partially educated, whether he can read or not. The boy that has seen his father plow, mow, and gather the fruits of the field will do it without special instruction; not so with an Indian. He must be taught how to hold the plow, how to prepare and keep in order his scythe, when to put in and when to harvest his crop, and a thousand things acquired by farmers' sons by observation must be taught specially to an Indian youth. But, above all, the Indian boy must be taught the value of steady, continuous labor. He must be trained to do what he has never seen done and what he has been taught it is not manly to do. I want to impress on your mind that if you must neglect either, it should be his literary studies, and not his manual labor exercises. I much prefer to know that he can plow, sow, and harvest, than to know that he has made great attainments in a literary way. I write this because I fear there is a very general disposition to overlook the great advantage of the instruction intended to enable him to support himself.

I desire also to call your attention to the necessity of strict economy in the management of your financial affairs. The limit per capita will be doubtless in the vicinity of one hundred and seventy-five dollars. It appears to me that with the advantages of the farm you ought to be able to keep within that sum, and still furnish all that is required for the proper care and improvement of the children. You must remember that the children have not come from luxurious homes, and when they leave school they will return to the reservation to take care of themselves. Great care should be exercised that they do not acquire habits of living that will be so far above their ability to meet, that they will become discouraged and fail to be benefited by their schooling. They will have plenty of good land, and if they have acquired habits of industry and economy, they will be able to take care of themselves in comfort, but not in luxury. I think all the appointments about the school should be plain and inexpensive. They should be accustomed to plain clothes and plain living, having only occasionally enough of the luxuries of life to stimulate them to endeavor to secure for themselves all the advantages of civilization.

I want as little as possible done with machinery, and I shall be pleased to know that you do your farm labor without the use of mowing-machines and reapers if possible. Very few Indians will be able to purchase expensive machinery with which to carry on farming operations, and they should be taught to sow grain by hand, cultivate corn with plow and hoe, and cut grass with scythe and grain with hand cradle, and to care for it after it is cut.

I also suggest that you should teach both boys and girls to milk cows. The girls should be taught to make butter, cheese, and curds, as well as do all the household work, such as cooking, washing, and making and mending clothes.

Very respectfully,
H. M. Teller
Secretary

(17)

Chief Flying Hawk Describes Custer's Last Battle*

Surely the most famous battle of the Indian Wars was Custer's Last Stand, immortalized in paintings, songs, stories, articles, movies, television and radio shows. The battle came about because, in 1874, Custer found gold on land belonging to the Sioux and held sacred by them; the Indians refused to sell the land and whites, rushing into the

* Chief Flying Hawk, "The True Story About Custer's Last Fight," as told to M. I. McCreight (Tchanta Tanka), *Chief Flying Hawk's Tales* (New York: Alliance Press, 1936).

area, refused to leave. The government finally ordered the Indians
onto reservations, in violation of
the Treaty of 1868, and sent soldiers in to force them. Custer attacked a large encampment of Indians on the Little Big Horn River.
In this account, Chief Flying Hawk
describes how he and Crazy Horse
fought Custer's troops.

Crazy Horse and I left the crowd and rode down along
the river. We came to a ravine; then we followed up the
gulch to a place in the rear of the soldiers that were making
the stand on the hill. Crazy Horse gave his horse to me to
hold along with my horse. He crawled up the ravine to
where he could see the soldiers. He shot them as fast as he
could load his gun. They fell off their horses as fast as he
could shoot. (Here the chief swayed rapidly back and forth
to show how fast they fell.) When they found they were
being killed so fast, the ones that were left broke and ran as
fast as their horses could go to some other soldiers that were
further along the ridge toward Custer.

By that time all the Indians in the village had got their
horses and guns and watched Custer. When Custer got
nearly to the lower end of the camp, he started to go down
a gulch, but the Indians were surrounding him, and he tried
to fight. They got off their horses and made a stand but it
was no use. Their horses ran down the ravine right into the
village. The squaws caught them as fast as they came. One
of them was a sorrel with white stocking. Long time after
some of our relatives told us they had seen Custer on that
kind of a horse when he was on the way to the Big Horn.

When we got them surrounded the fight was over in one
hour. There was so much dust we could not see much, but
the Indians rode around and yelled the war-whoop and shot
into the soldiers as fast as they could until they were all
dead. One soldier was running away to the east but Crazy
Horse saw him and jumped on his pony and went after him.
He got him about a half a mile from the place where the
others were lying dead. The smoke lifted so we could see a

little. We got off our horses and went and took the rings and money and watches from the soldiers. We took some clothes off too, and all the guns and pistols. We got seven hundred guns and pistols. Then we went back to the women and children and got them together that were not killed or hurt.

It was hard to hear the women singing the death-song·for the men killed and for the wailing because their children were shot while they played in the camp. It was a big fight; the soldiers got just what they deserved this time. No good soldiers would shoot into the Indian's tepee where there were women and children. These soldiers did, and we fought for our women and children. White men would do the same if they were men.

We did not mutilate the bodies, but just took the valuable things we wanted and then left. We got a lot of money, but it was of no use.

We got our things packed up and took care of the wounded the best we could, and left there the next day. We could have killed all the men that got into the holes on the hill, but they were glad to let us alone, and so we let them alone too.

(18)

Vine Deloria, Jr., Writes a Satirical History*

> Vine Deloria, Jr., is one of the young and articulate Indians who are rising to leadership within the Indian community. In this article, written for *Indian Voices,* Deloria presents a version of American history as it might have been if Indians had written it.

FROM THE ARCHIVES OF THE NATIONAL CONGRESS OF AMERICAN INDIANS

February 12, 1510 We had a real crisis today. Another "Big Canoe" pulled up on the beach and another European

---

* "Satirical History," Vine Deloria, Jr., *Indian Voices* (Jan., 1966).

got out. He is from Italy like Chris Columbus was and his
name is Americus Vespucci. We have been running into
quite a few Italians lately and they seem to share this Indian
kick. Anyway the horrible thought suddenly occurred to the
tribal council. It seems that since Columbus landed everyone has been calling us "Indians." We have pretty well convinced them that it is not India, but we know that sooner or
later they will find a name for our country. They might do
some nutty thing like name it after one of these Europeans,
such as our guest. Then I suppose they would call it "America" and since they still insist on calling us Indians we could
end up with the tab of "American Indians" instead of our
tribal names. That is something to contemplate but the
council thinks it will never happen.

February 19, 1510 More news than ever. Today was a
special meeting of the coast tribes to lay down some ground
rules on these immigrants. We passed a resolution for some
Immigration legislation at the next NCAI [National Council of American Indians] convention. Many believe that we
will have to impose strict quotas on these people and keep
this land for the Redman. We call these people Birch-
barkers as they raise cain at every meeting with their bark-
ing until even the birches are swaying. We can't help feeling
that we might be setting all kinds of bad precedents. One
chief wanted to limit immigration to those with skills, but
we can't find any with skills, none can hunt, few can fish,
the rest simply tear up the forests and glades, throw up
dams, kill the fish, pollute the streams. One saw a town of
ours and wanted to buy up the land for a "shopping
center." Another wanted to start "suburbs" and the whole
thing got so complicated that we simply moved the town to
another part of the coast. Then one showed up and com-
plimented us on "urban renewal." It seems that they are so
restless and feel that if they are not doing something they
are being sinful. I should relate an experience that I had so
that future generations will know how crazy these people
are. I was sitting on the bank fishing when one of them

came up and started talking to me about work. He pointed out that I had made no preparations for the future, and I replied that I had everything I wanted. He suggested that I work and save and pretty soon I would have great riches. So I asked him why I should have great riches and he said that then I would retire from my work and have a vacation. I asked what I would do on a vacation and he said hunt and fish. I replied, "I'm doing that now."

(19)

Devil's Lake Sioux,* 1965

> Homer Bigart's account, in the *New York Times,* of his visit to Fort Totten Reservation, is a matter-of-fact, unemotional description of what Bigart describes as a "new, native American slum." The article was written in 1965, but it could have been done in 1970 as well.

Among the Devil's Lake Sioux, at Fort Totten, there is almost a total lack of employment. Even the members of the tribal council, with the exception of the chairman, Louis Goodhouse, are on relief.

The Fort Totten Reservation, poor in land and sparse in population, runs south and west of Devil's Lake, a huge salty slough that collects drainage from the surrounding countryside. Lacking an outlet, the stagnant lake is evil-smelling in summer; Indians recall that in 1934 the stench was so bad that some lakeside dwellers moved away. A barrage of low, wooded hills marks the southern shore. . . .

On the plain is the hamlet of Tokio, a group of white clapboard houses nagged by the March winds, huddling for warmth beside the Great Northern Railway track. Tokio has been deserted by its white population except for a few farmers, and the Indians have moved into Main Street,

* "Devil's Lake Sioux," Homer Bigart, *New York Times,* as reprinted in *Indian Voices* (Feb. & Mar., 1966).

converting the old bank, the grocery and the dry goods store into dwellings.

The tribal chairman, Mr. Goodhouse, and Richard H. Cavanaugh, former chief judge of the tribal court, escorted a visitor through this new, native American slum. Down by the railroad track, half-hidden by snowdrifts, was the shell of an old Great Northern coach. Mr. Goodhouse called out and, getting no reply, kicked open the door. A naked light bulb glowed at the far side of the coach revealing a sign: "What's home Without a Mother?" Three beds, littered with dirty blankets, hugged a wood stove in the center of the room. Mr. Goodhouse said the place was occupied by a Mrs. Katie DeWolf and two sons and that they were apparently gathering wood.

The DeWolfs had endured the winter by stuffing rags in the coach windows and patching the door with pieces of tin. They had fashioned a kitchen annex out of old boards. Snow from the last blizzard had sifted through the cracks and lay a foot deep around an old refrigerator. Three cats and two dogs leaped from the beds and gathered expectantly around a battered cupboard that Mr. Goodhouse opened. "Flour, dry milk, cornmeal," he announced over the mewing and whimpering of the animals. It was dank, cold and sour smelling inside the coach.

The visitors left quickly and drove to the other side of Tokio where, in a bleak, one-room shack on a hilltop, Albert Roy and his crippled wife were sitting by the stove. "They got money to keep those things spinning around all the time," grumbled Mr. Roy, his hand making an orbit, "but they say they haven't money enough to give us a house . . ."

The room was clean and warm enough. Mrs. Roy had put an old rug on the floor but it had worn through in big spots, revealing the damp, rotting boards. There were religious pictures on the walls and a portrait of President Kennedy with the designation: "A Leader Lost to This World."

Mr. Roy produced a letter. He had asked the Farmers Home Administration for a loan and now he had his reply.

The letter, couched in bureaucratic jargon, seemed unnecessarily cruel.

It said: "In reaching a decision on each application, the county committee takes into consideration the applicant's debts, integrity, reputation for industry and repayment of debts, and the amount of credit needed.

"In your case the committee feels that you lack character and honesty, and have no way of repaying a loan.

"If you have any questions concerning this action or desire further information, we shall be glad to discuss it with you. Our office day is Monday. Very truly yours."

Mr. Roy conceded that he had been arrested for drunkenness. "But he's a scholar and a gentleman," the former chief judge concurred.

Next stop was the cabin of Dick Walking Bull, a Sioux whose rambling shack was on a wooden hill near a ski jump for non-Indians. Walking Bull was not home, but his wife, holding the youngest of her five children, silently escorted visitors through the hovel.

It had turned warm. Melted snow dribbled through the roof, coming so fast that the kitchen looked like the inside of a shower bath. Mrs. Walking Bull had abandoned the kitchen and was cooking on the heating stove of her bedroom. In the adjacent room, crowded with beds, her children waited to be fed. George Washington, Abraham Lincoln, and John F. Kennedy looked down from the walls.

(20)

An Indian Youth Asks His Peers: "Which One Are You?"*

The profound changes taking place among the young Indians today have resulted in the creation of new organizations which make new

* "Which One Are You?," by Clyde Warrior, in Stan Steiner, *The New Indians* (New York: Harper & Row, 1968).

demands upon the Indians themselves and the white society. Pride
in "Indianness" and a willingness
to reject the values of the dominant society are two of the characteristics which separate these
new Indians from the older generations. Clyde Warrior, who was
president of the National Indian
Youth Council, analyzes five different types of young Indians living in America today.

Among American Indian youth today there exists a
rather pathetic scene, in fact, a very sick, sad, sorry scene.
This scene consists of the various types of Indian students
found in various institutions of learning throughout American society. It is very sad that these institutions, and whatever conditioning takes place, creates these types. For these
types are just what they are, types, and not full, real human
beings, or people.

Type A—SLOB OR HOOD. This is the individual who receives his definition of self from the dominant society, and
unfortunately, sees this kind in his daily relationships and
associations with his own kind. Thus, he becomes this type
by dropping out of school, becomes a wino, steals, eventually becomes a court case, and is usually sent off. If lucky,
he marries, mistreats his family, and becomes a real pain to
his tribal community as he attempts to cram that definition
[of himself] down the society's throat. In doing this, he
becomes a Super-Slob. Another Indian hits the dust through
no fault of his own.

Type B—JOKER. This type has defined himself that to be
an Indian is a joke. An Indian does stupid, funny things.
After defining himself, from cues society gave him, he
proceeds to act as such. Sometimes he accidentally goofs-
up, sometimes unconsciously on purpose, after which he
laughs, and usually says, "Well, that's Indian." And he goes
through life a bungling clown.

Type C—REDSKIN "WHITE-NOSER" OR THE SELL-OUT.
This type has accepted and sold out to the dominant so-

ciety. He has accepted that definition that anything Indian is dumb, usually filthy, and immoral, and to avoid this is to become a "LITTLE BROWN AMERICAN" by associating with everything that is white. He may mingle with Indians, but only when it is to his advantage, and not a second longer than is necessary. Thus, society has created the fink of finks.

Type D—ULTRA-PSEUDO-INDIAN. This type is proud that he is Indian, but for some reason does not know how one acts. Therefore he takes his cues from non-Indian sources, books, shows, etc., and proceeds to act "Indian." With each action, which is phony, we have a person becoming unconsciously phonier and phonier. Hence, we have a proud, phony Indian.

Type E—ANGRY NATIONALIST. Although abstract and ideological, this type is generally closer to true Indianness than the other types, and he resents the others for being ashamed of their own kind. Also, this type tends to dislike the older generation for being "Uncle Tomahawks" and "yes men" to the Bureau of Indian Affairs and whites in general. The "Angry Nationalist" wants to stop the current trend toward personality disappearance, and institute changes that will bring Indians into contemporary society as real human beings; but he views this, and other problems, with bitter abstract and ideological thinking. For thinking this [he] is termed radical, and [he] tends to alienate himself from the general masses of Indians, for speaking what appears, to him, to be truths.

None of these types is the ideal Indian. . . .

It appears that what is needed is genuine contemporary creative thinking, democratic leadership to set guidelines, cues and goals for the average Indian. The guidelines and cues have to be *based on true Indian philosophy geared to modern times*. This will not come about without nationalistic pride in one's self and one's own kind.

This group can evolve only from today's college youth. Not from those who are ashamed, or those who have sold out, or those who do not understand true Indianism. Only from those with pride and love and understanding of the

People and the People's ways from which they come can this evolve. And this appears to be the major task of the National Indian Youth Council—for without a people, how can one have a cause?

This writer says this because he is fed up with religious workers and educationalists incapable of understanding, and pseudo-social scientists who are consciously creating social and cultural genocide among American Indian youth.

I am fed up with bureaucrats who try to pass off "rules and regulations" for organizational programs that will bring progress.

I am sick and tired of seeing my elders stripped of dignity and low-rated in the eyes of their young.

I am disturbed to the point of screaming when I see American Indian youth accepting the horror of "American conformity," as being the only way for Indian progress. While those who do not join the great American mainstream of personalityless neurotics are regarded as "incompetents and problems."

The National Indian Youth Council must introduce to this sick room of stench and anonymity some fresh air of new Indianness. A fresh air of new honesty, and integrity, a fresh air of new Indian idealism, a fresh air of a new Greater Indian America.

How about it? Let's raise some hell!

(21)

An Indian Review of "Stalking Moon"*

> More than any other art form, the movies have created an image of Indians held by millions and millions of people all over the world. Here, in an Indian newspaper, a young Indian girl reviews a contemporary film about her people.

* "Stalking Moon," a movie review by Annette Little Horn, *The Native Nevadan* (July, 1969).

Well, I was not too thrilled by this so-called "thriller," but I was somewhat bewildered. As the story goes, according to the blushing confession of the leading lady, she submitted to the "ferocious savage" Salvaje in order to save her life. She became his wife and bore his son. Now right away this confuses me. If he was such a ferocious savage, then why didn't he just have his way with the dear lady and then simply kill her. How come he made her his wife and allowed her to have his child? Well, anyhow—this pitiful little white woman went along for ten years, watching her son grow up, pretending not to hate. But suddenly, after ten years, she meets up with her own kind of people, that is to say, the civilized whites. She promptly seeks asylum for herself and her son, begging a good old army scout to take them along, which he does.

Meantime, Salvaje realizes his son has taken an unexplained trip with the little mother, and for some reason he sets out after them. Surely not because he loves them. Meanwhile we see that the good old scout and the little white lady have set up housekeeping and they're going to keep the little half-savage son also, presumably to teach him the niceties of life. There are a couple of fights along the way; in one, Salvaje emerges as a hateful fiend after wiping out several able-bodied white men at the stagecoach station; in the other fight, a weary, bedraggled but oh so heroic scout succeeds in killing that same ferocious fiend. After which the two pure lilywhites, all virtuously victorious, fade off into the sunset with Salvaje's son and the beautiful civilized prospect of the boy to be raised by his father's killer.

The way I see it, Salvaje risked his life and lost it, to try to regain his son, who was taken from him by an irresponsible, selfish woman. It seems quite natural for a man to get furious when his wife takes his child, deserts him, and goes off to play house with another man.

I really liked the little boy.

(22)

Proclamation to the Great White Father and All His People*

In November of 1969, a group of Indians seized the island of Alcatraz in San Francisco Bay, which was occupied only by some caretakers on the old prison site. In the first pan-tribal effort in the 20th century, they made arrangements to stay there indefinitely, refusing the orders of government officials to leave. The following proclamation sets forth their claim to the island.

PROCLAMATION:
TO THE GREAT WHITE FATHER AND ALL HIS PEOPLE

We, the native Americans, re-claim the land known as Alcatraz Island in the name of all American Indians by right of discovery.

We wish to be fair and honorable in our dealings with the Caucasian inhabitants of this land, and hereby offer the following treaty:

We will purchase said Alcatraz Island for twenty-four dollars ($24) in glass beads and red cloth, a precedent set by the white man's purchase of a similar island about 300 years ago. We know that $24 in trade goods for these 16 acres is more than was paid when Manhattan Island was sold, but we know that land values have risen over the years. Our offer of $1.24 per acre is greater than the 47¢ per acre that the white men are now paying the California Indians for their land.

We will give to the inhabitants of this island a portion of that land for their own, to be held in trust by the American Indian Affairs and by the bureau of Caucasian Affairs to

* Proclamation: To the Great White Father and All His People, Indians of all Tribes, San Francisco, California.

hold in perpetuity—for as long as the sun shall rise and the rivers go down to the sea. We will further guide the inhabitants in the proper way of living. We will offer them our religion, our education, our life-ways, in order to help them achieve our level of civilization and thus raise them and all their white brothers up from their savage and unhappy state. We offer this treaty in good faith and wish to be fair and honorable in our dealings with all white men.

****

We feel that this so-called Alcatraz Island is more than suitable for an Indian Reservation, as determined by the white man's own standards. By this we mean that this place resembles most Indian reservations in that:

1. It is isolated from modern facilities, and without adequate means of transportation.
2. It has no fresh running water.
3. It has inadequate sanitation facilities.
4. There are no oil or mineral rights.
5. There is no industry and so unemployment is very great.
6. There are no health care facilities.
7. The soil is rocky and non-productive; and the land does not support game.
8. There are no educational facilities.
9. The population has always exceeded the land base.
10. The population has always been held as prisoners and kept dependent upon others.

Further, it would be fitting and symbolic that ships from all over the world, entering the Golden Gate, would first see Indian land, and thus be reminded of the true history of this nation. This tiny island would be a symbol of the great lands once ruled by free and noble Indians.

THE BLACKS

*T*he Chronicles have been written, but not all goes by
the legend. We must hurry to invent a few new myths."
                                    Pablo Armando Fernández,
                                    Barracks and Nets

"The Nation has not yet found peace from its sins. . . ."
                                    W. E. B. Du Bois,
                                    The Souls of Black Folk

"The crisis in race relations," reported the editors of *Fortune* in 1968, "is of manageable proportions."[1] The optimistic spokesmen for perhaps the most socially conscious segment of American business reassured their readers that "the gloom that enshrouded our cities after the 1967 riots was based partly on an overstatement of the problem and partly on an underestimate of the resources we could bring to bear on it."

Their optimism rested, in part, on the conclusion that "things were not as bad as they seemed. Negroes' incomes,

[1] *Fortune, The Negro and the City,* Time–Life Books, 1968, p. 153.

jobs, housing, and education have been getting significantly better in recent years—and Negroes, in general, know it." The *Fortune* editors then called for "systematic thinking" about the problem, including the active participation of the business community in coping with problems government agencies had been unable to resolve. The reader finished the report with the happy thought that businessmen had at last joined the fight for better race relations, that America's worst racial crises were over, and the outlook for the future bright.

The *Fortune* argument, one expressed by liberal integrationists, assumes that since the statistics indicate improvements for blacks, their rebellious fervor will abate accordingly. It postulates that the more miserable and oppressed a people are, the more revolutionary their behavior will be.

Just the opposite is the case. At no time in American history have blacks been freer or "better off." Yet at no time have they been more militant, more willing to express their deep hatreds. The more they acquire, the more they understand American racism. They have become more open to new ideas and more politically active as a people.

The editors of *Fortune* were confident of their view because a 1967 survey of more than 300 blacks in 13 cities showed that more people trusted Martin Luther King than Stokely Carmichael and that more blacks felt violence was unnecessary in achieving Negro objectives. Actually the figures in the 1967 survey showed that 49 percent of the people trusted Stokely Carmichael, from "very much" to a "little," and that 44 percent of northern blacks felt violence was necessary to achieve their objectives. Furthermore, only 12 percent of those interviewed saw total integration as a desirable goal. In 1970 even fewer blacks view integration as desirable or feasible. If a survey were done today on what percentage of blacks participate, or would participate, in direct action, or any action, the results might indicate a larger promilitant percentage than expected.

Liberalism has proved itself incapable of offering a program or solution that deals effectively with even the most superficial aspects of American race relations. Lip service is paid to the "raw deal" blacks got in the past, but "that's over and done with" and now the attitude is that "we can wipe the slate clean" and start afresh, especially if "they" will be "reasonable."

For the American black to be "reasonable" meant first slavery, then systematic exclusion from the benefits of the American way of life. Yet it turns out that only when they behave "unreasonably" are some of their demands met with quick and direct action. So rather than accepting slow and gradual improvements, they have turned more and more to demanding everything—now. And the more they demand the more they see how incapable the American system is of providing.

In 1960 integration was an acceptable goal among most politically conscious blacks and whites, both inside and outside the Establishment. But by the late 1960s, as the *Fortune* survey actually revealed, only 12 percent of blacks thought of full integration as desirable—to say nothing of possible. The fact that most blacks now reject integration as an objective indicates that accommodation is no longer important. This does not mean, however, that black separatism or nationalism can or will provide an adequate program for the needs of blacks. But whites can no longer dictate the terms for blacks, even though blacks are still a long way from achieving the full equality set out in the Declaration of Independence almost 200 years ago.

By the late 1960s Americans were willing to acknowledge a racial problem with roots as deep as that of American society itself. Racism, hatred, and brutality have been transmitted through men and institutions for more than 300 years. The importance of slavery and racism in America's past should be obvious to everyone. But we are not a people who are conscious of our past. We have been hypnotized by the celebration of democracy, frontier individualism, and our ever expanding destiny, all couched in changing liberal rhetoric.

In recent years a "shock of recognition" has led blacks to

try to separate their history from American history. Black studies programs and Negro history courses—now changed to black history—are offered by many colleges and universities. They were often forced by strikes and demonstrations—or the threat of them—for inclusion in the curriculum.

There is neither black history, nor white history in America. American history is, in part, the unfolding of the relationship between two transplanted peoples: the white Europeans who came to the New World to find wealth and religious freedom and the blacks who were brought here as slaves. To understand today's racial crisis, we must look not only at the present conflicts as expressed in opposing demands and cries, but into the past that laid the foundation for the current American dilemma.

The early colonists came to found a civilization in a barbarous land where they hoped they could worship God in peace, and flourish. The white Christians saw themselves as God's highest creations, the closest thing to angels on an imperfect earth. But they had decided that the black man did not fit this image. He did not look the same, act the same, speak the same language, or worship the same God. He was associated with filth and his color was attributed to God's punishment for his earlier sins. This black man, born in the land of the apes, had been brought to the New World, the colonists rationalized, for the sole purpose of laboring for the white man in a manner that befitted his low level of culture and his heathenism. He was an object, worthy only of hatred.

The first blacks arrived in 1619 on a Dutch slaver and were sold as slaves in Virginia. Most historians believe that these blacks were originally treated as indentured servants who could earn their freedom. Legal slavery did not exist at that time. But with the 1640 tobacco boom and the urgent need for labor, the southern colonies began to see the advantages of, even the "necessity" for, a legalized system of slavery to ensure their expanding economy. By 1663, after forty-four years of involuntary service in the southern fields, the blacks had proved themselves valuable, indeed necessary if the land was to be worked for large profits.

The legislature of Maryland put into law what had already been established in fact: that black slaves, and those who shall be imported, "shall serve *durante vita;* and all children born of any Negro or other slave, shall be slaves as their fathers were for the term of their lives." Sexual intercourse was forbidden between whites and blacks. No black was permitted to carry firearms, and certain restrictions were placed on everyday behavior. The economic need for slavery was paramount. Rationalizations for slavery began pouring forth from pulpits and legislatures. Few outright critics of this "peculiar institution" were heard. Only the Quakers protested against it.

Rules and regulations for white and black behavior were written into the colonial laws, sanctified by colonial churches, and philosophically rationalized in the early universities. What began as an economic arrangement became a complex way of life.

The American colonists, however, unlike other slaveholders, shared the English tradition of the rights of man. This made it impossible for them easily to accept slavery as part of "the nature of things," as for example some Arab cultures had done. American slavery had to be woven into a primitive democratic fabric, thus joining together direct opposites. What the establishment of slavery did to American democracy is perhaps clearer today than ever before. It embedded a racism into the laws, institutions, and ideology of the new country that is still evident today.

Resistance to slavery and racism became a tradition of American morality, from the early Quakers to the late Dr. Martin Luther King, Jr. Set against this tradition is the fact that slavery brutalized everyone involved with it, black and white. This brutalization continues more than one hundred years after slavery was abolished. Gunnar Myrdal wrote a book about the conflict and called it *An American Dilemma*. One hundred and fifty years earlier, John Quincy Adams and other moralists expressed a similar concern when they saw the power of the young nation being distorted by the racism being woven into its democratic fabric.

Because slavery worked so well, the Southern economy became dependent upon it, not only as the means to huge profits, but later on as an end in itself. The economic development of the South in the colonial period was based on tobacco, indigo, and other crops, which required a durable labor force. As indentured servants became harder to obtain—and more costly than slaves—use of the cheaper blacks became an economic imperative.

"A rational man," wrote a South Carolinian in 1682, "will certainly inquire 'when I have land, what shall I do with it? What commodities shall I be able to produce, that will yield me money in other countrys, that I may be inabled to buy Negro-slaves, without which a planter can never doe any great matter?' "[2]

"To live in Virginia without slaves is morally impossible," explained Reverend Peter Fontaine in a letter to his brother in 1757. Slavery had shaped the economy and society to such an extent that "we have no merchants, traders or artificers of any sort but what become planters in a short time."[3]

English and American slave traders profited from their human cargoes "that lie as close together as it is possible to be crowded."[4]

Padlocks "for blacks and dogs" were advertised by an English merchant. The brutalization of slaves began when they were sold or kidnapped in Africa and increased during the voyage to America. For the black, the nightmare had just begun. It is estimated that as many as 10,000,000 died or committed suicide during the voyages. At the New Orleans and Charleston auction blocks, the nightmare con-

---

[2] Stanley M. Elkins, *Slavery, A Problem in American Institutional and Intellectual Life*. The Universal Library, Grosset & Dunlap, N.Y., 1959, p. 48.

[3] Thomas A. Bailey, *The American Spirit*. Vol. I, Chapter 1, p. 18, D. C. Heath & Co., Boston, 1963.

[4] Gilbert Osofsky, *The Burden of Race*. Harper & Row, 1967, p. 2.

tinued. For example, if a slave had been lucky enough to be kidnapped or sold with another member of his family, he was often separated.

But the brutalization was not limited to the American continent or the ships at sea. Slavery also had its lasting effects on the African people left behind. African tribes who had previously enslaved their conquered enemies and extracted from them a kind of tribute, could now sell their victims to white traders. A good example of the horror of the process and some reactions to it is provided by Joseph Hawkins, who made a voyage to the African coast in 1793 to look for slaves. Hawkins described how the Ebo tribes, who had defeated the Golos, offered their prisoners for sale:

We found them confined in a large area within a thin stockade, on the outside of which was a trench: the inside was divided into parcels, and huts irregularly constructed, and at the entrance . . . was guarded by men with spears. . . . In the scene before me, the ear was not indeed dinned with the clanking of heavy fetters, but was horrible in its peculiar way. The captives were destitute . . . and bound indiscriminately together by the hands and legs, the cords being again fastened to the ground by stakes; they were loosed a few at a time once every day, when each was permitted to eat the only meal they were allowed, consisting of rice and palm oil. . . .[5]

Hawkins was horrified, but rationalized that the blacks would be better off in America:

I had often in the course of the voyage, and of the journey, rebuked myself for having embarked in the African trade, but found a consolation in the reflection, that it was not from a malicious inclination or avaricious disposition, that I had embarked on it, but from the pressing call of necessity, and at a time when my dissent could not alter or obstruct the undertaking. On the present occasion, however, I was fully convinced the removal of these poor wretches even into the slavery of the

[5] Joseph Hawkins, *Voyage to the Coast of Africa, 1797*, reprinted in Elizabeth Donnan, *Documents Illustrative of the History of the Slave to America*, Washington, D.C., 1935, Vol. IV, p. 495–96, published by Carnegie Institution of Washington.

West Indies, would be an act of humanity, rather than one exposed to censure.[6]

This argument was not uncommon even in the early days of slavery.

Hawkins also reported on what he saw of the blacks' reactions to their white captors: "The slaves that I had purchased were young men, many of whom being eager to escape from their bondage in Ebo, preferred the evil they 'knew not of' to that which they then felt; but the majority were evidently affected with grief at their approaching departure."[7]

Hawkins did not realize then, as most Americans still fail to do, that western slavery's impact on Africa was as great, if not greater, than its impact on America. Whatever the virtues or failings of African tribal culture before the opening of the American slave trade, the western system of slavery led to the destruction of those indigenous cultures and paved the way for colonization.[8]

Africa entered the world market and its product was human beings. Her mineral and animal treasures were nothing compared to the riches of slave trading. Some of the finest black men and women were sold to a culture that wanted only their labor. Whether the enslaved Golos had heard what their fate would be at the hands of the white man is unknown, but Hawkins described their reactions as being full of "sudden melancholy and deep sighs. Often did they look back with eyes flowing with tears, turn sudden round and gaze, seeming to part with reluctance, even from their former bondage." The fact that it was their land on which they were gazing, even though they had been captives there, did not occur to Hawkins. The slaves' melancholy "was excessively affecting to me . . . and I endeavoured to reconcile them to their condition, by representing flattering accounts of the country to which they were going; that the bonds they then bore were only to

6 *Ibid.,* p. 496.
7 *Ibid.,* p. 497.
8 Philip Curtin, *Africa Remembered.* University of Wisconsin Press, Madison, 1967.

prevent their flight; that they should be at liberty where they were going, and have plenty to eat and drink, etc."[9]

Hawkins was not an evil man, as the slave trader is usually portrayed. He was not cruel or sadistic. He described the scene in which the slaves were transferred to the ships " . . . necessarily in irons brought for the purpose. This measure occasioned one of the most affecting scenes I ever witnessed: their hopes with my assurances had buoyed them up on the road; but a change from the cordage to iron fetters, rent their hopes and hearts together: their wailings were torturing beyond what words can express: but delay at this crisis would have been fatal. . . ."[10]

Hawkins' descriptions provide insight, not only into the desensitizing of the character of white men connected with slavery, but also into the first indications of black resistance. He described the first reaction of passive resistance: "The slaves seemed every hour to feel their situation more grievously, and I ordered them each a dram of liquor which for a while exhilarated their spirits and quieted their cares. . . . We furnished the slaves with provisions, but whether through grief or sullenness, very few of them would partake of any refreshment beside water."[11]

Hawkins saw the blacks' efforts at resistance as spontaneous responses to their conditions, but in his report of their behavior it appears as though some kind of organized rebellion may have been planned. Organized slave rebellion was one of the planters' great fears, and the system of restraints they put on blacks was based on this fear. (Toussaint L'Ouverture's successful revolt in Haiti only intensified this fear.) Hawkins' report described the first rebellion of slaves as they were being transferred from small river boats to a larger ocean vessel:

They appeared generally more quiet, and willing to act as we directed by the interpreter than usual. . . . When we had got under weigh, and were passing through a narrow part of the

9 Donnan, *op. cit.,* p. 498.
10 *Ibid.*
11 *Ibid.*

river, two of them found means to jump overboard; a sailor . . . seized one of them by the arms. . . . The others, who had been at the oars, seeing their fellows, one of them seized and the other struck on the head with a pole, set up a scream, which was echoed by the rest below; those that were loose made an effort to throw two of the sailors overboard.[12]

Hawkins described in some detail the ensuing struggle in which he lost a finger. But the interesting thing about the struggle was the fact that it demonstrated the courage of the slaves. Although locked in irons, they tried to assist their comrades "by holding our legs, encouraging their companions, and shouting whenever those above did anything that appeared likely to overcome one or other of us."[13] The revolt was unsuccessful and all the slaves were locked in double irons. From then on Hawkins displayed none of his earlier compassion and appeared to have fully conditioned himself to the brutalities of his trade. "The officers had all provided themselves with three or four wives each, and rebuked me for not bringing mine along, alleging that they would . . . bring a good price when we arrived in America."[14]

There are few accounts of these early revolts from the slaves' points of view; few of them had learned to write. But the experience, orally transmitted to generations of slaves, must have intensified their feelings of hopelessness and helplessness—and the desire for freedom. Some of these feelings are expressed in spirituals. Analysis of early black music often reveals strong feelings about salvation (freedom) after death or the liberation of oppressed peoples by Biblical heroes.

Overseas slave trade was officially suppressed by Congress in 1807, but it continued illicitly as the market for field hands grew in the western states. The domestic slave trade, however, became a flourishing business and the transportation of blacks from the Eastern Seaboard to New

---

[12] *Ibid.*, pp. 498–99.
[13] *Ibid.*, p. 499.
[14] *Ibid.*

Orleans was as grisly as that of the Atlantic crossings. William Wells Brown, a slave who later escaped, described how the slaves were fixed up, like produce, for the New Orleans market:

In the course of eight or nine weeks Mr. Walker had his cargo of human flesh made up. There was in this lot a number of old men and women, some of them with grey locks. We left St. Louis in the steamboat . . . bound for New Orleans. . . . I had to prepare the old slaves for market. I was ordered to have the old mens' whiskers shaved off, and the grey hairs plucked out where they were not too numerous, in which case we had a preparation of blacking to color it. . . .[15]

Every slave received similar treatment, or worse, at some time in his life, or at least knew of others who did. Nothing was sacred; the slave had no rights and no security. And the people who subjected him to this treatment were Christians and democrats, and as fierce believers in their religion and political creed as any who existed in the world.

The brutalization of everyday life carried over into theology and politics, so that no area of human existence was untouched by the "peculiar institution." "Baptism," declared the Virginia Legislature in 1667, "makes no difference as to bondage or freedom."[16] This settled the religious question of the propriety of enslaving believers. The masters could now reveal the word of God to slaves and still keep them as chattels. (Later on the masters were very careful about which parts of the Bible they revealed to the slaves.)

Christianity was adjusted to the purposes of the masters, and then used to justify the enslavement of Africans because it saved their heathen souls.

In the seventeenth and eighteenth centuries, Puritan theologians concluded that the Lord permitted blacks to be slaves, but that did not preclude their hearing the Revealed Word. In fact, Cotton Mather opened a school for slaves

[15] "The Narrative of William Wells Brown: A Fugitive Slave," reprinted in Osofsky, *op. cit.*, p. 13.
[16] Benjamin Quarles, *Negro in the Making of America.* New York: Macmillan, 1964, p. 36.

and in 1706 published *The Negro Christianized: An Essay to Excite and Assist that Good Work, the Instruction of Negro-Servants in Christianity*. By 1710 Judge John Saffin of Massachusetts was convinced that "God . . . hath ordained different degrees and orders of men, some to be High and Honourable, some to be Low and Despicable . . . yes some to be born Slaves and so to remain during the rest of their lives, as hath been proved. Otherwise there would be a mere parity among men. . . ."[17] The Puritan theory of predestination was further adjusted *ad absurdum* by a magistrate whose ultimate reflection on slavery was the following question: whether those who have slaves "ought in Conscience to set them free, and so lose all the money they cost?"[18]

White society in the South shaped its laws, religion, and institutions around slavery, and the blacks shaped their lives as best they could around surviving in a society that denied them the fundamental rights of manhood and womanhood: the right to marry, to be parents, to have sexual choice. Human beings, even slaves, had enjoyed these rights in almost every other civilization known in the history of the world.

As the framers of the Declaration of Independence—many of them slaveholders—were drafting the most liberating political document yet known to man, black Americans were living in the most oppressive police state ever devised. White southerners, and many northerners, functioned as policemen, specifically charged with preventing blacks from escaping bondage and with maintaining constant vigilance over them to prevent uprisings.

The eighteenth century is called the Age of Enlightenment. History texts devote countless pages to analyzing the influence of Locke, Montesquieu, Rousseau, and the revolutionary European philosophers on the rights of man, on equality and freedom. Yet the foremost American advo-

---

[17] Williams Sumner Jenkins, *Proslavery Thought in the Old South*. Chapel Hill: University of North Carolina Press, 1955, p. 5.

[18] Arthur Zilversmit, *The First Emancipation*. Chicago: University of Chicago Press, 1967, p. 60.

cates of enlightenment were slave owners, some of whom practiced on their plantations the very opposite of what they preached in the colonial legislatures.

The continuation of slavery depended on keeping the blacks ignorant. In *My Bondage and My Freedom*, Frederick Douglass wrote:

> To make a contented slave, you must make a thoughtless one. It is necessary to darken his moral and mental vision, and, as far as possible to annihilate his power of reason. He must be able to detect no inconsistencies in slavery. The man that takes his earnings, must be able to convince him that he has a perfect right to do so. It must not depend on mere force; the slave must know no Higher Law than his master's will. The whole relationship must not only demonstrate, to his mind, its necessity, but its absolute rightfulness.[19]

The fact that there were enlightened or kind masters—some of whom taught their slaves to read and even freed them in their wills—is irrelevant. The kind and the sadistic masters, both, had entered into a brutal relationship with black men, women and children, whereby they *possessed* them whether they abused them or not. The very existence of slavery destroyed the humanity of the planter and the slave alike. Few American whites felt any guilt while slavery existed. Few blamed themselves for the plight of the black man, nor did many recognize the manifold effects of slavery upon themselves as well as their slaves.

The important fact about slavery was that its existence sanctioned almost any abuse practiced by one man upon another. For the master, it represented the destruction of the "inherent features of man" expressed in the Declaration of Independence. The "natural rights" of man Jefferson wrote into our nation's first document did not apply to slaves, for Jefferson did not recognize blacks as men. (He thought he was a kind master and freed all his slaves when he died.) For the slave, it meant that his very identity, even

[19] Frederick Douglass, *My Bondage and My Freedom,* cited in Gilbert Osofsky, *The Burden of Race: A Documentary History of Negro-White Relations in America.* New York & Evanston: Harper & Row, 1967, p. 1.

his name, was given to him by his master, and that legally every move he made was dictated by his master. Slave owners even practiced eugenics and often watched the "scientific breeding" experiments.

The psychological effects of slavery were not to be brushed aside with emancipation. Only a complete social revolution could have swept away its brutal legacy, and as Reconstruction fell far short of that, the effects of slavery persist to this day. To the extent that these effects of slavery are not recognized (although slavery has been abolished by law and in fact), they remain embedded in the American psyche. The American black is still not accepted as a moral and intellectual being. Frederick Douglass wrote:

It is only when we contemplate the slave as a moral and intellectual being, that we can adequately comprehend the unparalleled enormity of slavery, and the intense criminality of the slaveholder. . . . Mr. Covey succeeded in *breaking* me in body, soul and spirit. My natural elasticity was crushed; my intellect languished, the disposition to read departed, the cheerful spark that lingered about my eye died out; the dark night of slavery closed in upon me; and behold a man transformed to a brute.[20]

Douglass understood the essence of the slave system, not from an economic base, but from the point of view of its effect on human character.

SLAVE REVOLTS AND AMERICAN MYTHS

Some slaves rebelled alone. Some organized rebellions that were mostly small and ineffective. Nat Turner, like Frederick Douglass, recognized that a crime was being committed against his people and set out to dispense retribution.

[20] Cited in Bailey, *op. cit.* Vol. I, pp. 353–55.

It is surprising that there were rebellions at all given the experience of those who survived the Middle Passage, the strange land, an incomprehensible language, the auction block, the separation of families and tribesmen, a police force that included every white man.

Historians of slavery tend to divide into three schools. One argues that slaves were militant and rebellious, and that not only did more than 1,200 recorded uprisings occur, but that the blacks sabotaged production and resisted their oppressors whenever possible. This school also believes that the field hands were more militant because they did not share the privileges and rewards of the house slaves.

The counter argument, of course, is that the slaves were by nature docile and accepting, and that slavery was not all that bad. This is the *Gone With the Wind* school of history.

Finally, a more sophisticated analysis compares southern slavery to modern concentration camps, and argues that there was resistance, but that it was limited by the police, by breaking the will of the slaves, and by making them live in constant terror of beatings, deprivation, and separation from their families.

Since organized resistance was difficult to mount and usually foredoomed, other forms of resistance developed, such as malingering, destroying machinery, abusing animals, stealing hams from the shed and chickens from the coop, pretending to be stupid and awkward. Thus slaves prevented the southerners from getting any more than the bare minimum of their labor power. This prevented diversification of agriculture, and industrialization. At the same time the blacks lived up to the stereotype their masters had created for them. It was the easiest way to get along and still rebel against the master's will. It was the kind of rebellion that the masters expected and understood, but in the end it only served to further emasculate the blacks.

American slave rebellions did not equal in intensity those of Cuba, Brazil, and especially Haiti. This was due to the structure of the American slavery system, as opposed to that of the Spanish and Portuguese. It was not necessarily that Americans were more physically cruel, but rather because American slavery proved so much more rigorous and ideological.

There was considerable harmony, as well as antagonism, within the slave system, but this harmony did not alleviate the brutality of the system. Actually it complicated the political economy of slavery, and made simple interpretations of black and white behavior difficult to substantiate. Recent writings by liberal and radical historians have tended to glorify resistance during the slave period, thus exaggerating the role of slave rebellions and impeding an understanding of much that underlies our racial crisis today. The social mores in liberal and radical circles have made it ". . . virtually sacrilege—or at least white chauvinism—to suggest that slavery was a social system within which whites and blacks lived in harmony as well as antagonism."[21]

The black rebellion of the 1960s has sought heroes from the past around whom they could build a movement with a glorious tradition of resistance. But as Prof. Eugene Genovese suggests, "there is little evidence of massive, organized opposition" in the days of slavery. "The blacks did not establish a revolutionary tradition of much significance," says Prof. Genovese, and rather than exaggerate the role of the few rebels, "our main problem is to discover the reasons for the widespread accommodation and, perhaps more important, the long term effects both of accommodation and of that resistance which did occur."

Without exaggerating the role of today's organized and militant resistance it is still possible to point to its origins in slavery, as opposed to that other strain in current black political thought which derives from the Christian accommodationist point of view. When the Civil War broke out no concurrent black insurrections were reported, although some slaves did drive their masters from their plantations. Black leadership at that time was, by and large, Christian

[21] Eugene D. Genovese, "The Legacy of Slavery and the Roots of Black Nationalism," *Studies on the Left,* Vol. 6, 1966, pp. 3–26.

and accommodating, and the blacks relied on the Union
Army to protect and care for them.

———————

AFTER EMANCIPATION—
FROM SLAVERY TO
FREEDOM

Whether the Civil War was fought because of slavery is
not an issue to be argued here, but no historian will deny
the stake the southerners had in their institution, from the
plantation lords to aspiring small farmers and artisans
whose ultimate goal was to own slaves. As Reverend Fontaine said back in the eighteenth century, "It is morally
impossible" to live in the South and not own slaves.

The planters' ideology had become the dominant one for
the entire South. The pseudoaristocracy and genteel culture
of the plantations had become the ideal for every white
man, rich or poor. Success meant owning slaves. It is not
possible to understand the slave system and the desire to
fight a war for it unless one comprehends the economic and
social stake white southerners of *all* classes had in it. And
the blacks knew that all whites, whether slave owners or
not, had to maintain the system. Their only white friends
were the Abolitionists.

In the South the Abolitionists were known as "outside
agitators"; in the North they were called fanatics. But their
tradition is almost as old as slavery on this continent, and
they used the Bible to prove the opposite of what the pro-
slavery preachers taught. The Civil War led to Emancipation. But the work of the Abolitionists over some two
hundred years had helped create the political and emotional
climate in which Lincoln could proclaim freedom for the
slaves.

In the end, though, it was men like John Brown who

understood how deeply entrenched the slave system was in the minds, hearts, and values of the body politic. Only violence could bring it down. By the same token, slave owners had concluded that only warfare could maintain it. The story of John Brown's raid on Harpers Ferry is familiar, and sympathetic recounters of it underscore the lack of slave response to it as a tragedy. Whether Brown actually believed that masses of slaves would join his effort is perhaps not the interesting point. It is possible that he saw his attack on Harpers Ferry as a dramatic act designed to awaken every slave to question the dominance of his white master.

After the Civil War, the United States had its first opportunity to integrate the newly freed black man, but it did so only on paper. Those who argued that the black man was not ready for full citizenship were not aware that in the few areas where blacks served in state legislatures and local councils and in the Freedmen's Bureau, they performed as well as legislators anywhere. The argument that the blacks were as corrupt as the carpetbaggers and scallywags was nonsense. The entire nation was breaking out in a rash of graft and corruption, in the North and South, and there was no evidence that blacks were any worse than northern city bosses. But in literature and movies, the stories put forth by the Ku Klux Klan about incompetent and corrupt black officials lives on as "true history."

The chance for America to absolve herself of her past sins against the black man meant, first of all, that her sin be admitted and atoned for. Lincoln, after all, like Christ, had died for the sins of America, Reverend Henry Ward Beecher liked to remind his flock. That meant America could now go about God's business, which happened to be business.

The problem was that most Americans felt neither guilt about the blacks nor sympathy for their demands for full equality. They were not Abolitionists. Lincoln himself wrote in the *Emancipation Proclamation* that the freeing of slaves was "sincerely believed to be an act of justice, war-

ranted by the Constitution upon military necessity. . . ."[22]
At no time had official northern war goals included a
commitment to full black equality. Lincoln never became
an Abolitionist, although his early racist views were modi-
fied by his increased contact with Abolitionism during the
war.

The Abolitionists, in their moral and political war against
slavery, had caused a polarization in the country. They had
not convinced the mass of northern whites, however. Like
Lincoln, the majority of northerners opposed slavery's expansion into other states, and when the war was over, they
hoped the Negroes would disappear. But the Radicals
pushed the 13th, 14th, and 15th amendments through Congress, as well as other laws guaranteeing the rights of
Negroes.

But such programs as were embodied in the Freedmen's
Bureau and the few measures pushed through the state
legislatures in the South were hardly able to stem the tide of
postwar reaction. What was needed was a mass of sup-
portive whites or an organized black constituency, which
did not exist. So strong was the American myth and the
tradition of democracy that America's greatest and most
sophisticated black historian blamed the failure of Reconstruction on faulty leadership and pragmatic compromises.
Writing in 1935, when the democratic ideal was at its
strongest, W. E. B. Du Bois summed up American black history from its origins through Reconstruction:

The most magnificent drama in the last thousand years of human
history is the transportation of ten million human beings out of
the dark beauty of their mother continent into the new-found El
Dorado of the West. They descended into Hell; and in the third
century they arose from the dead, in the finest effort to achieve
democracy for the working millions which this world has ever
seen. It was a tragedy that beggared the Greek; it was an upheaval of humanity like the Reformation and the French Revolution. Yet we are blind and led by the blind. We discern in it no

22 Henry Steele Commager, *Documents of American History*. N.Y.:
Appleton-Century-Crofts, Inc., 1958.

part of our labor movement; no part of our industrial triumph; no part of our religious experience. Before the dumb eyes of ten generations of ten million children, it is made mockery of and spit upon, a degradation of the eternal mother; a sneer at human effort; with aspiration and art deliberately and elaborately distorted. And why? Because in a day when the human mind aspired to a science of human action, a history and psychology of the mighty effort of the mightiest century, we fell under the leadership of those who would compromise with truth in the past in order to make peace in the present and guide policy in the future.[23]

Dr. Du Bois was writing about the betrayal of the promise of Reconstruction. He was also talking about the lies which have come down to us as "history and tradition," lies rooted in what the moralists have called the unredeemed sin of the American past.

One of the great problems in dealing with Reconstruction is the kind of history that has been written about it, much of it in the twentieth century. For years Reconstruction belonged only to southern history's version, best summed up by the title of Claude Bowers' account, *The Tragic Era.* Popular versions of the age have also been expressed in such novels as *Gone With the Wind* and in films like David Wark Griffith's *Birth of a Nation.* Adults have been fed the propaganda of historians, novelists, and filmmakers, and children have read similar material in their textbooks. During the 1930s some southern and midwestern states children still read that all Negroes "were ignorant of public business" and were "unfit to govern themselves"[24] during Reconstruction.

The stereotype of the ignorant, lazy, dishonest, and extravagant Negro found its way into history via books: "These men knew not only nothing about the government,

---

[23] W. E. B. Du Bois, *Black Reconstruction in America.* New York: Russell & Russell, 1935, p. 2.

[24] Woodburn and Moran, *Elementary American History and Government;* Everett Barnes, *American History for Grammar Grades.* Both cited in W. E. B. Du Bois, *Black Reconstruction in America.* New York: Russell & Russell, 1935, p. 711.

but also cared for nothing except what they could gain for themselves."[25]

"Legislatures were often at the mercy of Negroes, childishly ignorant, who sold their votes openly, and whose 'loyalty' was gained by allowing them to eat and drink, and clothe themselves at the state's expense."[26]

"Legislative expenses were grotesquely extravagant; the colored members in some states engaging in a saturnalia of corrupt expenditure."[27]

"Thinking that slavery meant toil and that freedom meant idleness, the slave after he was set free was disposed to try out his freedom by refusing to work."[28]

"Foolish laws were passed by the black lawmakers. The public money was wasted terribly and thousands of dollars were stolen straight. Self-respecting Southerners chafed under the horrible regime."[29]

A great whitewash began with the first apology for slavery by the first white man who felt guilt, and continued after the Civil War ended. Those who had been oppressed, and those whites who had spoken out against slavery or acted to end that oppression, were blamed for the war and the "tragic era" that followed. If not for the presence of the blacks, there would have been no conflict, went the popular theory, and if not for the Abolitionists, the conflict would have been peacefully settled.

Through the 1950s, historians of Reconstruction, with few exceptions, continued to treat the period as a southern phenomenon in which ignorant blacks subjected the defeated whites to humiliation and corruption. The importance of this distortion of American history is that moral

[25] Helen F. Giles, *How the United States Became a World Power,* cited in W. E. B. Du Bois, *ibid.,* p. 711.

[26] William J. Long, *America—a History of Our Country,* cited in W. E. B. Du Bois, *ibid.,* p. 712.

[27] Frederick Jackson Turner, in the *Encyclopaedia Britannica,* 14th ed., Vol. 22, cited in W. E. B. Du Bois, *ibid.,* p. 713.

[28] S. E. Forman, *Advanced American History* (revised edition), cited in W. E. B. Du Bois, *ibid.,* p. 712.

[29] Emerson David Fite, *These United States,* cited in W. E. B. Du Bois, *ibid.,* p. 712.

questions are avoided. The Civil War and Reconstruction, like slavery, became minor blights on a near perfect record of democracy. Extremism was to blame. The role of the black man in American history was reduced to a stereotype. In the end he was still just a nigger.

The myth of the old South was resurrected after the war and with it came the darkie of bygone days happily twanging his banjo, crooning his spirituals in the cotton fields; the fat mammy comforting the little blond girl after her first upsetting experience; the bent-over, balding darkies weeping at the grave of their beloved master and singing "All de darkies am a weepin' massa's in de col' col' groun'." "That's how it used to be," the planters told their children and the rest of the country as well, "and it will never be quite the same, but we ought to try anyway . . ."

To help re-establish white supremacy, the new southern rulers enacted ordinances to curtail the Negroes' new-found freedom. Black Codes were set up to control the unruly and shiftless niggers.

Fantasy and a kind of pseudopsychiatry also entered the picture. ". . . All they wanted was to deflower some white women. And maybe deep down in their hearts, all white women wanted was to be raped by a big black nigger."

"We're too civilized to give the delicate Southern women what they really need."

"Damn those niggers, those savages," say the descendants of the slave owners.

"The Freedmen's Bureau was run by a bunch of carpet-baggers who told the blacks they were equal . . . which was a lie and gave them a false sense and caused them to be uppity."

"Look at them in our legislatures, in our court houses, walking down our streets . . . impolite . . . and those Abolitionist Radicals, with their coarse invective, just victimizing us for their own money-grubbing ends . . . poor South, poor we all!"

Charles and Mary Beard wrote about Reconstruction as though it were a poetic epoch, with the forces of manufacturing and industry clashing with those of romantic agrarian feudalism—with the victory, of course, going to the forces of material progress. W. E. B. Du Bois, on the other hand, looked on Reconstruction as a great experience in democracy and denounced American historians for distorting it:

. . . there is no room for the real plot of the story, for the clear mistake and guilt of rebuilding a new slavery of the working class in the midst of a fateful experiment in democracy; for the triumph of sheer moral courage and sacrifice in the abolition crusade; and for the hurt and struggle of degraded black millions in their fight for freedom and their attempt to enter democracy.[30]

The blacks had a role in the fighting of the Civil War, with 20,000 (many of them ex-slaves) fighting in the Union Army against the Confederacy. But this part of their history is as little known in textbooks and popular lore as their contributions to the rebuilding of the nation after the war. Compare a monument to Confederate soldiers in North Carolina which read, "They died fighting for their liberty!", with W. E. Woodward's comment which stated that blacks were ". . . the only people in the history of the world . . . that ever became free without any effort of their own. . . ."[31]

Blacks today know little about their ancestors' efforts in the Civil War. The going myths prevail for them also. To be sure, some truth went into their making, as with all myths. But the heroic tradition, the fighting tradition—dating back to the first resistance to being sold into slavery through the revolts of Gabriel, Vesey, and Turner, and some 200 Civil War battles in which blacks fought—was not passed down to modern blacks and whites. Instead, there is the vulgar tradition of the planters' stereotype.

The black man was not properly organized to face Reconstruction; he was poorly advised and often manipulated by white men, and by black petty bourgeois entrepreneurs and hustlers as well. The situation was ripe for corruption.

---

[30] W. E. B. Du Bois, *ibid.*, p. 715.
[31] W. E. Woodward, *Meet General Grant,* cited in W. E. B. Du Bois, *ibid.,* p. 716.

The startling fact is that there was far less evidence of black corruption in the South than of white corruption in the North, where millions were stolen from the public in the building of the railroads and the great swindles of the political bosses. The very people today who have foundations named after them, were guilty of stealing and cheating far more wealth than were the handful of corrupt blacks. The "Robber Barons" emerged as "Industrial Statesmen" and the blacks were written off as lazy, shiftless scoundrels.

THE WHITE REACTION TO ITS OWN MYTH OF "THE TRAGIC ERA"

The period following Reconstruction—with its repeal of laws protecting blacks, the Supreme Court decision upholding black disfranchisement, and the establishment of the "Separate but Equal" doctrine—has been presented in countless texts. What is often omitted is the connection between the growth of twentieth-century racism and its justification for the semislavery of modern blacks and the spread of overseas American imperialism.

The official racism of the United States Government, from the 1890s through the "Big Stick" period, went hand in hand with the new Jim Crow laws. America's "manifest destiny" abroad, with its assumptions of the inferiority of all colored races, bolstered racism and racist violence at home. The blacks, who emerged from the Civil War into a state of poverty, no longer had even the support of the patriarchal family tradition to strengthen them in their resistance to white reaction everywhere. The majority of blacks were illiterate and without experience in political organization. Authorities tended to reinforce white hatred for blacks—as well as black self-hatred. Congressmen, senators, and the President of the United States made continual references to the inferiority of Negroes, while the black man experienced a way of life hardly designed to promote self-esteem, much less militant political organization. American history books often discuss the Gay Nineties with barely a reference to the degradation suffered by blacks during the years from 1877 (the end of Reconstruction) through World War I.

The institution of lynching is also treated sketchily in most American histories. The rush to the frontier, the building of railroads, industrialization, and America's emergence as a world power in the years following Reconstruction, are the subjects generally emphasized. The farmer rebellions, the Populist movement, and labor violence are also included in our recorded past. But Jim Crow, lynchings, disfranchisement of the newly enfranchised blacks, black exclusion from most areas of American life, are relegated to small, insignificant chapters. Is it so strange then that blacks are finally demanding black studies programs to find out about their past? Is it so strange that they ignore the glorious "nation-building" strain in American history?

The political corruption of this period is not as well known as its glorious conquests. More often than not the black man found himself at the receiving end of some political fraud. For example, his vote would be bought or cajoled from him—then he would be blamed for fraudulent voting. C. Vann Woodward reported a growing fear "that corruption in political life would contaminate business and social relations. The remedy, declared the reformers, was the disfranchisement of the Negro."[32]

The paradox of further punishing the already downtrodden is hardly limited to the post–Civil War period. This has been part of America's racial history all along. Indians, Mexicans, Orientals, almost every minority group, has been submitted to the same injustices. (We cannot understand the attitudes of nonwhite people today without recognizing what they have been told over the years by society, the law, legislators, trustees, and gentlemen—"You are bad, child-

---

[32] C. Vann Woodward, *Origins of the New South, 1877–1913*. Baton Rouge: Louisiana State University Press, 1951, p. 327.

ish, lazy, violent, savage, and stupid. You are inferior and we can punish you when and where we like"—and that they have been treated accordingly.)

In order to continue disfranchisement of the blacks, devices were invented to get around one of the fundamental principles of the Declaration of Independence—"All men are created equal." Such devices as grandfather clauses, poll taxes, literacy and property tests were adopted for that purpose. Ben Tillman of South Carolina argued that "Some have said there is fraud in this understanding clause.[33] Some poisons in small doses are very salutary and valuable medicines . . . Ah, you grin."[34]

The Democratic Party led the fight for disfranchisement, but the Republicans also acted by forming "lily-white" Republican groups. By the end of the 1880s, the color lines were drawn and even those northern churches that had once carried out missionary work among the newly freed blacks abandoned the ex-slaves. Race dominated political loyalties. "I will not vote to make a negro my ruler," said a white southern Republican. "I was a white man before I was a Republican."

For the blacks, without any real support from such former friends as the Radicals, who had either passed from political life by the 1880s or had altered their views, the situation became desperate once again. The old terror blacks had felt as slaves returned as a daily part of their lives. During slavery blacks had been unprotected from the whims of sadistic whites, but at least they were considered valuable property by many. After Reconstruction, all safeguards to life and security were removed. Between 1885 and 1894, for example, an estimated 1700 blacks were lynched. "Each death a scar on my soul," wrote Dr. Du Bois.[35] There seemed to be only one thing safe for blacks

[33] Referring to the requirement that voters must be able to understand and interpret all passages of the State Constitution, a requirement used to keep blacks from the polls.

[34] Woodward, op. cit., p. 333.

[35] W. E. B. Du Bois in Lerone Bennett, Jr., Before the Mayflower. New York: Penguin Books, 1966, p. 280.

to do; many of them could and did move out of the South and into the new ghettos in northern cities.

The turn of the century brought no great improvement in black life. Several southern cities passed ordinances enforcing neighborhood segregation; in 1913 President Woodrow Wilson segregated federal employees in Washington; department stores in New York advertised "Nigger Brown" shoes, a new color. Lynchings continued, with at least 79 reported in 1913 alone, as blacks continued to march northward by the millions.

World War I was fought to make the world safe for democracy, but democracy became no safer for the blacks at home. The race war the black GI left behind to go fight in Europe was still going strong when he returned home. In Europe some blacks fought by cleaning latrines and serving as orderlies; others were assigned to the most dangerous combat. (400,000 blacks were drafted[36] and some 200,-000 saw overseas duty.) When they returned home, after fighting in the most ideological war since the Crusades, they found that racism had increased. Blacks living in northern (particularly Harlem) as well as southern ghettos were turning, increasingly, to what James Weldon Johnson called "racial radicalism":

With the close of the war went most of the illusions and high hopes American Negroes had felt would be realized when it was seen that they were doing to the utmost their bit at home and in the field. Eight months after the armistice, with black men back fresh from the front, there broke the Red Summer of 1919, and the mingled emotions of the race were bitterness, despair and anger. There developed an attitude of cynicism which was a characteristic foreign to the Negro. There developed also a spirit of defiance born of desperation. These sentiments found varying degrees of expression in the Negro publications throughout the country; but Harlem became the center where they were formulated and voiced to the Negroes of America and the world. Radicalism in Harlem, which had declined as the war ap-

[36] Gunnar Myrdal, *An American Dilemma, The Negro Problem and American Democracy.* New York and London: Harper & Bros. Publishers, 1944, Vol. 2, p. 745.

proached, burst out anew. But it was something different from the formal radicalism of pre-war days; it was a radicalism motivated by a fierce race consciousness.[37]

By the end of World War I, America's racial problem also existed in every large city in the North. The blacks had become the bottom layer of the proletariat. At the same time, a black elite, already existent on a small scale, took on new meaning as black intellectuals groped for political solutions to racial oppression.

BLACK POLITICS

The traditional history book usually begins the section on black politics with Booker T. Washington, Jr. and the conflict in Negro politics (usually attributed to the differences between Washington and Dr. W. E. B. Du Bois). Actually black politics began in Africa. In America, black politics went largely unreported, since slaves did not keep records on organizations designed to free them. Among free blacks two trends emerged: the integrationist-accommodationist, and separatist-nationalist ideologies.

The integrationist trend began as a strong public position with Frederick Douglass and continues into the present with the National Association for the Advancement of Colored People. The separatist idea originated back in the eighteenth century, but became a clearly defined movement with Martin R. Delany's "Back to Africa" dream in 1859.

Delany, the grandson of slaves, was an antislavery writer and Harvard-trained physician who lived in Pennsylvania. "Where shall we go?" he asked in his book *Destiny of the Colored Race*. ". . . We desire the civilization and enlightenment of Africa—the high and elevated position of Liberia among the nations of the earth."[38] Delany's con-

[37] James Weldon Johnson, *Black Manhattan*. New York: Arno Press, 1968, p. 246.

[38] Martin R. Delany, *Destiny of the Colored Race*. Philadelphia, 1852, pp. 160–61.

clusion, that only a return to Africa would afford independence to American black men, was based on his judgment of American white men. After passage of the Fugitive Slave Act in 1850, Delany concluded that the plight of the black man was hopeless in America. "A people capable of originating and sustaining such a law as this are not the people to whom we are willing to entrust our liberty at discretion."

His argument was based on a sound premise: that racism —and slavery—were written into the laws and into the moral structure of America and that since "there are no people who ever lived, love their country and obey their laws as the Americans,"[39] there was no future for blacks in the U.S. Delany's bitterness is evident. "Their country is their Heaven. . . . It is the most consummate delusion and misdirected confidence to depend upon them for protection; and for a moment suppose even our children are safe while walking in the streets among them."

For Delany the situation was clear: white Americans would never accept the black man, nor would the black man want to walk among them. This applied to slaves, but even more to those blacks with the status of "free Negroes" (like Delany himself). He rejected the moral ideals of the Abolitionists, feeling, as many black intellectuals do today, that the white man could never adequately think or speak for the black. As long as the black man remained in America he would feel insecure and unwanted, whether slave or free. But, Delany wrote, "the slave is more secure than we; he knows who holds the heel upon his bosom—we know not the wretch that may grasp us by the throat."[40]

During the period Delany was exhorting free blacks to pursue the "Back to Africa" idea, Frederick Douglass, who had joined forces with the radical Abolitionists, was propounding the integrationist solution. The two were friends, however, and collaborated on the magazine *The North Star,* an Abolitionist organ founded in 1847. Their

[39] *Ibid.,* p. 156.
[40] *Ibid.,* p. 155.

opposing ideas were stated in the same magazine. They were responses to two strains in American history, racism and democracy. Delany saw the true character of white Americans in their treatment of all nonwhites and believed their attitude was embedded in the country's laws and institutions. Douglass, coming from the same slave heritage, did not deny the racism, but looked at democracy with its ideals of equality, reason, and justice, and felt they also were woven into America's social, political, and moral fabric.

With the work of W. E. B. Du Bois the contradictory ideas of Delany and Douglass "nearly merged into a new synthesis, for Du Bois, in addition to being a founder of the NAACP integrationist trend was also a leading exponent of the Pan Africanism that had its origins with Martin R. Delany."[41]

In traditional history survey courses one-half of one lecture is devoted to the differences between Booker T. Washington and W. E. B. Du Bois. Students are taught that Booker T. Washington believed that Negroes should withdraw from the political arena and concentrate on learning trades and skills. They learn that he was willing to accommodate to white rule in the hope that Negroes would develop enough economic strength to earn a place in the power structure.

Modern students learn in freshman survey courses that Dr. Du Bois opposed Washington's self-help idea and argued for more militant tactics. Du Bois is described as a socialist and Marxist who founded the NAACP to achieve equal rights on all levels. In their historic confrontation there is no winner, although Washington's influence over Negroes during his years as a leader was extremely powerful. Since the New Deal, though, Washington has been the butt of liberal historians, mostly white, who attack him for advocating accommodation and for directing blacks to withdraw

---

[41] Harold Cruse, *Crisis of the Negro Intellectual*. N.Y.: Morrow, 1967, p. 6.

from direct political struggle. He is accused of having been in league with wealthy white industrialists, of having sold out, and of being the classic Uncle Tom.

Du Bois' own judgment of Washington and the essence of the conflict between them were far more complex and important than the treatment generally given them in traditional American history courses. Conor Cruise O'Brien wrote of a meeting with Du Bois during the last years of his life in Ghana. Du Bois took issue when someone accused Washington of being "a stooge for the bosses." Here are O'Brien's notes on Du Bois:

He said that he had in his youth spoken slightingly of Booker T. Washington and had been memorably reprimanded by his aunts, who told him that it ill became one who had been born free to speak disrespectfully of a man whose back bore the marks of the lash. . . . In the circumstances of the South in Washington's day, he could not have done anything effective in any other way. He [Du Bois], with his Northern and relatively privileged background, had been able to take a different stance and had been obliged to enter into public controversy with Washington. He did not want that controversy to obscure the merits of what Washington had achieved. . . .[42]

If Washington's effort at self-help is seen as a way for black people to establish a sense of self-worth and Du Bois' idea of agitation and stress on black nationalism and African heritage are seen as different means toward the same end, the controversy is better understood. But it must be pointed out that Du Bois was not averse to accepting white help—or money—and in fact saw that an alliance between progressive white intellectuals and the black and white working class could serve to bring about social justice in America. He wished to abolish the intertwined evils of capitalism and racism, while Washington, accepting the prevailing economic system, was concerned with making a place within the power structure that existed. Washington and Du Bois also differed on their estimate of what blacks were prepared to do, based on what they had done during

[42] Conor Cruise O'Brien to Eugene Genovese, in *Studies on the Left*, Vol. 6, No. 6, 1966, p. 59.

Reconstruction. Du Bois tended to glorify the efforts of blacks after the Civil War, while Washington, the ex-slave, felt the black masses were ignorant about organized political efforts and still helpless before the power of white paternalism. The question for Washington was how to establish self-reliance and self-worth without engaging in a political struggle he felt would result in even more repression for the black man than he was already experiencing. (Between the late 1880s and the 1920s all blacks were subject to racism, repression, and lynching unparalleled in American history.) Washington was even willing to rely on the older southern classes at the time when they were being replaced in the political arena by the Populists with their super brand of racism. "Somehow he meant to destroy the effects of paternalism in the long run by strengthening paternalism in the short run."[43] Du Bois' public stance, on the other hand, was that of a militant agitator.

Neither of these strains in black politics accomplished much in themselves. But from them developed the integrationist and the black nationalist aims. At certain times one or the other was the more dominant. In the 1920s black nationalism under Marcus Garvey grew into the largest black mass movement in American history, while the NAACP and the integrationist forces had little appeal for the black proletariat. At other times prominent integrationists, like Du Bois himself, were also strong nationalists. Or vice versa. For example, although Malcolm X and Washington had radically different styles, the aim of Malcolm's exhortations, especially before he broke with the Muslims, was the establishment of a self-help, self-discipline organization.

When Booker T. Washington is seen, not through the eyes of intellectuals and scholars, but rather as a man speaking to a barely literate people, his influence is best understood. Work and money, he stressed, should be the goals of black people. This economic nationalism was also included in Marcus Garvey's Back to Africa Movement.

[43] Genovese, *Studies on the Left*, Vol. 6, No. 6, 1966, p. 15.

However, it spelled the doom of Garvey's vision because it fostered the growth of a black bourgeoisie that could never acquire enough wealth and power to alter the American social structure. What developed, instead, from this emphasis on earning money was a pathetic imitation of white society, further deepening class cleavages within black society.

Du Bois was aware of this, and as much as he hoped for racial consciousness he never fostered the illusion that black capitalism alone could remedy the effects of American racism. Du Bois belonged, at one and the same time, to the world of white intellectuals and to the world of black soul. When a white writer approached Du Bois shortly before World War I with the idea of writing sympathetic articles on blacks, Du Bois told him point blank that Negroes "do not wish to be written about by white men, even when they know they will be treated sympathetically. Perhaps especially then, they do not desire it."[44]

American history survey courses notwithstanding, Du Bois cannot be classified as an integrationist. His literary and historical writings emphasize black soul and the right of black people to their own culture, their own propaganda, and their own esthetic. In 1926 he told a black audience that they had a right to "believe black blood human, lovable and inspired with new ideals for the world."[45] Du Bois, in one paragraph, defined the black man's cultural role in America, encompassing in it the political and social goals that have defined both the integrationist and nationalist movements:

We want to be Americans, full-fledged Americans, with all the rights of other American citizens. But is that all? Do we simply want to be Americans? Once in a while through all of us there flashes some clairvoyance, some clear idea, of what America really is. We who are dark can see America in a way that white

[44] Hutchins Hapgood, *A Victorian in the Modern World*. New York: Harcourt, Brace, 1939, pp. 344–45, quoted in Cruse, *op. cit.,* p. 39.

[45] Cruse, *op. cit.,* p. 39.

Americans can not. And seeing our country thus, are we satisfied with its present goals and ideals?[46]

The largest and most popular of all black mass movements, whose record is still unsurpassed today, was the Universal Negro Improvement Association under President General (and Provisional President of Africa) Marcus Garvey. Garvey's movement constituted more than an answer to the illusions of integration built up during World War I. It was a call to all blacks to do the obvious, and to Garvey the obvious was to establish a significant self-help program that would carry blacks to freedom, justice, dignity, and wealth—in Africa. He carried on an ideological struggle with all the black leaders who advocated cultural assimilation by calling them "opportunists, liars, thieves, traitors, and bastards."[47] Garvey enrolled hundreds of thousands of blacks in his organization.

Before Garvey, prestige points were won by having light skin. In Garvey's movement it was blackness, for a change, that counted. Prosperity also counted. "Poverty is no virtue," said the West Indian Black Moses, "it is a crime." Garvey urged blacks to go back to Africa, their homeland. His newspaper, *Negro World,* had "Africa for the Africans" as its slogan. Garvey, in effect, said "black is beautiful." He also spelled out early versions of black power and Muslim doctrines. "Be as proud of your race today as our fathers were in the days of yore. We have a beautiful history, and we shall create another in the future that will astonish the world."[48]

A strong Africa, Garvey felt, would protect and be a source of pride for all blacks everywhere. His inspiration came from Booker T. Washington. "I read *Up From Slavery*—and then my doom, if I may so call it—of being a race

---

[46] From "Criteria of Negro Art," in *Crisis,* October, 1926, pp. 290–97 and cited in Cruse, *ibid.,* p. 43.

[47] Myrdal, *op. cit.,* Vol. 2, p. 746.

[48] Edmund David Cronon, *Black Moses.* Madison, Wisconsin: University of Wisconsin Press, 1955, p. 170.

leader dawned upon me—I asked: 'Where is the black man's government? Where is his King, his Kingdom? Where is his President, his country, and his ambassador, his army, his navy, his men of affairs?' I could not find them, and then I declared, 'I will help to make them.' "[49]

Garvey, with his elaborate uniforms, rituals, and titles, was the most important black man in America in the early 1920s. He emphasized blackness in everything and tried to restore in blacks, whose souls had been shattered by World War I and the life in northern urban ghettos, a sense of worth and power. "Up you mighty race!" he cried. "You can accomplish what you will. . . . No one knows when the hour of Africa's redemption cometh. . . . One day, like a storm, it will be here."[50] He harangued from the sidewalks and rode through the streets of Harlem in fancy autos. He demanded Negro be spelled with a capital N. He asserted that Christ was neither white nor Jewish but pure black, and he never spoke without referring to the vision of a future black society. Like Booker T. Washington, he felt that economic success could lead to increased power for blacks. Through the Black Star Steamship Company, which he began and financed by means of contributions from the black community, he attempted to prove that black business could succeed if blacks supported it. Inexperienced management and fraud by some of Garvey's associates who were new to business and wealth, crippled the company and ultimately led to a prison sentence for Garvey.

Garvey is often treated in traditional texts as if he were something of a clown, even though the Shriners and the American Legion indulge in more bizarre behavior. He was termed "dangerous to the comfort and security" of society by a New York legislative committee which obviously did not include blacks. At the time that stock market shenanigans had reached undreamed-of heights during the mid-1920s Marcus Garvey was indicted by the federal govern-

49 *Ibid.,* p. 16.
50 In Langston Hughes and Milton Meltzer, *A Pictorial History of the Negro in America.* New York: Crown Pub., 1956, p. 270.

ment on a charge of mail fraud. After two years in Atlanta Prison, he was deported, and eventually died in 1940 in London.

Considered the father of modern black nationalism, Garvey wrote a message to his followers in 1925 which must be read symbolically: "My work has just begun. . . . I planted well the seed of Negro or black nationalism which cannot be destroyed. . . . If I die . . . I shall rise with God's grace and blessing to lead the missions up the heights of triumph. . . . I shall come and bring with me countless millions of black slaves who have died in America and the West Indies and the millions in Africa to aid you in the fight for Liberty, Freedom and Life."[51]

Dr. Du Bois, whom Garvey had "excluded" from the black race, said in retrospect of Garvey's plans, "It was a grandiose and bombastic scheme, utterly impracticable as a whole, but it was sincere and had some practical features; and Garvey proved not only an astonishing popular leader, but a master of propaganda."[52]

Edmund David Cronon, Garvey's white biographer, concluded in 1955 that "Garvey's passionate interest in Africa was a logical development of his firm conviction that Negroes could expect no permanent progress in a land dominated by white men."[53] This conclusion was shared by more blacks than had ever affiliated with, or felt active sympathy for, any other black mass organization.

Garvey preached strength (power) and attempted to strike fear "into the hearts of the oppressors." He did, was prosecuted, and deported. But the failure of the Universal Negro Improvement Association did not mean that Garvey's influence or ideology had failed, although he is often written off in standard texts as a mildly interesting and perhaps quaint historical figure. The Muslims and Malcolm X, for example, incorporated and elaborated on the strongest points of Garvey's nationalism. President Johnson's house

[51] Cronon, *op. cit.*, pp. 136–37.
[52] Du Bois, *Dusk of Dawn*. New York: Schocken Books, 1968.
[53] Cronon, *op. cit.*, p. 187.

historian, Eric Goldman, however, passed him off in typical liberal fashion, neither understanding what Garvey was doing nor his importance to black men. "The leader never quite got around to mundane details. He was too busy making his ornate offices still more ornate, supporting a bevy of very nationalistic and very good-looking women, equipping, gazetting, and knighting the aristocracy of the coming black empire."[54] James Weldon Johnson, on the other hand, understood Garvey's power and importance. "He stirred the imagination of the Negro masses as no Negro had before. He raised more money in a few years than any other Negro organization had ever dreamed of."[55]

Garvey's movement came along with the Harlem Renaissance and the emergence of socialist thought among black intellectuals. Garvey preached, as had Washington, that "capitalism is necessary to the progress of the world," and those who opposed it, like Du Bois, were "enemies of human advancement."[56] At the same time, A. Philip Randolph and Du Bois embarked on a campaign for militance and socialism which included criticism of Garvey in several magazines, such as *Messenger* and *Crusader.* Randolph, then a socialist, sought to ally Negro protest with radical white labor activity. However, this attempt failed, so Randolph formed a militant organization, the Brotherhood of Sleeping-Car Porters, an all-Negro trade union.

Du Bois, who continued to edit *Crisis,* maintained the position he articulated in his attack on Washington in the early 1900s. "It is impossible," wrote Du Bois, "that nine millions of men can make effective progress in economic lines if they are deprived of political rights . . ."[57] Also, Du Bois never abandoned his Pan Africanism, which blended into the flourishing black art of the twenties. The poems of Claude McKay and Langston Hughes, the writ-

---

[54] Eric F. Goldman, *Rendezvous with Destiny.* New York: Vintage, 1958, p. 233.

[55] James Weldon Johnson, *Black Manhattan,* p. 256.

[56] Marcus Garvey, *Philosophy and Opinions.* New York: Universal Publishing House, 1925, Vol. II, p. 72.

[57] W. E. B. Du Bois, *Souls of Black Folk,* p. 51.

ings of the older James Weldon Johnson, and the music and dance of black artists came into vogue.

But no cultural identity emerged from this Renaissance. When the Depression hit, Garvey was in exile and Du Bois was an isolated intellectual feared by many black intellectuals. Randolph was, by this time, completely absorbed· in black unionism and his socialism now sounded rhetorical. The hopes that black artists and intellectuals had in the early and mid-twenties dissolved along with their prosperity. "Unable to arrive at any philosophical conclusions of their own as a *black intelligentsia,* the leading literary lights of the 1920's substituted the Communist left-wing philosophy of the 1930's, and thus were intellectually sidetracked for the remainder of their productive years."[58]

Dr. Du Bois felt great optimism in the thirties and forties, despite setbacks and lack of real progress. He watched the civil rights movement develop, even though he witnessed the continual failure of blacks to win even the most. elementary rights. The white leadership, liberal and conservative, maintained a democratic veneer over its racism. Two world wars and Korea, all fought in the name of democracy, were seen as gains toward integration in Du Bois' eyes. But he saw no fundamental change in the minds or hearts of American whites. The Communist Party, which at first seemed to represent to Du Bois an agency for the kind of change he envisioned and which he deeply respected for many years, switched its lines to those of Moscow. Du Bois, then in his nineties, had to quit America. He went to Ghana, became its "First Citizen," and died there in 1963.

Du Bois' self-exile represents the highest symbolic condemnation of American society. He was the greatest militant black intellectual, who believed that reason and democracy could conquer capitalism and racism. Martin Luther King, Jr., also believed. His brutal death taught yet another lesson to American blacks: that the American traditions of reason and democracy are no match for the violent racism that developed along with them. Colored people

[58] Cruse, *op. cit.,* p. 63.

have never been able to use reason and democracy to win their rights. After both world wars, riots broke out in cities throughout the country. (And again in the 1960s. "We will burn it down," screamed angry blacks. The fire, indeed, was *this* time, but it was their own ghettos they were burning down.) Du Bois had hoped for a socialist revolution with blacks—and whites—overthrowing capitalism and racism. The Black Panthers and several militant black groups today still hold to his ideal.

The black community is still, in general, unorganized and brutalized as it was a hundred years ago, even two hundred years ago. Even so, it has finally rejected white paternalism. Now only black solutions are acceptable. What these solutions will be, and who will lead the blacks, and whether white society will allow an independent black movement to gain power without bloodshed—these are the unknowns. What is known, at least to local police, is that the so-called "crisis in the cities" is no longer manageable without the aid of the National Guard. The Establishment position, however, has not wavered, despite riot after riot, assassination after assassination. It clings fervently to its rhetoric of democracy and reason; and in its publications and speeches the traditional American myths persist.

C. Vann Woodward raised an important point when he warned scholars with partisan sentiments about the danger of counter-mythmaking: "The scholarly community, indeed the whole intellectual community, from left to right, has gotten itself in a bind over the race crisis. Because of our sympathy with the liberation movement, we have schooled ourselves meekly to swallow any amount of historical eye-wash as long as it bolsters the ego of the downtrodden and lacerates Mr. Charley. We have grown solemn and humorless in our piety and abandoned intellectual honesty for righteousness and conformity."[59]

Any movement seeks heroes and villains as it defines itself and its enemies and vies for the support of the masses. The history of black politics has not been one of unity. Like

[59] In *Studies on the Left*, Vol. 6, No. 6, 1966, pp. 40–41.

all other political struggles it has been a fight over ideas involving fundamental questions of human existence: how to survive in a white racist society, how to gain freedom (inside the society, outside it, or by destroying it?), and how to preserve one's identity within one of the most oppressive societies in the world.

THE FIRE EVERYWHERE

"Individualism is a luxury we can no longer afford."[60]
"If I was black I would be a waitress, scrub floors or anything else I had to do to send my kids to college."[61]

The civil rights movement, beginning in the 1950s and gaining momentum with the Freedom Rides, sit-ins, and the Mississippi summer of 1964, was perhaps the last liberal Great Awakening. Thousands of whites and blacks acted together in the belief that integration was an achievable and desirable goal. Indeed, the Movement proposed many reforms. Some were made into law and others were adopted by businesses and other groups. The beating, jailings, harassment, and murders of civil rights workers finally led to Congressional affirmation of what the Constitution had already guaranteed: the right of every citizen to vote.

But the effects of white racism, which liberals had assumed were found mainly in the South, proved to be far more widespread and more powerful than the moral and physical heroism of the civil rights workers everywhere. The legacies of slavery and oppression had not been overcome in the North, any more than they had been in the South; they had simply grown new roots in the northern ghettos. The white backlash, the reaction to the changes sought by the Movement, affected the North as much as the South. The extent of this reaction can be estimated by the number of George Wallace's northern votes in the 1968 presidential

---

[60] Stokely Carmichael, Tougaloo, Mississippi, 1967.
[61] A member of the Society of the Cincinnati, 1969.

election. So, by 1965 the majority of blacks in the Civil Rights Movement had concluded that the effort to bring full equality to blacks through reform, pressure, and moral persuasion of whites, had failed.

True, there had been some gains. Because of the Movement it was easier for educated blacks to get good jobs. But the mass of blacks continued to go uneducated. It was easier for middle-class blacks to rent or buy good homes. But the vast majority could afford only segregated housing. Blacks began to appear in commercials, and in movies and TV shows, as extras and even heroes. But the downtown area of every city exhibited a façade of integration that masked a burgeoning black ghetto.

By the mid-1960s blacks had been granted full equality by the President, Congress, and the courts, in decrees, laws, and decisions. But this did not change the racist structure of the American society. Blacks remained the lowest paid on the work force and, even more important, became an increasingly irrelevant factor in the economy. Token reforms could not answer black needs, nor could they turn back the effects of 300 years of racism. The kind of sacrifices required to bring about full equality for blacks were unthinkable for the majority of white Americans. Their characteristic answer to black demands for equality, better housing, schools, and jobs, was to refer to the Puritan ethic and American individualism: "If they worked hard . . . if they only saved a little . . . if they only lived the way we do. . . ." The idea that any individual could, by applying the Puritan ethic, raise himself and his family up the social scale became one of the reinforcements of continued racism. Attacks on welfare systems and other doles increased, especially in white lower, middle, and working-class communities. American individualism—in the largest mass society in the world—was the white answer to black demands.

Black activists, who had gained new awareness from their experiences in the civil rights movement, turned away from liberalism. If more evidence was needed to prove the futility of liberal, reformist methods, the murder of Dr. Martin Luther King provided it. Black activists concluded that America was still, after 300 years, violent and racist and that integration was neither possible nor desirable. They began to urge that blacks work for black interests—outside the mainstream.

Stokely Carmichael, then the Chairman of the Student Non-Violent Coordinating Committee, was the first to announce "Black Power" as the objective of black politics. It became the slogan for many black political groups and politicians. Excited by the growing number and intensity of race riots in large, medium, and small cities, black leaders proclaimed the "Black Power" slogan through the mass media. But the definitions of "Black Power" differed.

By 1968 black leadership was divided, especially over the role of government aid programs. Floyd McKissick, then head of the Congress of Racial Equality, opted for a program crudely labeled as black capitalism. The program was no more than a watered-down rehash of proposals lying somewhere between the teachings of Booker T. Washington and Marcus Garvey. It called for capital investment in the ghettos and support of black merchants. The ultimate goal was black economic control in their own communities. Some middle-class blacks and businessmen, with government and corporate aid, began a few projects. But most of the projects were doomed to failure before they started. There was no room for black capitalists, who possessed neither large amounts of capital nor a great deal of experience. Black capitalism had little substance in its programs, and only a few companies experimented in financing black industries in the ghettos.

Cultural nationalism was another activist tactic taken in reaction to the failure of liberalism. A "Hate Whitey," "Black Is Beautiful" ideology developed to help blacks gain a sense of self-worth, and as a rallying cry to organize all blacks on the basis of race. "Still a brother," Carmichael said of the black bourgeoisie in February, 1968. Some nationalists claimed that the black bourgeoisie, despite their class and privilege, were still subject to racial oppression and needed to gain control of all agencies and property within the black community.

High schools and universities, under pressure from militant Black Student Unions, often led by ex-civil rights workers or people who had gained awareness during the Movement days, began to adopt black studies programs.

Blackness, Africa, soul food, natural hairdos, and ghetto street language, all were glorified—not only by blacks, but also by hip, white advertising companies and "in" white commentators. What began in the Movement as means to develop black identity, were adopted by the culture-makers and marketed as a new style. But this development did not negate the effects of the black cultural renaissance on black youth. Many gained from it not only a pride in being black but a more revolutionary consciousness. The beginnings of a socialist revolutionary approach to all of American society appeared. According to the new approach, racism went hand in hand with capitalism and imperialism. In order to eradicate racism, a struggle had to be waged against the profit system and overseas aggression. A renaissance of the works of Marx, and especially those of Fidel Castro, "Che" Guevara, and Chairman Mao, began to spread among black militants.

Many blacks remained in the narrow, cultural nationalist camp, but a growing movement, led by the Black Panther Party, denounced all racism and called for unity with revolutionary whites and all oppressed people in the world. The Panthers and similar groups recognized America as an imperialist nation and announced solidarity with North Vietnam, the National Liberation Front, Cuba, China, and the new African revolutions. They called for a socialist revolution, an overthrow of traditional American institutions, and the establishment of an egalitarian society. Police were labeled as "pigs," the agents of imperialism at home.

Initially the Panthers made great strides in recruiting poor black youth and forming a semi-military party they hoped would be able to organize and control life in the ghettos. The Panthers resisted local police and the federal government and were harassed, jailed, and murdered, sometimes by the police, sometimes by rival black groups jealous of their success. Beginning as an armed, self-defense group in 1966, the Panthers developed into what they called the vanguard of the revolutionary movement, with an explicitly socialist program that included whites and blacks. By 1969, despite harassment, dead leaders, prison, and exile, Panthers had become the focus of attention for white radicals as well as growing numbers of ghetto youth.

But building a revolutionary party is extremely difficult, as the Panthers soon discovered. They had to build an organization that would not crack under pressure, but most of their cadres were poorly educated and possessed few of the skills necessary for organized revolutionary activity.

The birth of the Panthers, however, is testimony to the determination of many blacks to free themselves from the legacy of inequality. Whether they will succeed in building a revolutionary movement able to win power is still an unanswerable question. But these blacks have recognized what police forces throughout the country have known for years: that they are an enemy within the gates that can no longer be controlled by mere promises of reform; that they are no longer willing to be absorbed into American society; that they must fight for their survival.

"Individualism," Stokely Carmichael said, "is a luxury we can no longer afford," and in response thousands of black youths have come together in riots and in demonstrations in the universities and in the offices where they work, to assert black collectivity.

Some still see only black solutions to black problems, but if white revolutionaries prove themselves reliable allies the black movement may move to a more meaningful alliance with them under the guidelines of a revolutionary theory.

White America's final response to the mounting pressures from blacks remains an unknown. Repression has weakened the Movement, but not its determination. Poor, uneducated blacks have no place in modern capitalist America; to win a place blacks must participate with whites in completely changing society. Most Americans are far from sympathetic to this idea, no matter what their feelings are about racial equality. And so, as the pressure mounts, many whites may act on the racism that has been America's sickness since the founding of the colonies.

Introduction to Black Documents

The amount of material that exists depicting the condition of blacks in America from 1619 to the present is enormous. Almost all the documents portray brutality and oppression, a historic relationship of tension and fear between blacks and whites. But much material remains in the category of folklore or oral history, and has not yet been recorded or analyzed. We have selected a few documents designed mainly to show black responses to slavery and to post-emancipation oppression. What the documents also show is that the current black militant leaders have clear antecedents in the 19th century.

(1)

Slaves Petition for Freedom, 1774*

The "happy, ignorant slave" myth is adequately disproved by a slave petition for freedom in 1774. The petition also indicates that the revolutionary ideals had spread to black slaves inside the colonies.

To his Excellency Thomas Gage Esq. Captain General and Governor in Chief in and over this Province.
To the Honourable his Majestys Council and the Hon-

---

* Joanne Grant, *Black Protest: History, Documents and Analysis from 1619 to the Present* (Fawcett World Library, New York, 1968).

*ourable House of Representatives in General Court as-
sembled May 25, 1774*

The Petition of a Grate Number of Blacks of this Province who by divine permission are held in a state of Slavery
within the bowels of a free and Christian Country

Humbly Shewing

That your Petitioners apprehind we have in common
with all other men a naturel right to our freedoms without
Being depriv'd of them by our fellow men as we are a free-
born Pepel and have never forfeited this Blessing by aney
compact or agreement whatever. But we were unjustly
dragged by the cruel hand of power from our dearest frinds
and sum of us stolen from the bosoms of our tender Parents
and from a Populous Pleasant and plentiful country and
Brought hither to be made slaves for Life in a Christian
land. Thus we are deprived of every thing that hath a tendency to make life even tolerable, the endearing ties of
husband and wife we are strangers to for we are no longer
man and wife than our masters or mistresses thinkes proper
marred or onmarred. Our children are also taken from us
by force and sent maney miles from us wear we seldom or
ever see them again there to be made slaves of for Life
which sumtimes is vere short by Reson of Being dragged
from their mothers Breest Thus our Lives are imbittered to
us on these accounts By our deplorable situation we are
rendered incapable of shewing our obedience to Almighty
God how can a slave perform the duties of a husband to a
wife or parent to his child How can a husband leave master
to work and cleave to his wife How can the wife submit
themselves to there husbands in all things How can the child
obey thear parents in all things. There is a great number of
us sencear . . . members of the Church of Christ how can
the master and the slave be said to fulfil that command Live
in love let Brotherly Love contuner and abound Beare yea
onenothers Bordenes How can the master be said to Beare
my Borden when he Beares me down whith the Have
chanes of slavery and operson against my will and how can
we fulfill our parte of duty to him whilst in this condition

and as we cannot searve our God as we ought whilst in this situation. Nither can we reap an equal benefet from the laws of the Land which doth not justifi but condemns Slavery or if there had bin aney Law to hold us in Bondage we are Humbely of the Opinion ther never was aney to inslave our children for life when Born in a free Countrey. We therfor Bage your Excellency and Honours will give this its deer weight and consideration and that you will accordingly cause an act of the legislative to be pessed that we may obtain our Natural right our freedoms and our children be set at lebety at the yeare of twenty one for whoues sekes more petequeley your Petitioners is in Duty ever to pray.

(2)

Benjamin Banneker Writes to Thomas Jefferson, 1791*

> One of the outstanding black intellectuals of the Revolutionary period was Benjamin Banneker, an astronomer and mathematician. In 1791, he wrote to Thomas Jefferson, entreating him to remember the Declaration of Independence and end the hypocrisy by ending slavery.

Suffer me to recall to your mind that time, in which the arms of the British crown were exerted, with every powerful effort, in order to reduce you to a state of servitude; look back, I entreat you . . . you were then impressed with proper ideas of the great violation of liberty, and the free possession of those blessings, to which you were entitled by nature; but, sir, how pitiable is it to reflect that although you were so fully convinced of the benevolence of the Father of Mankind, and of his equal and impartial distribution of these rights and privileges which he hath conferred upon

* "Letter from Banneker to Jefferson," Lerone Bennett, Jr., *Before the Mayflower: A History of the Negro in America, 1619–1964* (Baltimore: Penguin Books, Revised Edition, 1966).

them, that you should at the same time counteract his mercies, in detaining by fraud and violence, so numerous a part of my brethren under groaning captivity and cruel oppression, that you should at the same time be found guilty of that most criminal act, which you professedly detested in others.

(3)

Rep. Pinckney Upholds Slavery, 1820*

By 1820, the problem of slavery was the source of major political divisions. Representative Charles Pinckney of South Carolina, one of the framers of the Constitution, articulates the major southern justifications for maintaining slavery.

. . . A great deal has been said on the subject of slavery: that it is an infamous stain and blot on the states that hold them, not only degrading the slave, but the master, and making him unfit for republican government; that it is contrary to religion and the law of God; and that Congress ought to do everything in their power to prevent its extension among the new states.

Now, sir, . . . is there a single line in the Old or New Testament either censuring or forbidding it (slavery)? I answer without hesitation, no. But there are hundreds speaking of and recognizing it. . . . Hagar, from whom millions sprang, was an African slave, brought out of Egypt by Abraham, the father of the faithful and the beloved servant of the Most High; and he had, besides, three-hundred-and-eighteen male slaves. The Jews, in the time of the theocracy, and the Greeks and Romans, had all slaves; at that time there was no nation without them.

* "Rep. Pinckney Upholds Slavery, 1820," in *The American Spirit— United States History as Seen by Contemporaries,* Vol. 1, ed. Thomas A. Bailey (Boston: D. C. Heath & Co., 1963 & 1968).

If we are to believe that this world was formed by a great and omnipotent Being, that nothing is permitted to exist here but by his will, and then throw our eyes throughout the whole of it, we should form an opinion very different indeed from that asserted, that slavery was against the law of God. . . .

It will not be a matter of surprise to anyone that so much anxiety should be shown by the slaveholding states, when it is known that the alarm, given by this attempt to legislate on slavery, has led to the opinion that the very foundations of that kind of property are shaken; that the establishment of the precedent is a measure of the most alarming nature. . . . For, should succeeding Congresses continue to push it, there is no knowing to what length it may be carried.

Have the Northern states any idea of the value of our slaves? At least, sir, six-hundred millions of dollars. If we lose them, the value of the lands they cultivate will be diminished in all cases one half, and in many they will become wholly useless. And an annual income of at least forty millions of dollars will be lost to your citizens, the loss of which will not alone be felt by the non-slaveholding states, but by the whole Union. For to whom, at present, do the Eastern states, most particularly, and the Eastern and Northern, generally, look for the employment of their shipping, in transporting our bulky and valuable products (cotton), and bringing us the manufactures and merchandises of Europe?

Another thing, in case of these losses being brought on us, and our being forced into a division of the Union, what becomes of your public debt? Who are [sic] to pay this, and how will it be paid? In a pecuniary view of this subject, therefore, it must ever be the policy of the Eastern and Northern states to continue connected with us.

(4)

Frederick Douglass:
A Mulatto Boy Learns a Lesson, 1827*

Frederick Douglass learned to read and write while a slave, taught by the naive wife of his master. He escaped and wrote about his life under slavery. The selected passage indicates that slave owners wanted slaves to know only certain parts of the Bible, and feared that if they read it all, it would lead to rebellion.

The frequent hearing of my mistress reading the Bible aloud—for she often read aloud when her husband was absent—awakened my curiosity in respect to this mystery of reading, and roused in me the desire to learn. Up to this time I had known nothing whatever of this wonderful art, and my ignorance and inexperience of what it could do for me, as well as my confidence in my mistress, emboldened me to ask her to teach me to read.

With an unconsciousness and inexperience equal to my own, she readily consented, and in an incredibly short time, by her kind assistance, I had mastered the alphabet and could spell words of three or four letters. My mistress seemed almost as proud of my progress as if I had been her own child, and supposing that her husband would be as well pleased, she made no secret of what she was doing for me. Indeed, she exultingly told him of the aptness of her pupil, and of her intention to persevere in teaching me, as she felt her duty to do, at least to read the Bible. . . .

Master High was astounded beyond measure, and probably for the first time proceeded to unfold to his wife the true philosophy of the slave system, and the peculiar rules necessary in the nature of the case to be observed in the

* "A Mulatto Boy Learns a Lesson," in *The American Spirit—United States History as Seen by Contemporaries,* Vol. 1, ed. Thomas A. Bailey (Boston: D. C. Heath & Co., 1963 and 1968).

management of human chattels. Of course, he forbade her to give me any further instruction, telling her in the first place that to do so was unlawful, as it was also unsafe. "For," said he, "if you give a nigger an inch, he will take an ell. Learning will spoil the best nigger in the world. If he learns to read the Bible, it will forever unfit him to be a slave. He should know nothing but the will of the master, and learn to obey it. As to himself, learning will do him no good, but a great deal of harm, making him disconsolate and unhappy. If you teach him how to read, he'll want to know how to write, and this accomplished, he'll be running away with himself."

(5)

Affray and Murder: Slave Revolt in Ohio, 1829*

Since almost all slaves were illiterate there are few accounts of actual resistance from the slaves' point of view. This account from a Portsmouth, Ohio, paper, August 22, 1829, indicates that the slaves had either planned their assault on their captives, or spontaneously acted in consort. In either case the spirit of armed resistance resulted from a common hatred of white oppressors.

A most shocking outrage was committed in Kentucky, about eight miles from this place, on 14th inst. . . . The men [about sixty slaves] were handcuffed and chained together, in the usual manner for driving those poor wretches, while the women and children were suffered to proceed without incumbrance. It appears that, by means of a file the negroes, unobserved, had succeeded in separating the iron which bound their hands, in such a way as to be able to throw them off at any moment. About 8 o'clock in the morning,

* "Affray and Murder, Portsmouth, Ohio, August, 1829," in *David Walker's Appeal to the Colored Citizens of the World, 1829–1830* (New York: Humanities Press for the American Institute for Marxist Studies, 1965).

while proceeding on the state road leading from Greenup to
Vanceburg, two of them dropped their shackles and commenced a fight, when the wagoner (Petit) rushed in with
his whip to compel them to desist. At this moment, every
negro was found to be perfectly at liberty; and one of them
seizing a club, gave Petit a violent blow on the head, and
laid him dead at his feet; and Allen, who came to his assistance, met a similar fate, from the contents of a pistol fired
by another of the gang. Gordon was then attacked, seized
and held by one of the negroes, whilst another fired twice at
him with a pistol, the ball of which each time grazed his
head, but not proving effectual, he was beaten with clubs,
and left for dead. They then commenced pillaging the
wagon, and with an axe split open the trunk of Gordon, and
rifled it of the money, about $2,400. Sixteen of the negroes
then took to the woods; Gordon, in the mean time, not being
materially injured, was enabled, by the assistance of one of
the women, to mount his horse and flee; pursued, however,
by one of the gang on another horse, with a drawn pistol;
fortunately, he escaped with his life barely, arriving at a
plantation, as the negro came in sight; who then turned
about and retreated.

The neighbourhood was immediately rallied, and a hot
pursuit given—which, we understand, has resulted in the
capture of the whole gang and the recovery of the greatest
part of the money. Seven of the negro men and one woman,
it is said were engaged in the murders, and will be brought
to trial at the next court in Greenupsburg.

(6)

David Walker's Appeal to the Colored Citizens of the World, 1829*

> David Walker was born in North
> Carolina in 1785, the son of a
> black slave and a free mother,

* David Walker's Appeal to the Colored Citizens of the World, 1829–
1830 (New York: Humanities Press for the American Institute for
Marxist Studies, 1965).

which made him a free man. He traveled throughout the country, and gathered his thoughts and observations into a document he called the *Appeal*. Its impact, because it was written by a black, was enormous. A group of whites in Georgia conspired to murder Walker, and the Mayor of Boston asked him to suppress his book. The *Appeal* reached both free blacks and slaves; copies were found throughout the South, where they were declared "seditious literature." Walker was the first black man to write a sustained assault upon slavery and racism in the United States.

. . . I will ask one question here. —Can our condition be any worse?—Can it be more mean and abject? If there are any changes, will they not be for the better, though they may appear for the worst at first? Can they get us any lower? Where can they get us? They are afraid to treat us worse, for they know well, the day they do it they are gone. But against all accusations which may or can be preferred against me, I appeal to Heaven for my motive in writing— who knows that my object is, if possible, to awaken in the breasts of my afflicted, degraded and slumbering brethren, a spirit of inquiry and investigation respecting our miseries and wretchedness in this *REPUBLICAN LAND OF LIB-ERTY!!!!!!*

My Beloved Brethren:—The Indians of North and of South America—the Greeks—the Irish, subjected under the king of Great Britain—the Jews, that ancient people of the Lord—the inhabitants of the islands of the sea—in fine, all the inhabitants of the earth (except however, the sons of Africa) are called *men,* and of course are, and ought to be free. But we (colored people) and our children are *brutes!!* and of course are, and *ought to be* SLAVES to the American people and their children forever!! to dig their mines and work their farms; and thus go on enriching them, from one generation to another with our *blood* and our *tears!!!!* . . .

The whites have always been an unjust, jealous, unmerciful, avaricious, and bloodthirsty set of beings, always seeking after power and authority. . . .

. . . In fact, take them as a body, they are ten times more cruel, avaricious, and unmerciful [as Christians] than ever they were; for while they were heathens, they were bad enough it is true, but it is positively a fact that they were not quite so audacious as to go and take vessel loads of men, women, and children, and in cold blood, and through devilishness, throw them into the sea, and murder them in all kinds of ways. While they were heathens, they were too ignorant for such barbarity. But being Christians, enlightened, and sensible, they are completely prepared for such hellish cruelties. . . .

The whites want slaves, and want us for their slaves, but some of them will curse the day they ever saw us. As true as the sun ever shone in its meridian splendor, my color will root some of them out of the very face of the earth. They shall have enough of making slaves of, and butchering, and murdering us in the manner which they have. . . .

Though I should like to see the whites repent peradventure God may have mercy on them, some however, have gone so far that their cup must be filled. . . .

. . . I must truly say, that ignorance, the mother of treachery and deceit, gnaws into our very vitals. Ignorance, as it now exists among us, produces a state of things, Oh my Lord! too horrible to present to the world. Any man who is curious to see the full force of ignorance developed among the colored people of the United States of America, has only to go into the southern and western states of this confederacy, where, if he is not a tyrant, but has the feelings of a human being, who can feel for a fellow creature, he may see enough to make his very heart bleed! He may see there, a son take his mother, who bore almost the pains of death to give him birth, and by the command of a tyrant, strip her as naked as she came into the world, and apply the cowhide to her, until she falls a victim to death in the road! He may see a husband take his dear wife, not unfrequently in a pregnant state, and perhaps far advanced, and beat her for an unmerciful wretch, until his infant falls a lifeless lump at her feet!

My observer may see fathers beating their sons, mothers their daughters, and children their parents, all to pacify the passions of unrelenting tyrants. He may also, see them telling news and lies, making mischief one upon another. . . . He may see some of my brethren in league with tyrants, selling their own brethren into *hell upon earth,* not dissimilar to the exhibitions in Africa, but in a more secret, servile, and abject manner. . . . My observer may see some of those ignorant and treacherous creatures (coloured people) sneaking about in the large cities, endeavoring to find out all strange colored people, where they work and where they reside, asking them questions, and trying to ascertain whether they are runaways or not, telling them at the same time, that they always have been, are, and always will be friends to their brethren; and perhaps, that they themselves are absconders, and a thousand such treacherous lies to get the better information of the more ignorant!!! There have been and are at this day in Boston, New-York, Philadelphia, and Baltimore, coloured men, who are in league with tyrants, and who receive a great portion of their daily bread, of the moneys which they acquire from the blood and tears of their more miserable brethren, whom they scandalously delivered into the hands of our *natural enemies!!!!!!* . . .

What the American preachers can think of us, I aver this day before my God, I have never been able to define. They have newspapers and monthly periodicals, which they receive in continual succession, but on the pages of which, you will scarcely ever find a paragraph respecting slavery, which is ten thousand times more injurious to this country than all the other evils put together; and which will be the final overthrow of its government, unless something is very speedily done; for their cup is nearly full.—Perhaps they

will laugh at or make light of this; but I tell you Americans!
that unless you speedily alter your course, *you* and your
Country are gone!!!!!! For God Almighty will tear up the
very face of the earth!!!

(7)

Life Under Slavery

Few records exist written by blacks
of life under slavery. The following excerpts, the first by Frederick
Douglass written in 1834, and the
second by Solomon Northrup, a
free Negro from New York, in
1859, reveal how slave masters
tried to break the spirit of slaves
and at the same time breed them
for profit. The Northrup excerpt
tells how slaves were inspected at
auction (Northrup, like many other
free blacks, was kidnapped in
Washington, D.C., but unlike most
kidnapped blacks, he managed to
escape and write of his experiences). The third excerpt, from the
autobiography of Louis Hughes,
does not express the kind of bitterness that other ex-slaves felt. But
even from his account the horror of slave life and the bestialities
of slave-master relations become
clear.

"COHABITATION IN THE CABINS, 1834"*

In pursuit of this object [wealth], pious as Mr. Covey
was, he proved himself as unscrupulous and base as the
worst of his neighbors. In the beginning he was only able—
as he said—"to buy one slave"; and scandalous and shocking as is the fact, he boasted that he bought her simply "as a
breeder." But the worst of this is not told in this naked
statement. This young woman (Caroline was her name)

* "Cohabitation in the Cabins, 1834," in *The American Spirit—United
States History as Seen by Contemporaries,* Vol. 1, ed. Thomas A. Bailey
(Boston: D. C. Heath & Co., 1963 & 1968).

was virtually compelled by Covey to abandon herself to the object for which he had purchased her; and the result was the birth of twins at the end of the year. At this addition to his human stock Covey and his wife were ecstatic with joy. No one dreamed of reproaching the woman or finding fault with the hired man, Bill Smith, the father of the children, for Mr. Covey himself had locked the two up together every night, thus inviting the result.

But I will pursue this revolting subject no farther. No better illustration of the unchaste, demoralizing, and debasing character of slavery can be found than is furnished in the fact that this professedly Christian slaveholder, amidst all his prayers and hymns, was shamelessly and boastfully encouraging and actually compelling, in his own house, undisguised and unmitigated fornication, as a means of increasing his stock. It was the system of slavery which made this allowable, and which condemned the slaveholder for buying a slave woman and devoting her to this life no more than for buying a cow and raising stock from her and the same rules were observed, with a view to increasing the number and quality of the one as of the other. . . .

"HUMAN CATTLE FOR SALE, 1850"*

Next day many customers called to examine Freeman's "new lot" [of slaves]. The latter gentleman was very loquacious, dwelling at much length upon our several good points and qualities. He would make us hold up our heads, walk briskly back and forth, while customers would feel of our hands and arms and bodies, turn us about, ask us what we could do, make us open our mouths and show our teeth, precisely as a jockey examines a horse which he is about to barter for or purchase.

Sometimes a man or woman was taken back to the small house in the yard, stripped, and inspected more minutely.

* "Human Cattle for Sale," in *The American Spirit—United States History as Seen by Contemporaries,* Vol. 1, ed. Thomas A. Bailey (Boston: D. C. Heath & Co., 1963 & 1968).

Scars upon a slave's back were considered evidence of a rebellious or unruly spirit, and hurt his sale.

One old gentleman, who said he wanted a coachman, appeared to take a fancy to me. From his conversation with Freeman, I learned he was a resident of the city [New Orleans]. I very much desired that he would buy me, because I conceived it would not be difficult to make my escape from New Orleans on some Northern vessel. Freeman asked him $1,500 for me. The old gentleman insisted it was too much, as times were very hard. Freeman, however, declared that I was sound and healthy, of a good constitution, and intelligent. He made it a point to enlarge upon my musical attainments. The old gentleman argued quite adroitly that there was nothing extraordinary about the nigger, and finally, to my regret, went out, saying he would call again.

THIRTY YEARS A SLAVE: AUTOBIOGRAPHY OF LOUIS HUGHES*

Mrs. McGee was naturally irritable. Servants always got an extra whipping when she had any personal trouble, as though they could help it. Every morning little Kate, Aunt Delia's little girl, would have to go with the madam on her rounds to the different buildings of the establishment, to carry the key basket. So many were the keys that they were kept in a basket especially provided for them, and the child was its regular bearer. The madam, with this little attendant, was everywhere—in the barn, in the hennery, in the smokehouse—and she always made trouble with the servants wherever she went. Indeed, she rarely returned to the house from these rounds without having whipped two or three servants, whether there was really any cause for the punishment or not. She seldom let a day pass without beating some poor woman unmercifully. The number and severity of these whippings depended more upon the humor of the madam than upon the conduct of the slaves. Of

* Louis Hughes, *Thirty Years a Slave: Autobiography of Louis Hughes* (Milwaukee: South Side Printing Co., 1897).

course, I always came in for a share in this brutal treatment. She continued her old habit of boxing my jaws, pinching my ears; no day ever passing without her indulging in this exercise of her physical powers. So long had I endured this, I came to expect it, no matter how well I did my duties; and it had its natural effect upon me, making me a coward, even though I was now growing into manhood. . . . Her usual morning greeting was: "Well, Lou, have you dusted the parlors?" "Oh, yes," I would answer. "Have the flowers been arranged?" "Yes, all is in readiness," I would say. Once I had stoned the steps as usual, but the madam grew angry as soon as she saw them. I had labored hard, and thought she would be pleased. The result, however, was very far from that. She took me out, stripped me of my shirt and began thrashing me, saying I was spoiled. I was no longer a child, but old enough to be treated differently. I began to cry, for it seemed to me my heart would break. But, after the first burst of tears, the feeling came over me that I was a man, and it was an outrage to treat me so—to keep me under the lash day after day. . . .

Sometimes when the farm hands were at work, peddlers would come along; and, as they were treated badly by the rich planters, they hated them, and talked to the slaves in a way to excite them and set them thinking of freedom. They would say encouragingly to them: "Ah! You will be free some day." But the down-trodden slaves, some of whom were bowed with age, with frosted hair and furrowed cheek, would answer, looking up from their work: "We don't b'lieve dat; my grandfather said we was to be free, but we aint free yet." It had been talked of (this freedom) from generation to generation. Perhaps they would not have thought of freedom, if their owners had not been so cruel. Had my mistress been more kind to me, I should have thought less of liberty. I know the cruel treatment which I received was the main thing that made me wish to be free. Besides this, it was inhuman to separate families as they did. Think of a mother being sold from all her children—separated for life! This separation was common, and many died heart-broken, by reason of it. Ah! I cannot forget the cruel separation from my mother. I know not what became of her, but I have always believed her dead many years ago. Hundreds were separated, as my mother and I were, and never met again. Though freedom was yearned for by some because the treatment was so bad, others, who were bright and had looked into the matter, knew it was a curse to be held a slave—they longed to stand out in true manhood—allowed to express their opinions as were white men. Others still desired freedom, thinking they could then reclaim a wife, or husband, or children. The mother would again see her child. All these promptings of the heart made them yearn for freedom. . . .

My wife Matilda was born in Fayette county, Kentucky, June 17th, 1830. . . . I remember well the day she came. The madam greeted her, and said: "Well, what can you do, girl? Have you ever done any cooking? Where are you from?" Matilda was, as I remember her, a sad picture to look at. She had been a slave, it is true, but had seen good days to what the slaves down the river saw. Any one could see she was almost heartbroken—she never seemed happy. . . . Matilda had been there three years when I married her. The Boss had always promised that he would give me a nice wedding, and he kept his word. He was very proud, and liked praise. The wedding that he gave us was indeed a pleasant one. All the slaves from their neighbor acquaintances were invited. One thing Boss did was a credit to him, but it was rare among slave-holders—he had me married by their parish minister. . . . Things went on as usual after this. The madam grew more irritable and exacting, always finding fault with the servants, whipping them, or threatening to do so, upon the slightest provocation, or none at all. There was something in my wife's manner, however, which kept the madam from whipping her—an open or implied threat perhaps that such treatment would not be endured without resistance or protest of some kind. This the madam regarded as a great indignity, and she hated my wife for it, and, at times, was ready to crush her, so great was her anger. In a year there were born to us twin babies; and the madam now thought she had my wife tied, as the babies would be a barrier to anything like resistance on her part, and there would be no danger of her running away. She, therefore, thought that she could enjoy, without hindrance, the privilege of beating the woman of whose womanhood she had theretofore stood somewhat in fear. Boss said from the first that I should give my wife assistance, as she needed time to care for the babies. Really he was not as bad as the madam at heart, for she tried to see how hard she could be on us. She gave me all the extra work to do that she could think of, apparently to keep me from helping my wife in the kitchen. She had all the cooking to do for three heavy meals each day, all the washing and ironing of the finest clothes, besides caring for the babies between times. In the morning she would nurse the babies, then hurry off to the kitchen to get breakfast while they were left in charge of a little girl. Again at noon she repeated her visit to the babies, after cooking the dinner, then in the evening, after supper, she would go to nurse them again. After supper was over, dishes all washed and kitchen in order, she would then go to the little ones for the night. . . . My heart was sore and heavy, for my wife was almost run to death with work. The children grew puny and sickly for want of proper care. . . . Our trial went on, until one morning I heard a great fuss in the house, the madam calling for the yard man to come and tie my wife, as she could not manage her. My wife had always refused to allow the madam to whip her; but now, as the babies were here, mistress thought she would try it once more. Matilda resisted, and madam called for Boss. In a minute he came, and, grabbing my wife, commenced choking her, saying to her: "What do you mean? Is that the way you talk to ladies?" My wife had only said to her mistress: "You shall not whip me." This made her furious, hence her call for Boss. I was in the dining room, and could hear everything. My blood boiled in my veins to see my wife so abused; yet I dare not open my mouth. After the fuss, my wife went straight to the laundry. I followed her there, and found her bundling up her babies' clothes, which were washed but not ironed. I knew at a glance that she was going away . . . and I did not know what to say, but I told her to do the best she could. Often when company came and I held the horses, or did an errand for them, they would tip me to a quarter or half a dollar. This money I always saved, and so had a little change, which I now gave to Matilda, for her use in her effort to get away from her cruel treatment. She started at once for Forrest's trader's yards, with the babies in her arms and, after she got into Memphis, she stopped outside the yard to rest. While she was sitting on the curbstone, Forrest came out of the yard by the back gate and saw her. Coming up to her he said: "My God! Matilda, what are you doing here? You have changed so I would not have known you. Why have you come here?" Matilda said: "I came back here to be sold again." . . . Word was then sent McGee that his cook was in the yard and had come to be sold. He went in haste to the yard. . . . She was brought back, and as they rode along in the rockaway, Boss said: "When I am through with you I guess you won't run away again." As they drove up I saw the madam go running out to meet them. She shouted to Matilda: "Ah! madam, you put up at the wrong hotel." They at once went to the barn where my wife was tied to the joist, and Boss and the madam beat her by turns. After they had finished the whipping, Boss said, tauntingly: "Now I am buying you and selling you—I want you to know that I never shall sell you while my head and yours is hot." I was trembling from head to foot, for I was powerless to do anything for her. My twin babies lived only six months after that, not having had the care they needed, and which it was impossible for their mother to give them while performing the almost endless labor required of her, under threats of cruel beatings. . . .

Ever since the beginning of the war, and the slaves had heard that possibly they might some time be free, they seemed unspeakably happy. They were afraid to let the masters know that they ever thought of such a thing, and they never dreamed of speaking about it except among

themselves. They were a happy race, poor souls! notwithstanding their downtrodden condition. They would laugh
and chat about freedom in their cabins; and many a little
rhyme about it originated among them, and was softly sung
over their work. I remember a song that Aunt Kitty, the
cook at Master Jack's, used to sing. It ran something like
this:

> There'll be no more talk about Monday, by and by,
> But every day will be Sunday, by and by.

The old woman was singing, or rather humming, it one
day, and old lady McGee heard her. She was busy getting
her dinner, and I suppose never realized she was singing
such an incendiary piece, when old Mrs. McGee broke in
upon her: "Don't think you are going to be free; you
darkies were made by God and ordained to wait upon us."

(8)

Destiny of the Colored Race: Martin R. Delany, 1852*

Martin Delany, a free black physician educated at Harvard, was born in 1812 in what is now Charleston, West Virginia; he died in 1885.

He was the foremost advocate of black emigration from the United States, though he was bitterly opposed to Liberia as a possible home. His reasoning is strikingly similar to that of those blacks who today see no possibility of resolving America's racial problem within the country's borders. The following are excerpts from his book, *Destiny of the Colored Race*, published in 1852. The first describes his reaction as a black free man to the Fugitive Slave Law; the second, thoughts about emigration.

* Martin R. Delany, *The Condition, Elevation, Emigration and Destiny*

By the provisions of this bill, the colored people of the United States are positively degraded beneath the level of the whites—are made liable at any time, in any place, and under all circumstances, to be arrested—and upon the claim of any white person, without the privilege, even of making a defence, sent into endless bondage. Let no visionary nonsense about *habeas corpus,* or a *fair trial,* deceive us; there are no such rights granted in this bill, and except where the commissioner is too ignorant to understand when reading it, or too stupid to enforce it when he does understand, there is no earthly chance—no hope under heaven for the colored person who is brought before one of these officers of the law. Any leniency that may be expected, must proceed from the whims or caprice of the magistrate—in fact, it is optional with them; and *our* rights and liberty entirely at their disposal.

We are slaves in the midst of freedom, waiting patiently, and unconcernedly—indifferently, and stupidly, for masters to come and lay claim to us, trusting to their generosity, whether or not they will own us and carry us into endless bondage.

The slave is more secure than we; he knows who holds the heel upon his bosom—we know not the wretch who may grasp us by the throat. His master may be a man of some conscientious scruples; ours may be unmerciful. Good or bad, mild or harsh, easy or hard, lenient or severe, saint or satan—whenever that master demands any one of us—even our affectionate wives and darling little children, *we must go into slavery*—there is *no alternative*. The *will* of the man who sits in judgment on our liberty, is the law. To him is given *all power* to say, whether or not we have a right to enjoy freedom. This is the power over the slave in the South—this is now extended to the North. The will of the man who sits in judgment over us is the law; because it is explicitly provided that the *decision* of the commissioner

of the Colored People of the United States (Arno Press and the New York Times, New York, 1968).

shall be final, from which there can be no appeal. . . .

. . . We must abandon all vague theory, and look at
facts as they really are; viewing ourselves in our true
political position in the body politic. To imagine ourselves
to be included in the body politic, except by express legislation, is at war with common sense, and contrary to fact.
Legislation, the administration of the laws of the country,
and the exercise of rights by the people, all prove to the
contrary. We are politically . . . aliens to the laws and
political privileges of the country. These are truths—fixed
facts, that quaint theory and exhausted moralising, are
impregnable to, and fall harmlessly before.

It is useless to talk about our rights in individual States:
we can have no rights there as citizens, not recognised in our
common country; as the citizens of one State, are entitled
to all the rights and privileges of an American citizen in all
the States—the nullity of the one necessarily implying the
nullity of the other. These provisions then do not include
the colored people of the United States; since there is no
power left in them, whereby they may protect us as their
own citizens. Our descent, by the laws of the country,
stamps us with inferiority—upon us has this law worked
corruption of blood. We are in hands of the General Government, and no State can rescue us. The Army and Navy
stand at the service of our enslavers, the whole force of
which, may at any moment—even in the dead of night, as
has been done—when sunk in the depth of slumber, called
out for the purpose of forcing our mothers, sisters, wives,
and children, or ourselves, into hopeless servitude, there to
weary out a miserable life, a relief from which, death would
be hailed with joy. . . .

What then shall we do?—what is the remedy—is the important question to be answered? . . .

THAT there have been people in all ages under certain
circumstances, that may be benefited by emigration, will be
admitted; and that there are circumstances under which
emigration is absolutely necessary to their political eleva-

tion, cannot be disputed. . . .

Where shall we go? This we conceive to be all-important
—of paramount consideration, and shall endeavor to show
the most advantageous locality; and premise the recom-
mendation, with the strictest advice against any countenance whatever, to the emigration scheme of the so-called
Republic of Liberia.

THAT we desire the civilization and enlightenment of
Africa—the high and elevated position of Liberia among
the nations of the earth, may not be doubted, as the writer
was among the first, seven or eight years ago, to make the
suggestion and call upon the Liberians to hold up their
heads like men; take courage, having confidence in their
own capacity to govern themselves, and come out from
their disparaging position, by formally declaring their
Independence. . . .

We have but a single object in view, and that is, to
inform the minds of the colored people at large, upon many
things pertaining to their elevation, that but few among us
are acquainted with. Unfortunately for us, as a body, we
have been taught to believe, that we must have some person
to think for us, instead of thinking for ourselves. So accustomed are we to submission and this kind of training,
that it is with difficulty, even among the most intelligent of
the colored people, an audience may be elicited for any
purpose whatever, if the expounder is to be a colored
person; and the introduction of any subject is treated with
indifference, if not contempt, when the originator is a
colored person. Indeed, the most ordinary white person, is
almost revered, while the most qualified colored person is
totally neglected. Nothing from them is appreciated.

We have been standing comparatively still for years,
following in the footsteps of our friends, believing that what
they promise us can be accomplished, just because they say
so, although our own knowledge should long since, have
satisfied us to the contrary. Because even were it possible,
with the present hate and jealousy that the whites have

towards us in this country, for us to gain equality of rights with them; we never could have an equality of the exercise and enjoyment of those rights—because, the great odds of numbers are against us. We might indeed, as some at present, have the right of the elective franchise—nay, it is not the elective franchise, because the *elective franchise* makes the enfranchised, *eligible* to any position attainable; but we may exercise the right of *voting* only, which to us, is but poor satisfaction; and we by no means care to cherish the privilege of voting somebody into office, to help to make laws to degrade us.

In religion—because they are both *translators* and *commentators,* we must believe nothing, however absurd, but what our oppressors tell us. In Politics, nothing but such as they promulge; in Anti-Slavery, nothing but what our white brethren and friends say we must; in the mode and manner of our elevation, we must do nothing, but that which may be laid down to be done by our white brethren from some quarter or other; and now, even on the subject of emigration, there are some colored people to be found, so lost to their own interest and self-respect, as to be gulled by slave owners and colonizationists, who are led to believe there is no other place in which they can become elevated, but Liberia, a government of American slave-holders, as we have shown—simply, because white men have told them so.

Go or stay—of course each is free to do as he pleases—one thing is certain; our Elevation is the work of our own hands. And Mexico, Central America, the West Indies, and South America, all present now, opportunities for the individual enterprise of our young men, who prefer to remain in the United States, in preference to going where they can enjoy real freedom, and equality of rights. Freedom of Religion, as well as of politics, being tolerated in all these places.

Let our young men and women, prepare themselves for usefulness and business; that the men may enter into merchandise, trading, and other things of importance; the young women may become teachers of various kinds, and otherwise fill places of usefulness. . . .

A GLANCE AT OURSELVES—
With broken hopes—and devastation;
A race *resigned* to DEGRADATION!

We have said much to our young men and women, about their vocation and calling; we have dwelt much upon the menial position of our people in this country. Upon this point we cannot say too much, because there is a seeming satisfaction and seeking after such positions manifested on their part, unknown to any other people. There appears to be, a want of a sense of propriety or *self-respect,* altogether inexplicable; because young men and women among us, many of whom have good trades and homes, adequate to their support, voluntarily leave them, and seek positions, such as servants, waiting maids, coachmen, nurses, cooks in gentlemen's kitchen, or such like occupations, when they can gain a livelihood at something more respectable, or elevating in character. And the worse part of the whole matter is, that they have become so accustomed to it, it has become so "fashionable," that it seems to have become second nature, and they recall becoming offended, when it is spoken against. . . .

We have nothing to say against those whom *necessity* compels to do these things, those who can do no better; we have only to do with those who can, and will not, or do not do better. The whites are always in the advance, and we either standing still or retrograding; as that which does not go forward, must either stand in one place or go back. The father in all probability is a farmer, mechanic, or man of some independent business; and the wife, sons and daughters, are chamber-maids, on vessels, nurses and waiting-maids, or coachmen and cooks in families. This is retrogradation. The wife, sons, and daughters should be elevated above this condition as a necessary consequence.

If we did not love our race superior to others, we would not concern ourself about their degradation; for the greatest desire of our heart is, to see them stand on a level with the most elevated of mankind. No people are ever elevated above the condition of their *females;* hence, the condition of the *mother* determines the condition of the child. To know the position of a people, it is only necessary to know the *condition* of their *females;* and despite themselves, they cannot rise above their level. Then what is our condition? Our *best ladies* being washerwomen, chamber-maids, children's traveling nurses, and common house servants, and menials, we are all a degraded, miserable people, inferior to any other people as a whole, on the face of the globe.

These great truths, however unpleasant, must be brought before the minds of our people in its true and proper light, as we have been too delicate about them, and too long concealed them for fear of giving offence. It would have been infinitely better for our race, if these facts had been presented before us half a century ago—we would have been now proportionably benefitted by it.

As an evidence of the degradation to which we have been reduced, we dare premise, that this chapter will give offence to many, very many, and why? Because they may say, "He dared to say that the occupation of a *servant* is a degradation." It is not necessarily degrading; it would not be, to one or a few people of a kind; but a *whole race of servants* are a degradation to that people. . . .

Though we are servants; among ourselves we claim to be *ladies* and *gentlemen,* equal in standing, and as the popular expression goes, "Just as good as any body"—and so believing, we make no efforts to raise above the common level of menials; because the *best* being in that capacity, all are content with the position. We cannot at the same time, be domestic and lady; servant and gentleman. We must be the one or the other.

In our own country, the United States, there are *three million five hundred thousand slaves;* and we, the nominally free colored people, are *six hundred thousand* in number; estimating one-sixth to be men, we have *one hundred thousand* able bodied freemen, which will make a powerful auxiliary in any country to which we may become adopted

—an ally not to be despised by any power on earth. We love our country, dearly love her, but she don't love us—she despises us, and bids us begone, driving us from her embraces; but we shall not go where she desires us; but when we do go, whatever love we have for her, we shall love the country none the less that receives us as her adopted children.

For the want of business habits and training, our energies have become paralyzed; our young men never think of business, any more than if they were so many bondmen, without the right to pursue any calling they may think most advisable. With our people in this country, dress and good appearances have been made the only test of gentleman and ladyship, and that vocation which offers the best opportunity to dress and appear well, has generally been preferred, however menial and degrading, by our young people, without even, in the majority of cases, an effort to do better; indeed, in many instances, refusing situations equally lucrative, and superior in position; but which would not allow as much display of dress and personal appearance. This, if we ever expect to rise, must be discarded from among us, and a high and respectable position assumed.

One of our great temporal curses is our consummate poverty. We are the poorest people, as a class, in the world of civilized mankind—abjectly, miserably poor, no one scarcely being able to assist the other. To this, of course, there are noble exceptions; but that which is common to, and the very process by which white men exist, and succeed in life, is unknown to colored men in general. In any and every considerable community may be found, some one of our white fellow-citizens, who is worth more than all the colored people in that community put together. We consequently have little or no efficiency. We must have means to be practically efficient in all the undertakings of life; and to obtain them, it is necessary that we should be engaged in lucrative pursuits, trades, and general business transactions. In order to be thus engaged, it is necessary that we should occupy positions that afford the facilities for such pursuits.

To compete now with the mighty odds of wealth, social and religious preferences, and political influences of this country, at this advanced stage of its national existence, we never may expect. A new country, and new beginning, is the only true, rational, politic remedy for our disadvantageous position; and that country we have already pointed out, with triple golden advantages, all things considered, to that of any country to which it has been the province of man to embark.

Every other than we, have at various periods of necessity, been a migratory people; and all when oppressed, shown a greater abhorrence of oppression, if not a greater love of liberty, than we. We cling to our oppressors as the objects of our love. It is true that our enslaved brethren are here, and we have been led to believe that it is necessary for us to remain, on that account. Is it true, that all should remain in degradation, because a part are degraded? We believe no such thing. We believe it to be the duty of the Free, to elevate themselves in the most speedy and effective manner possible; as the redemption of the bondman depends entirely upon the elevation of the freeman; therefore, to elevate the free colored people of America, anywhere upon this continent; forebodes the speedy redemption of the slaves. We shall hope to hear no more of so fallacious a doctrine—the necessity of the free remaining in degradation, for the sake of the oppressed. Let us apply, first, the lever to ourselves; and the force that elevates us to the position of manhood's considerations and honors, will cleft the manacle of every slave in the land. . . .

The offsprings of slaves and peasantry, have the general characteristics of their parents; and nothing but a different course of training and education, will change the character.

The slave may become a lover of his master, and learn to forgive him for continual deeds of maltreatment and abuse; just as the Spaniel would couch and fondle at the feet that kick him; because he has been taught to reverence them, and consequently, becomes adapted in body and mind to his condition. Even the shrubbery-loving Canary, and lofty-soaring Eagle, may be tamed to the cage, and learn to love it from habit of confinement. It has been so with us in our position among our oppressors; we have been so prone to such positions, that we have learned to love them. . . .

The Irishman and German in the United States, are very different persons to what they were when in Ireland and Germany, the countries of their nativity. There their spirits were depressed and downcast; but the instant they set their feet upon unrestricted soil; free to act and untrammeled to move; their physical condition undergoes a change, which in time becomes physiological, which is transmitted to the offspring, who when born under such circumstances, is a decidedly different being to what it would have been, had it been born under different circumstances.

A child born under oppression, has all the elements of servility in its constitution; who when born under favorable circumstances, has to the contrary, all the elements of freedom and independence of feeling. Our children then, may not be expected, to maintain that position and manly bearing; born under the unfavorable circumstances with which we are surrounded in this country; that we so much desire. To use the language of the talented Mr. Whipper, "they cannot be raised in this country, without being stoop shouldered." Heaven's pathway stands unobstructed, which will lead us into a Paradise of bliss. Let us go on and possess the land, and the God of Israel will be our God.

(9)

Frederick Douglass Opposes Colonization*

Frederick Douglass believed that American blacks could fight for and win equality in the United States. For that reason he opposed Delany's colonization ideas, arguing that free blacks ought to devote their energy to freeing the slaves and reforming American society.

* A speech by Frederick Douglass, published in *The North Star,* January 26, 1849, reprinted in *Apropos of Africa,* compiled by Adelaide Cromwell Hill and Martin Kilson (New York: Humanities Press, 1969).

We are of opinion that the *free* colored people generally mean to live in America, and not in Africa; and to appropriate a large sum for our removal, would merely be a waste of the public money. We do not mean to go to Liberia. Our minds are made up to live here if we can, or die here if we must; so every attempt to remove us, will be, as it ought to be, labor lost. Here we are and here we shall remain. While our brethren are in bondage on these shores; it is idle to think of inducing any considerable number of the free colored people to quit this for a foreign land.

For two hundred and twenty-eight years has the colored man toiled over the soil of America, under a burning sun and a driver's lash—plowing, planting, reaping, that white men might roll in ease, their hands unhardened by labor, and their brows unmoistened by the waters of genial toil, and now that the moral sense of mankind is beginning to revolt at this system of foul treachery and cruel wrong, and is demanding its overthrow, the mean and cowardly oppressor is mediating plans to expel the colored man entirely from the country. Shame upon the guilty wretches that dare propose, and all that countenance such a proposition. We live here— have lived here—have a right to live here, and mean to live here.

(10)

Racism in Virginia, 1847*

The Dred Scott Decision of 1857 clarified the status of slaves as property, which meant that masters could take slaves into non-slave territory with impunity. The decision by Chief Justice Taney was based on the "innate inferiority" of blacks, arguing that the Declaration of Independence did not mean

---

* "A Virginia Newspaper Gloats, 1847," in *The American Spirit— United States History as Seen by Contemporaries,* ed. Thomas A. Bailey (Boston: D. C. Heath & Co., 1963 & 1968).

all men, but only white men. Southern newspapers used the decision to further white supremacy. The following excerpt from an editorial in a Southern newspaper was typical of the daily racism that all Southerners were exposed to just before the Civil War.

Negro nuisances, in the shape of occupying promiscuous seats in our rail-cars and churches with those who are citizens, must be abated. Negro insolence and domineering arrogance must be rebuked; the whole tribe must be taught to fall back into their legitimate position in human society—the position that Divine Providence intended they should occupy. Not being citizens, they can claim none of the rights or privileges belonging to a citizen. They can neither vote, hold office, nor occupy any other position in society than an inferior and subordinate one—the only one for which they are fitted, the only one for which they have the natural qualifications which entitle them to enjoy or possess.

(11)

Lincoln's Thoughts on Emancipation and Colonization

President Abraham Lincoln believed in colonization as a rational solution to the "Negro problem." Although his racial beliefs changed between the 1850s and the War years he never became an abolitionist, nor was his thought freed from the contemporary racist attitudes. In his "Emancipation Proclamation" he states that the freeing of the slaves is "warranted by the Constitution upon military necessity," and "as a fit and necessary war measure for suppressing [the] rebellion. . . ."

Springfield, Illinois, October 11, 1854

If all earthly power were given me, I should not know what to do as to the existing institution. My first impulse would be to free all the slaves, and send them to Liberia, to their own native land. But a moment's reflection would convince me that whatever of high hope (as I think there is) there may be in this in the long run, its sudden execution is impossible. If they were all landed there in a day, they would all perish in the next ten days, and there are not surplus shipping and surplus money enough to carry them there in many times ten days. . . .

What next? Free them and make them politically and socially our equals. My own feelings will not admit of this and if mine would, we well know that those of the great mass of whites will not. Whether this feeling accords with justice and sound judgment is not the sole question, if indeed it is any part of it. A universal feeling, whether well or ill founded, cannot be safely disregarded.

Speech of Abraham Lincoln, Charleston, September 18, 1858.*

I will say, then, that I am not, nor ever have been, in favor of bringing about in my way the social and political equality of the white and black races (applause): that I am not, nor ever have been, in favor of making voters or jurors of negroes, nor of qualifying them to hold office, nor to intermarry with white people. . . .

And inasmuch as they cannot so live, while they do remain together there must be the position of superior and inferior, and as much as any other man am in favor of having the superior position assigned to the white race.

July 12, 1862—Appeal to Favor Compensated Emancipation. Read by the President to Border-State Representatives

I do not speak of emancipation at once, but of a decision at once to emancipate gradually. Room in South America for colonization can be obtained cheaply and in abundance,

* Henry Steele Commager, ed., *Documents of American History*. (New York: Appleton-Century-Crofts, Inc., 1958).

and when numbers shall be large enough to be company and encouragement for one another, the freed people will not be so reluctant to go.

December 1, 1862—Annual Message to Congress

Application have been made to me by many free Americans of African descent to favor their emigration, with a view to such colonization as was contemplated in recent acts of Congress. Other parties at home and abroad—some from interested motives, others upon patriotic considerations, and still others influenced by philanthropic sentiments—have suggested similar measures; while, on the other hand, several of the Spanish-American republics have protested against the sending of such colonies to their respective territories. Under these circumstances, I have declined to move any such colony to any state without first obtaining the consent of its government, with an agreement on its part to receive and protect such emigrants in all the rights of freemen; and I have at the same time offered to the several states situated within the tropics, or having colonies there, to negotiate with them, subject to the advice and consent of the Senate, to favor the voluntary emigration of persons of that class to their respective territories, upon conditions which shall be equal, just, and humane. Liberia and Hayti are as yet the only countries to which colonists of African descent from here could go with certainty of being received and adopted as citizens; and I regret to say such persons contemplating colonization do not seem so willing to migrate to those countries as to some others, nor so willing as I think their interest demands. I believe, however, opinion among them in this respect is improving; and that ere long there will be an augmented and considerable migration to both these countries from the United States. . . . I cannot make it better known than it already is, that I strongly favor colonization. And yet I wish to say there is an objection used against free colored persons remaining in the country which is largely imaginary, if not sometimes malicious.

It is insisted that their presence would injure and displace

white labor and white laborers. Labor is like any other
commodity in the market—increase the demand for it, and
you increase the price of it. Reduce the supply of black
labor by colonizing the black laborer out of the country,
and by precisely so much you increase the demand for, and
wages of, white labor.

But it is dreaded that the freed people will swarm forth
and cover the whole land? Are they not already in the land?
Will liberation make them any more numerous? Equally
distributed among the whites of the whole country, and
there would be but one colored to seven whites. Could the
one in any way greatly disturb the seven?

(12)

Freedman's Aspirations (1865)*

Contrary to the myths propagated
by many historians, the immediate
post-Civil War period was not
characterized by helpless blacks
waiting for carpetbaggers to tell
them what to do. While Freedman's Aid Societies, church groups,
and other agencies helped many of
the newly freed slaves, both previously free blacks and ex-slaves
got together, formulated demands,
and issued statements of their positions and their needs. One example
of such a statement is this excerpt
from the proceedings of a convention held in Alexandria, Virginia,
in 1865.

We, the undersigned members of a Convention of
colored citizens of the State of Virginia, would respectfully
represent that, although we have been held as slaves, and
denied all recognition as a constituent of your nationality
for almost the entire period of the duration of your govern-

* "Freedman's Aspirations (1865)," in *Reconstruction,* ed. Richard N.
Current (Englewood Cliffs, New Jersey: Prentice-Hall Publishing Co.,
1965).

ment, and that by *your permission* we have been denied either home or country, and deprived of the dearest rights of human nature: yet when you and our immediate oppressors met in deadly conflict upon the field of battle—the one to destroy and the other to save your government and nationality, *we,* with scarce an exception, in our inmost souls espoused your cause, and watched, and prayed, and waited, and labored for your success. . . .

When the contest waxed long, and the result hung doubtfully, you appealed to us for help, and how well we answered is written in the rosters of the two-hundred thousand colored troops now enrolled in your service; and as to our undying devotion to your cause, let the uniform acclamation of escaped prisoners, "whenever we saw a black face we felt sure of a friend," answer.

Well, the war is over, the rebellion is "put down" and we are *declared* free! Four-fifths of our enemies are paroled or amnestied, and the other fifth are being pardoned, and the President has, in his efforts at the reconstruction of the civil government of the States, late in rebellion, left us entirely at the mercy of these subjugated but unconverted rebels, in *everything* save the privilege of bringing us, our wives and little ones, to the auction block. . . . We *know* these men—know them *well*—and we assure you that, with the majority of them, loyalty is only "lip deep," and that their professions of loyalty are used as a cover to the cherished design of getting restored to their former relations with the federal government, and then, by all sorts of "unfriendly legislation," to render the freedom you have given us more intolerable than the slavery they intended for us.

We warn you in time that our only safety is in keeping them under governors of the *military persuasion* until you have so amended the federal Constitution that it will prohibit the States from making any distinction between citizens on account of race or color. In one word, the only salvation for us besides the power of the Government is in the *possession of the ballot*. Give us this, and we will protect ourselves. . . . But 'tis said we are ignorant. Admit it. Yet who denies we know a *traitor* from a loyal man, a gentleman from a rowdy, a friend from an enemy? . . . All we ask is an *equal chance* with the white *traitors* varnished and japanned with the oath of amnesty. Can you deny us this and still keep faith with us? . . .

(13)

"We Claim Exactly the Same Rights": A Black Convention in Alabama, 1867*

After the Civil War many blacks joined the Republican Party, and thereby entered the established political system for the first time in the South. In May, 1867, Alabama blacks convened in Mobile, Alabama and published the "Address of the Colored Convention to the People of Alabama." The content and style of the document demonstrate both an acute understanding of the difficulties involved in overcoming the traditional racism of America, as well as militant demands for immediate equality. Those historians who have described black participation in Reconstruction politics in terms of corruption and selfishness have ignored documents like this "Address of Alabama," which has parallels in several southern states.

As there seems to be considerable difference of opinion concerning the "legal rights of the colored man," it will not be amiss to say that we claim exactly *the same rights, privileges and immunities as are enjoyed by white men*—we ask nothing more and will be content with nothing less. *All legal* distinctions between the races are now abolished. The word white is stricken from our laws, and every privilege

* "Address of Alabama Colored Convention, 1867," in James S. Allen, *Reconstruction: the Battle for Democracy, 1865–1876* (New York, 1963).

which white men were formerly permitted to enjoy, merely because they were white men, now that word is stricken out, we are entitled to on the ground that we are men. *Color can no longer be pleaded for the purpose of curtailing privileges, and every public right, privilege and immunity is enjoyable by every individual member of the public.*—This is the touchstone that determines all these points. So long as a park or a street is a *public* park or street the entire public has the right to use it; so long as a car or a steamboat is a public conveyance, it must carry all who come to it, and serve all alike who pay alike. The law no longer knows white nor black, but simply men, and consequently we are entitled to ride in public conveyances, hold office, sit on juries and do everything else which we have in the past been prevented from doing solely on the ground of our color. . . .

We have said that we intend to claim all our rights, and we submit to our white friends that it is the height of folly on their part to withhold them any longer. One-half of the voters in Alabama are black men, and in a few months there is to be an entire reorganization of the State government. The new officers—legislative, executive and judicial —will owe their election largely, if not mainly to the colored people, and every one must see clearly that the voters will then be certain to require and the officers to compel a cessation of all illegal discriminations. The question which every man now illegally discriminating against us has to decide is, whether it is politic to insist upon gratifying prejudices during a few dull months, with the certainty by so doing, of incurring the lasting displeasure of one-half of the voting population of the State. We can stand it if they can, but we assure them that they are being watched closely, and that their conduct will be remembered when we have power.

There are some good people who are always preaching patience and procrastination. They would have us wait a few months, years, or generations, until the whites voluntarily give us our rights, but we do not intend to wait one day longer than we are absolutely compelled to. Look at our demands, and then at theirs. We ask of them simply that they surrender unreasonable and unreasoning prejudice; that they cease imitating dog in the manger; that they consent to allow others as well as themselves to prosper and be happy. But they would have us pay for what we do not get; tramp through the broiling sun or pelting rain, or stand upon a platform, while empty seats mockingly invite us to rest our wearied limbs; our sick must suffer or submit to indignity; we must put up with inconvenience of every kind; and the virtuous aspirations of our children must be continually checked by the knowledge that no matter how upright their conduct, they will be looked on as less worthy of respect than the lowest wretch on earth who wears a white skin. We ask you—only while in public, however—to surrender your prejudices,—nothing but prejudices; and you ask us to sacrifice our personal comfort, health, pecuniary interests, self-respect, and the future prospects of our children. The men who make such requests must suppose us devoid of spirit and of brains, but they will find themselves mistaken. Solemnly and distinctly, we again say to you, men of Alabama, that we will not submit voluntarily to such infamous discrimination, and if you will insist upon tramping on the rights and outraging the feelings of those who are so soon to pass judgment upon you, then upon your own heads will rest the responsibility for the effect of your course.

All over the state of Alabama—all over the South indeed—the colored people have with singular unanimity, arrayed themselves under the Republican banner, upon the Republican platform, and it is confidently predicted that nine-tenths of them will vote the Republican ticket.

It has gone on, step by step, doing first one thing for us and then another, and it now proposes to enfranchise our people all over the Union. It is the only party which has ever attempted to extend our privileges, and as it has in the past always been trying to do this, it is but natural that we should trust it for the future.

But, say some of the members of the opposition party,

"We intend to turn over a new leaf, and will hereafter give you all your rights." Perhaps they would, but we prefer not to put the new wine of political equality into the old bottles of "sectional animosity" and "caste feeling." We are somewhat fearful that those who have always opposed the extensions of rights are not sincere in their professions. . . .

It cannot be disguised that many men calling themselves conservatives are disposed to use unfair means to carry their points. The press of Mobile, and other parts of the State, contain numerous threats that those colored people who do not vote as their employers command, will be discharged; that the property-holders will combine, import white laborers, and discharge their colored hands, etc. Numerous instances have come to our knowledge of persons who have already been discharged because they attended Republican meetings, and great numbers more have been threatened. "Vote as we command, or starve," is the argument these men propose to make [use] of, and with it they expect to succeed.

In this expectation they will be mistaken, and we warn them before it is prosecuted any further, that their game is a dangerous one for themselves. The property which they hold was nearly all earned by the sweat of our brows—not theirs. . . .

Conservatives of Alabama, do you propose to rush upon certain destruction?

When the nation abolished slavery, you used your local governments to neutralize and defeat its action, and the nation answered by abolishing your governments and enfranchising us. If you now use your property to neutralize or defeat this, its last act, it will answer by taking away the property you are only allowed to retain through its unparalleled mercy and which you have proved yourselves so unworthy of retaining. . . .

So complete, indeed, will be our victory, that our opponents will become disheartened unless they can divide us. This is the great danger which we have to guard against. The most effectual method of preserving our unity will be for us to always act together—never to hold separate political meetings or caucuses. It may take some time for us to get to pulling together well, but perseverance and honest endeavor will overcome all obstacles. In nominations for office we expect that there will be no discriminations on account of color by either wing, but that the most capable and honest men will always be put in nomination. We understand full well that our people are too deficient in education to be generally qualified to fill the higher offices, but when qualified men are found, they must not be rejected for being black.

This lack of education, which is the consequence of our long servitude, and which so diminishes our powers for good, should not be allowed to characterize our children when they come upon the stage of action, and we therefore earnestly call upon every member of the Republican Party to demand the establishment of a thorough system of common schools throughout the State. It will benefit every citizen of the State, and, indeed, of the Union, for the well-being of each enures to the advantage of all.

(14)

Ku Klux Klan in Kentucky, 1871*

The Ku Klux Klan and other night-riding terrorists were ex-Confederates and white supremacists from border states, like Kentucky. Their object was to stop blacks, through the use of terror, from exercising their rights. Occasional black armed self-defense groups emerged to try to check the Klan, but blacks were not sufficiently organized, nor were they confident enough to break the terrorists' organization. Many blacks believed that it was up to Congress to stop the violence and were reluctant to resort to arms. A group of Kentucky blacks petitioned Congress in 1871 to stop the Klan.

* Bailey, *op. cit.*

To the Senate and House of Representatives in Congress assembled:

We would respectfully state that life, liberty, and property are unprotected among the colored race of this state. Organized bands of desperate and lawless men, mainly composed of soldiers of the late rebel armies, armed, disciplined, and disguised, and bound by oath and secret obligations, have, by force, terror, and violence, subverted all civil society among colored people; thus utterly rendering insecure the safety of persons and property, overthrowing all those rights which are the primary basis and objects of the government, which are expressly guaranteed to us by the Constitution of the United States as amended (by the 13th and 14th Amendments).

We believe you are not familiar with the description of the Ku Klux Klans riding nightly over the country, going from county to county, and in the county towns, spreading terror wherever they go by robbing, shipping, ravishing, and killing our people without provocation, compelling colored people to break the ice and bathe in the chilly waters of the Kentucky River.

The (state) legislature has adjourned. They refused to enact any laws to suppress Ku-Klux disorder. We regard them (the Ku-Kluxers) as now being licensed to continue their dark and bloody deeds under cover of the dark night. They refuse to allow us to testify in the state courts where a white man is concerned. We find their deeds are perpetrated only upon colored men and white Republicans. We also find that for our services to the government and our race we have become the special object of hatred and persecution at the hands of the Democratic Party. Our people are driven from their homes in great numbers, having no redress only (except) the United States court, which is in many cases unable to reach them.

We would state that we have been law-abiding citizens, pay our taxes, and in many parts of the state our people have been driven from the polls, refused the right to vote.

Many have been slaughtered while attempting to vote. We ask, how long is this state of things to last?

We appeal to you as law-abiding citizens to enact some laws that will protect us, and that will enable us to exercise the rights of citizens. . . .

The Democratic Party has here a political organization composed only of Democrats; not a single Republican can join them. Where many of these acts have been committed, it has been proven that they were the men, done with arms from the state arsenal.

We pray you will take some steps to remedy these evils.

(15)

John E. Bruce: Organized Resistance Is the Best Remedy, 1889*

> Armed resistance broke out sporadically against white oppression, beginning with the Africans first kidnapped or sold into bondage and continuing, intermittently, with slave rebellions, like those led by Denmark Vesey and Nat Turner. Two hundred thousand blacks fought in the Civil War, and armed self-defense groups arose in response to postwar terrorism. But by the 1880s, little armed resistance remained to prevent white supremacists from recapturing the South. John E. Bruce, a black journalist, believed that only organized and armed resistance could save the blacks' humanity and rights. His position was later adopted by men like Robert Williams in the 1950s and by many in the 1960s.

* "John E. Bruce Prophesy, 1889," in Robert F. Williams, *Negroes With Guns* (New York: Ed. by Marc Schleifer, Marzani & Munsell, 1962).

I fully realize the delicacy of the position I occupy . . . and know too well that those who are to follow me will largely benefit by what I shall have to say in respect to the application of force as one of the means to the solution of the problem known as the Negro problem. I am not unmindful of the fact that there are those living who have faith in the efficacy of submission. . . . Those who are thus minded will advise a pacific policy in order as they believe to effect a settlement of this question, with which the statesmanship of a century has grappled without any particularly gratifying results. Agitation is a good thing, organization is a better thing. . . .

Under the present condition of affairs the only hope, the only salvation for the Negro is to be found in a resort to force under wise and discreet leaders. . . . The Negro must not be rash and indiscreet either in action or in words but he must be very determined and terribly in earnest, and of one mind to bring order out of chaos and to convince southern rowdies and cutthroats that more than two can play at the game with which they have amused their fellow conspirators in crime for nearly a quarter of a century.

Organized resistance to organized resistance is the best remedy for the solution of the vexed problem of the century which to me seems practicable and feasible. . . .

(16)

The Black Rapist*

The stereotype of the black man as sexually insatiable was related in the ignorant and the educated southern mind to the potential destruction of the social order. (Or, perhaps this stereotype was only a cover for the white man's or woman's feelings of sexual inadequacy.) In the following excerpt, a

* "America's Race Problems," in Claude H. Nolen, *Negro's Image in the South* (Lexington: University of Kentucky Press, 1967).

19th Century southern college president gives an example of how
white communities punished a
black man accused of rape. Though
obviously revolted by the brutality
of the whites, he nevertheless justi-
fies it by resorting to the stereotype
of the black man as a sex-crazed
monster, a perpetual threat to the
virtue of white womanhood.

The Southern woman with her helpless little children in
solitary farm house no longer sleeps secure in the absence
of her husband with doors unlocked but safely guarded by
black men whose lives would be freely given in her defense.
But now, when a knock is heard at the door, she shudders
with nameless horror. The black brute is lurking in the
dark, a monstrous beast, crazed with lust. His ferocity is
almost demoniacal. A mad bull or a tiger could scarcely be
more brutal. A whole community is now frenzied with
horror, with blind and furious rage for vengeance. A stake
is driven; the wretched brute, covered with oil, bruised and
gashed, beaten and hacked and maimed, amid the jeers and
shouts and curses, the tears and anger and joy, the prayers
and the maledictions of thousands of civilized people, in the
sight of the schoolhouses, courthouses, and churches is
burned to death.

I do not hesitate to say that more horrible crimes have
been committed by the generation of Negroes that have
grown up in the South since slavery than by the six preceding generations in slavery. And also that the worst cruelties
of slavery all combined for two centuries were not equal to
the savage barbarities inflicted in retaliation upon the Negroes by the whites during the last twenty years.

(17)

Black Children in Schools*

Discrimination around the turn of the century reflected a national racism rather than a regional quirk. Horace Cayton recounts a conversation he and his sister had as children in Seattle; it shows how black children tried to comprehend and adjust to white racism.

"Madge," I asked, "why shouldn't we call the teacher 'ma'am'? Everyone else does."

"I don't know exactly," she replied, "but I think it's because Mom and Dad don't want us to feel inferior to anyone else."

"I don't feel inferior. How could I when our grandfather was a senator?"

"It's because we're colored, I think."

"But what's so bad about being colored?" Then, after a pause, I added, "Do the kids call you nigger?"

"Not very much, once in a while. I just pretend that I don't hear."

"But why should they? I don't know what to do when they call me that. I know I'm not supposed to like it but I don't know why. I asked Mother once and she said that I wasn't a nigger and just to call them nigger back because they were the real niggers. But it doesn't work. They just laugh and say they aren't niggers and that I am."

"I don't think our folks really know what to tell us," said the more worldly Madge. "They are all mixed up, too. I listen to what they say but I go right ahead and say, 'Yes, ma'am,' to the teacher. And when someone calls me nigger I just ignore it because I know I'm better than they are. They're nearly all white kids at school, and you have to be careful of them, though they are no better than we are—not

* Horace Cayton, *Long Old Road* (New York: Trident Press, 1965).

as good. But you have to be careful of the folks, too; they don't understand how things are at school. We have to figure things out for ourselves, I guess."

(18)

Race Riots, East St. Louis, 1919*

> The following passage from James
> Weldon Johnson's *Along This Way*
> provides a vivid description of the
> East St. Louis race riots in 1919,
> and of the intensity of white hatred
> of blacks.

. . . I rushed to Memphis to make an investigation of the burning alive of Ell Persons, a Negro, charged with being an "ax murderer." I was in Memphis ten days; I talked with the sheriff, with newspaper men, with a few white citizens, and many colored ones; I read through the Memphis papers covering the period; and nowhere could I find any positive evidence that Ell Persons was the man guilty of the crimes that had been committed. And, yet, without a trial, he was burned alive on the charge. . . .

On the day I arrived in Memphis, Robert R. Church drove me out to the place where the burning had taken place. A pile of ashes and pieces of charred wood still marked the spot. While the ashes were yet hot, the bones had been scrambled for as souvenirs by the mobs. I re-assembled the picture in my mind: a lone Negro in the hands of his accusers, who for the time are no longer human; he is chained to a stake, wood is piled under and around him, and five thousand men and women, women with babies in their arms and women with babies in their wombs, look on with pitiless anticipation, with sadistic satisfaction while he is baptized with gasoline and set afire. The mob disperses, many of them complaining, "They burned him too fast." I tried to balance the sufferings of the

---

* James Weldon Johnson, *Along This Way* (New York: Viking Press, 1933).

miserable victim against the moral degradation of Memphis, and the truth flashed over me that in large measure the race question involves the saving of black America's body and white America's soul. . . .

In the middle of this same summer, on July 2, the colored people of the whole country were appalled by the news of the East St. Louis massacres, a riot in which four hundred thousand dollars' worth of property was destroyed, nearly six thousand Negroes driven from their homes, hundreds of them killed, some burned in the houses set afire over their heads. This occurrence was the more bitterly ironical because it came when Negro citizens, as others, were being urged to do their bit to "make the world safe for democracy. . . . At a hearing before the Committee on Rules of the House of Representatives, Congressman Dyer, of Missouri, among other things, said:

I have visited out there and have interviewed a number of people and talked with a number who saw the murders that were committed. One man in particular who spoke to me is now an officer in the United States Army Reserve Corps, Lieut. Arbuckle, who is here in Washington somewhere, he having come here to report to the Adjutant General.

At the time of these happenings he was in the employ of the Government, but he was there on some business in East St. Louis. He said that he saw a part of this killing, and he saw them burning railway cars in yards, which were waiting for transport, filled with interstate commerce. He saw members of the militia of Illinois shoot Negroes. He saw policemen of the city of East St. Louis shoot Negroes. He saw this mob go to the homes of these Negroes and nail boards up over the doors and windows and then set fire and burn them up. He saw them take little children out of the arms of their mothers and throw them into the fires and burn them up. He saw the most dastardly and most criminal outrages ever perpetrated in this country, and this is undisputed. And I have talked with others; and my opinion is that over five hundred people were killed on this occasion.

. . . On July 28, nine or ten thousand Negroes marched silently down Fifth Avenue [in New York City] to the sound only of muffled drums. The procession was headed by children, some of them not older than six, dressed in white. These were followed by the women dressed in white, and bringing up the rear came the men in dark clothes. They carried banners; some of which read:

MOTHER, DO LYNCHERS GO TO HEAVEN?
GIVE ME A CHANCE TO LIVE.
TREAT US SO THAT WE MAY LOVE OUR COUNTRY MR.
PRESIDENT, WHY NOT MAKE AMERICA SAFE FOR DEMOC-
RACY?

Just ahead of the man who carried the American flag went a streamer that stretched half across the street and bore this inscription:

YOUR HANDS ARE FULL OF BLOOD

(19)

"Hue and Cry About Howard University"*

It is widely believed that student revolts are phenomena new to America. This article by Zora Neal Hurston about her days at Howard University reveals that the issues that caused the Howard revolt in 1968—and the revolts in other institutions, both black and integrated—were already present in the consciousness of some black students in 1919.

I went to Howard as a Prep in 1918–1919 . . .

The thrill Hannibal got when he finally crossed the Alps, the feeling of Napoleon when he finally placed upon his head the iron crown of Constantine, were nothing to the ecstasy I felt when I realized I was actually a Howard-ite. . . .

Howard was unutterably beautiful to me that spring. I

* "The Hue and Cry About Howard University," in Zora Neal Hurston, *The Messenger.*

would give a great deal to call back my Howard illusion of those days. . . .

A few days later and the first storm broke. A great number of students but not the entire body of students by any means were holding indignation meetings alleging that they had been forced or commanded by the president to sing "Spirituals." He was denounced as a despot, a tyrant, who was dragging us back into slavery. . . .

Though there were spokesmen among the students, various members of the faculty were credited as the real leaders. . . . The papers printed things down in the city and some members of the Senate denounced us as ingrates and accused us of being ashamed of ourselves and our traditions.

The president held a conference with the students one day after Chapel to find out how he had offended. There were speakers for and against the "Spirituals." . . .

The "Pro's" made the usual stand: *a*) The beauty and workmanship of the songs. *b*) Only American folk songs. *c*) Only beauty that came out of slavery. The "Anti's" held: *a*) They were low and degrading, being the product of slaves and slavery; *b*) not good grammar; *c*) they are not sung in white universities. . . .

After a few days of bluster this affair died down but not before a perceptible rift had been made in the faculty and student group.

A little later that same year, Senator Smoot arose on the floor of the Senate with a book in hand which he informed the Senators was a highly culpable bolshevistic volume which he had received from the hands of a Howard student. He understood it came from the university library and insinuated that it was in the curriculum. He held forth that a government-supported institution that was making bolshevists should be allowed to toddle along without government aid seeing that this was the U.S. and not Red Russia.

Rumors flew thick and fast among the students as to who had engineered the book into the Senator's hands. It is to be remembered that Smoot was head of the Appropriation Committee. Durkee [the president of Howard] hastened down to the Senate Committee room and explained that the book had been given by the Rand School and it was the policy of the university to accept all gifts. It was neither taught nor recommended. . . . He was denounced by some on the Hill and some off for having cringed before the Senate. He should have informed that body that we could teach what we liked and if the money was withheld we could have the satisfaction of being untrammeled. I even saw a typewritten, unsigned card on the bulletin board on the second floor of the main building to the effect: "It is better to lose $250,000 than our manhood." . . .

(20)

Joe Louis Uncovers Dynamite*

> When Joe Louis knocked out Max Baer in 1935, many whites and blacks interpreted the event in racial terms. Richard Wright, writing in *The New Masses,* describes the racial reaction to the fight.

"WUN-tuh-theee-fooo-fiiive-seex-seven-eight-niine-thuun!"
Then:
"JOE LOUIS—THE WINNAH!"
On Chicago's South Side five minutes after these words were yelled and Joe Louis' hand was hoisted as victor in his four-round go with Max Baer, Negroes poured out of beer taverns, pool rooms, barber shops, rooming houses, and dingy flats and flooded the streets.
"LOUIS! LOUIS! LOUIS!" they yelled and threw their hats away. They snatched newspapers from the stands of astonished Greeks and tore them up, flinging the bits into the air. They wagged their heads. Lawd, they'd never seen or heard the like of it before. They shook the hands of strangers. They clapped one another on the back. It was like a revival. Really, there was a religious feeling in the air. Well, it

* "Joe Louis Uncovers Dynamite," Richard Wright, *The New Masses* (October 8, 1935).

wasn't exactly a religious feeling, but it was the *thing,* and you could feel it. It was a feeling of unity, of oneness.

Two hours after the fight the area between South Parkway and Prairie Avenue on 47th Street was jammed with no less than twenty-five thousand Negroes, joy-mad and moving to they didn't know where. Clasping hands they formed long writhing snake-lines and wove in and out of traffic. They seeped out of doorways, oozed from alleys, trickled out of tenements, and flowed down the street, a fluid mass of joy. White storekeepers hastily closed their doors against the tidal wave and stood peeping through plate glass with blanched faces.

Something had happened, all right. And it had happened so confoundingly sudden that the whites in the neighborhood were dumb with fear. They felt—you could see it in their faces—that *something* had ripped loose, exploded. Something which they had long feared and thought was dead. Or if not dead at least so safely buried under the pretense of good-will that they no longer had need to fear it. Where in the world did it come from? And what was worst of all, how far would it go? Say, what's got into these Negroes?

And the whites and the blacks began to *feel* themselves. The blacks began to remember all the little slights, and discriminations and insults they had suffered; and their hunger too and their misery. And the whites began to search their souls to see if they had been guilty of something, some time, somewhere, against which this wave of feeling was rising.

As the celebration wore on, the younger Negroes began to grow bold. They jumped on the running boards of automobiles going east or west on 47th Street and demanded of the occupants:

"Who yuh fer—Baer or Louis?"

In the stress of the moment it seemed that the answer to the question marked out friend and foe.

A hesitating reply brought waves of scornful laughter. Baer, huh? That was funny. Now, hadn't Joe Louis just whipped Max Baer? Didn't think we had it in us, did you? Thought Joe Louis was scared, didn't you? Scared because Max talked loud and made boasts. We ain't scared either. We'll fight too when the time comes. We'll win, too.

A taxicab driver had his cab wrecked when he tried to put up a show of bravado.

Then they began stopping street cars. Like a cyclone sweeping through a forest, they went through them, shouting, stamping. Conductors gave up and backed away like children. Everybody had to join in this celebration. Some of the people ran out of the cars and stood, pale and trembling, in the crowd. They felt it, too.

In the crush a pocketbook snapped open and money spilled on the street for eager black fingers.

"They stole it from us, anyhow," they said as they picked it up.

When an elderly Negro admonished them, a fist was shaken in his face. Uncle Toming, huh?

"Whut in hell yuh gotta do wid it?" they wanted to know.

Something had popped loose, all right. And it had come from deep down. Out of the darkness it had leaped from its coil. And nobody could have said just what it was, and nobody wanted to say. Blacks and whites were afraid. But it was a sweet fear, at least for the blacks. It was a mingling of fear and fulfillment. Something dreaded and yet wanted. A something had popped out of a dark hole, something with a hydra-like head, and it was darting forth its tongue.

You stand on the border-line, wondering what's beyond. Then you take one step and you feel a strange, sweet tingling. You take two steps and the feeling becomes keener. You want to feel some more. You break into a run. You know it's dangerous, but you're propelled in spite of yourself.

Four centuries of oppression, of frustrated hopes, of black bitterness, felt even in the bones of the bewildered young, were rising to the surface. Yes, unconsciously they had imputed to the brawny image of Joe Louis all the balked dreams of revenge, all the secretly visualized moments of retaliation. AND HE HAD WON! Good Gawd Almighty! Yes, Jesus, it could be done! Didn't Joe do it? You see, Joe was the consciously-felt symbol. He was the concentrated essence of black triumph over white. And it comes so seldom, so seldom. And what could be sweeter than long nourished hate vicariously gratified? From the symbol of Joe's strength they took strength, and in that moment all fear, all obstacles were wiped out, drowned. They stepped out of the mire of hesitation and irresolution and were free! Invincible! A merciless victor over a fallen foe! Yes, they had felt all that—for a moment. . . .

And then the cops came.

Not the carefully picked white cops who were used to batter the skulls of white workers and intellectuals who came to the South Side to march with the black workers to show their solidarity in the struggle against Mussolini's impending invasion of Ethiopia; oh, no, black cops, but trusted black cops and plenty tough. Cops who knew their business, how to handle delicate situations. They piled out of patrols, swinging clubs.

"Git back! Gawddammit, git back!"

But they were very careful, very careful. They didn't hit anybody. They, too, sensed *something*. And they didn't want to trifle with it. And there's no doubt but that they had been instructed not to. Better go easy here. No telling what might happen. They swung clubs, but pushed the crowd back with their hands.

Finally, the street cars moved again. The taxis and automobiles could go through. The whites breathed easier. The blood came back to their cheeks.

The Negroes stood on the sidewalks, talking, wondering, looking, breathing hard. They had felt something, and it had been sweet—that feeling. They wanted some more of it, but they were afraid now. The spell was broken.

And about midnight down the street that feeling ebbed, seeping home—flowing back to the beer tavern, the pool room, the cafe, the barber shop, the dingy flat. Like a sullen river it ran back to its muddy channel, carrying a confused

and sentimental memory on its surface, like water-soaked
driftwood.

Say, Comrade, here's the wild river that's got to be
harnessed and directed. Here's that *something,* that pent-up
folk consciousness. Here's a fleeting glimpse of the heart of
the Negro, the heart that beats and suffers and hopes—for
freedom. Here's that fluid something that's like iron. Here's
the real dynamite that Joe Louis uncovered!

(21)

Elijah Muhammad: The Faith and the Future*

The Muslims are direct descendants of Marcus Garvey's movement, using religion as an ideology
to build a stable black community
and improve the sense of black
pride and identity. Elijah Muhammad was a serious student of Garvey and, like Garvey, demands
blind faith of his followers. The
Muslim political goals are obscure.
Their social program is somewhat
clearer: it is a mixture of black
capitalism and separatism, combined with an extremely rigorous
moral code.

You can't blame the government for not giving you
anything when you are not asking for anything. . . . It is
certainly evident by now that you were never intended to be
a full citizen. . . . Your role was that of a slave and today,
even . . . that intent underlies your role in the body
politic. . . .

Our oppressors are determined to keep our eyes in the
sky while they control the land under our feet, . . . smite
our cheeks and rob our pockets. . . .

To integrate with evil is to be destroyed with evil. What
we want—indeed, justice for us is to be set apart. We want,

* Eric C. Lincoln, *The Black Muslims in America* (Boston: Beacon
Press, 1961).

and must insist upon an area in this land that we can call our own, somewhere [where] we can hold our heads [up] with pride and dignity without the continued harassments and indignities of our oppressors. . . .

. . . let us carry in our hearts the doctrine of separation from our oppressors; let us demand a home we can call our own, support for ourselves until we are able to become self-sufficient. . . .

The best thing the white man can do is give us justice and stop giving us hell. I'm asking for justice. If they won't give us justice, then let us separate ourselves from them and live in four or five states in America, or leave the country altogether. . . .

Let us use the Moslem Crescent, which is the sign of LIFE . . . instead of the white man's cross, which is the sign of slavery, suffering and death. Tell the white man that since he has not given the Negro Christians justice in his Christian religion, you are now going back to the Islamic religion of your foreparents . . . a religion of TRUTH, in which we get freedom, justice and equality. . . . A religion that gives us dignity, unity, and makes us FEARLESS. . . ."

They say that I am a preacher of racial hatred, but the fact is that the white people don't like the truth, especially if it speaks *against* them. . . . It is a terrible thing for such people . . . to charge me with teaching race hatred when their feet are on my people's neck and they tell us to our face that they hate the black people. . . . Remember now, they even teach you that you must not hate them for hating you.

I have it from the mouth of God that the enemy had better try to protect my life and see that I continue to live. Because if anything happens to me, I will be the last one that they murder. And if any of my followers are harmed, ten of the enemy's best ones will be killed.

(22)

The Future of Black People*

William Edward Burghardt Du Bois' great-great grandfather "was kidnapped" on the African West Coast, brought to New York in 1735 and sold into slavery. Before W. E. B. Du Bois died in 1963 he had renounced the United States and taken the position of First Citizen in the Republic of Ghana. In all of his writings Du Bois stressed the cultural importance of Africa for American blacks. His own commitment to the freedom of black people and to Africa was tied together in the hope that American, West Indian and African blacks would merge some day in a freedom movement to crush imperialism abroad and bring socialism and justice to the United States.

Up until the close of the First World War, the "talented tenth" among Negroes had recognized leadership and the growing respect of the whites. But with the depression and the "New Deal," the American Negro intelligentsia began to lose ground. An economic and class differentiation took place and the race leadership began to shift to a new Negro bourgeoisie. Garvey, the sincere but uneducated and demagogic West Indian leader, had helped this change during his career in America. He promoted an African movement, but it was purely commercial and based on no conception of African history or needs. It was American and not African, and it failed. But American Negro business expanded. Negroes began to enter white industry. Curiously enough,

---

* W. E. B. Du Bois, "The American Negro Intelligentsia," *Présence Africaine*, N. S., 5 (Dec. 1955–Jan. 1956), pp. 34–51, reprinted in *Apropos of Africa*, compiled by Adelaide Cromwell Hill and Martin Kilson (New York: Humanities Press, 1969), pp. 320–21.

the propaganda of Booker Washington began with 1900 to change from effort to interest Negroes in "working with the hands" to inducing him to invest in business and profit by exploitation of labor. Thus insurance companies, retail business, distribution of goods and white collar work of all kinds increased among Negroes. By the time the Second World War opened, American Negro leadership was in the hands of teachers, writers, and social workers. Professional men joined this black bourgeoisie and the Negro began to follow white American display and conspicuous expenditure.

This new leadership had no interest in Africa. It was aggressively American. The Pan-African movement lost almost all support. It was only by my hard efforts that the last Congress in Britain in 1945 got American Negro notice. After that all interest failed.

Today the American interest in Africa is almost confined to whites. African history is pursued in white institutions and white writers produce books on Africa while Negro authors and scholars have shied away from the subject which in the twenties and thirties was their preserve.

As big business gained in power and promoted war, that war ostensibly against Communism was really for colonial aggression in Asia and Africa. In order to appease colored peoples, big business found it to its interest to yield ground on the color line in America. Race segregation in schools and travel was made illegal, although the law was not enforced in the former slave South. But this step toward the integration of Negroes into the American state greatly influenced American Negroes and led them to join in opposition to Communism, the Soviet Union and Socialism everywhere. While the right of the Negro to vote is still curtailed, yet it is growing in power and has to be courted. But big business dominates Negro business, including the Negro press. Negro soldiers form a considerable part of the military forces, and their integration into white units has further reconciled the American Negro to war even with colored peoples like the Koreans and Chinese.

But these fatal trends among us will not, must not, last. Leadership is arising which appreciates at its true value the great role which the Soviet Union and China are playing in the world and are destined to play. This leadership today is suffering persecution, but it will prevail.

As the world turns toward Africa as a great center of future activity and development and recognizes the ancient socialism of Africa, American Negroes, freed of their base-less fear of Communism, will again begin to turn their attention and aim their activity toward Africa. They will see how capitalistic exploitation, led by America, is exploiting and impoverishing Negroes of Africa and keeping them sick and ignorant, and thus indirectly encouraging the color line in America. They will realize how American Negroes are in position to help Africa; not only by their growing political power, but by their educational opportunities in the United States. They can when they will furnish guidance to Africa; they can give intellectual leadership working with and not for black Africa. When once the blacks of the United States, the West Indies, and Africa work and think together, the future of the black man in the modern world is safe.

(23)

Martin Luther King, Jr.*

> The murder of Dr. Martin Luther King, Jr. shocked the entire world and, for many, marked the end of the liberal hope for racial integra-tion through nonviolence. Dr. King was a deeply religious man, dedi-cated not only to Christ, but to the articulated ideals of American Democracy and equality. Like Frederick Douglass, he also had faith in the power of justice and reason. The following excerpts are from a speech that Dr. King de-

* "Martin Luther King—Hate Is Always Tragic" and "The Social Organization of Non-violence," Robert F. Williams, *Negroes With Guns* (New York: Ed. by Schleifer, Marzani & Munsell, 1962).

livered to the National Press Club in July 1962, and an article that he published in the October 1959 issue of *Liberation* magazine. Both appear in *Negroes With Guns* by Robert F. Williams.

Those who adhere to the method of nonviolent direct action recognize that legislation and court orders tend only to declare rights; they can never thoroughly deliver them. Only when the people themselves begin to act are rights on paper given lifeblood. The method of nonviolent resistance is effective in that it has a way of disarming the opponent; it exposes his moral defenses, it weakens his morale, and at the same time it works on his conscience.

Nonviolent resistance also provides a creative force through which men can channelize their discontent. It does not require that they abandon their discontent. This discontent is sound and healthy. Nonviolence saves it from degenerating into morbid bitterness and hatred. Hate is always tragic. It is as injurious to the hater as it is to the hated. It distorts the personality and scars the soul. Psychiatrists are telling us now that many of the inner conflicts and strange things that happen in the subconscious are rooted in hate. So they are now saying, "Love or perish." This is the beauty of nonviolence. It says you can struggle without hating; you can fight war without violence.

As a race, we must work passionately and unrelentingly for first-class citizenship, but we must never use second-class methods to gain it. If this happens, unborn generations will be the recipients of a long and desolate night of bitterness, and our chief legacy to the future will be an endless reign of meaningless chaos.

We have come to the day when a piece of freedom is not enough for us as human beings nor for the nation of which we are part. We have been given pieces, but unlike bread, a slice of which does diminish hunger, a piece of liberty no longer suffices. Freedom is like life. You cannot be given life in installments. You cannot be given breath but not body, nor a heart but no blood vessels. Freedom is one thing—you have it all, or you are not free.

Our destiny is bound up with the destiny of America— we built it for two centuries without wages, we made cotton king, we built our homes and homes for our masters, and suffered injustice and humiliation, but out of a bottomless vitality continued to live and grow. If the inexpressible cruelties of slavery could not extinguish our existence, the opposition we now face will surely fail. We feel that we are the conscience of America—we are its troubled soul.

. . . There is reason to believe that the Negro of 1959 will not accept supinely any such compromises [as token integration or partial citizenship] in the contemporary struggle for integration. His struggle will continue, but the obstacles will determine its specific nature. It is axiomatic in social life that the imposition of frustrations leads to two kinds of reactions. One is the development of a wholesome social organization to resist with effective, firm measures any efforts to impede progress. The other is a confused, anger-motivated drive to strike back violently, to inflict damage. Primarily, it seeks to cause injury to retaliate for wrongful suffering. Secondarily, it seeks real progress. It is punitive—not radical or constructive.

The current calls for violence have their roots in this latter tendency. Here one must be clear that there are three different views on the subject of violence. One is the approach of pure nonviolence, which cannot readily or easily attract large masses, for it requires extraordinary discipline and courage. The second is violence exercised in self-defense, which all societies from the most primitive to the most cultured and civilized, accept as moral and legal. The principle of self-defense, even involving weapons and bloodshed, has never been condemned, even by Gandhi, who sanctioned it for those unable to master pure nonviolence. The third is the advocacy of violence as a tool of advancement, organized as in warfare, deliberately and consciously. To this tendency many Negroes are being tempted today. There are incalculable perils in this approach. It is not the danger or sacrifice of physical being which is primary, though it cannot be contemplated without a sense of deep concern for human life. The greatest danger is that it will fail to attract Negroes to a real collective struggle, and will confuse the large uncommitted middle group, which as yet has not supported either side. Further, it will mislead Negroes into the belief that this is the only path and place them as a minority in a position where they confront a far larger adversary than it is possible to defeat in this form of combat. When the Negro uses force in self-defense he does not forfeit support—he may even win it, by the courage and self-respect it reflects. When he seeks to initiate violence he provokes questions about the necessity for it, and inevitably is blamed for its consequences. It is unfortunately true that however the Negro acts, his struggle will not be free of violence initiated by his enemies, and he will need ample courage and willingness to sacrifice to defeat this manifestation of violence. But if he seeks it and organizes it, he cannot win. . . .

There is more power in socially organized masses on the march than there is in guns in the hands of a few desperate men. Our enemies would prefer to deal with a small armed group rather than with a huge, unarmed but resolute mass of people. However, it is necessary that the mass-action method be persistent and unyielding. Gandhi said the Indian people must "never let them rest," referring to the British. He urged them to keep protesting daily and weekly, in a variety of ways. This method inspired and organized the Indian masses and disorganized and demobilized the British. It educates its myriad participants, socially and morally. All history teaches us that like a turbulent ocean beating great cliffs into fragments of rock, the determined movement of people incessantly demanding their rights always disintegrates the old order.

It is this form of struggle—non-cooperation with evil through mass actions—"never letting them rest"—which offers the more effective road for those who have been tempted and goaded to violence. It needs the bold and the

brave because it is not free of danger. . . . It requires
dedicated men because it is a backbreaking task to arouse,
to organize and to educate tens of thousands for disciplined,
sustained action. From this form of struggle more emerges
that is permanent and damaging to the enemy than from a
few acts of organized violence.

Our present urgent necessity is to cease our internal
fighting and turn outward to the enemy, using every form of
mass action yet known—create new forms—and resolve
never to let them rest. This is the social lever which will
force open the door to freedom. Our powerful weapons are
the voices, the feet, and the bodies of dedicated, united
people, moving without rest toward a just goal. Greater
tyrants than Southern segregationists have been subdued
and defeated by this form of struggle. We have not yet used
it, and it would be tragic if we spurn it because we have
failed to perceive its dynamic strength and power. . . .

(24)

Robert F. Williams: Negroes With Guns*

Robert Williams armed members
of the Monroe, N.C. chapter of
the NAACP with guns, and after
several scuffles with the law and
with white terrorists, he was
framed on a kidnapping charge.
Rather than stand trial, he left the
United States for exile first in
Cuba, then in China and Tanzania.
His thought evolved from advocacy
of self-defense to revolutionary
socialism. In 1969 Williams returned to the United States to
carry on his struggle. Williams' influence, even when in exile, was
considerable upon black militants
in the United States. The following passages are from *Negroes
With Guns,* written in Cuba in
1962.

* Robert F. Williams, *Negroes With Guns* (New York: Ed. by
Schleifer, Marzani & Munsell, 1962).

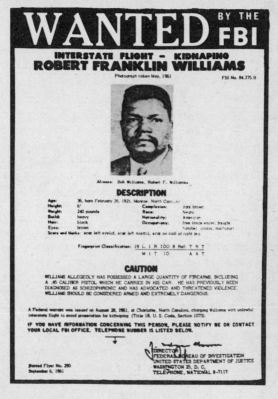

Why do I speak to you from exile?

Because a Negro community in the South took up guns in self-defense against racist violence—and used them. I am held responsible for this action, that for the first time in history American Negroes have armed themselves as a group, to defend their homes, their wives, their children, in a situation where law and order had broken down, where the authorities could not, or rather would not, enforce their duty to protect Americans from a lawless mob. I accept this responsibility and am proud of it. I have asserted the right of Negroes to meet the violence of the Ku Klux Klan by armed self-defense—and have acted on it. It has always been an accepted right of Americans, as the history of our Western states proves, that where the law is unable, or unwilling, to enforce order, the citizens can, and must, act in self-defense against lawless violence. I believe this right holds for black Americans as well as whites. . . .

The picket line continued.* On Sunday, on our way to the swimming pool, we had to pass through the same intersection (U.S. 74 and U.S. 601). There were about two or three thousand people lined along the highway. Two or three policemen were standing at the intersection directing traffic and there were two policemen who had been following us from home. An old stock car without windows was parked by a restaurant at the intersection. As soon as we drew near, this car started backing out as fast as possible. The driver hoped to hit us in the side and flip us over. But I turned my wheel sharply and the junk car struck the front of my car and both cars went into a ditch.

Then the crowd started screaming. They said that a nigger had hit a white man. They were referring to me. They were screaming, "Kill the niggers! Kill the niggers! Pour gasoline on the niggers! Burn the niggers!"

We were still sitting in the car. The man who was driving the stock car got out of the car with a baseball bat and started walking toward us and he was saying, "Nigger, what did you hit me for?" I didn't say anything to him. We just sat there looking at him. He came up close to our car, within arm's length with the baseball bat, but I still hadn't said anything and we didn't move in the car. What they didn't know was that we were armed. Under North Carolina state law it is legal to carry firearms in your automobile so long as these firearms are not concealed.

I had two pistols and a rifle in the car. When this fellow started to draw back his baseball bat, I put an Army .45 up in the window of the car and pointed it right into his face and I didn't say a word. He looked at the pistol and he

* Williams organized a picket line protesting the exclusion of blacks from a public swimming pool.

didn't say anything. He started backing away from the car.

Somebody in the crowd fired a pistol and the people again started to scream hysterically, "Kill the niggers! Kill the niggers! Pour gasoline on the niggers!" The mob started to throw stones on top of my car. So I opened the door of the car and I put one foot on the ground and stood up in the door holding an Italian carbine.

All this time three policemen had been standing about fifty feet away from us while we kept waiting in the car for them to come and rescue us. Then when they saw that we were armed and the mob couldn't take us, two of the policemen started running. One ran straight to me and he grabbed me on the shoulder and said, "Surrender your weapon! Surrender your weapon!" I struck him in the face and knocked him back away from the car and put my carbine in his face and I told him we were not going to surrender to a mob. I told him that we didn't intend to be lynched. The other policeman who had run around the side of the car started to draw his revolver out of the holster. He was hoping to shoot me in the back. They didn't know that we had more than one gun. One of the students (who was seventeen years old) put a .45 in the policeman's face and told him that if he pulled out his pistol he would kill him. The policeman started putting his gun back into the holster and backing away from the car, and he fell into the ditch.

There was a very old man, an old white man out in the crowd, and he started screaming and crying like a baby and he kept crying, and he said, "goddam, goddam, what is this goddam country coming to that the niggers have got guns, the niggers are armed and the police can't even arrest them!" . . .

The stranglehold of oppression cannot be loosened by a plea to the oppressor's conscience. Social change in something as fundamental as racist oppression involves violence. You cannot have progress here without violence and upheaval, because it's struggle for survival for one and a struggle for liberation for the other. Always the powers in command are ruthless and unmerciful in defending their position and their privileges. This is not an abstract rule to be meditated upon by Americans. This is a truth that was revealed at the birth of America, and has continued to be revealed many times in our history. The principle of self-defense is an American tradition that began at Lexington and Concord. . . .

Why do the white liberals ask us to be nonviolent? We are not the aggressors; we have been victimized for over 300 years! Yet nobody spends money to go into the South and ask the racists to be martyrs or pacifists. But they always come to the downtrodden Negroes, who are already oppressed and too submissive as a group, and they ask them not to fight back. There seems to be a pattern of some sort of strange coincidence of interest when whites preach a special doctrine to Negroes. Like the choice of theology when the plantation-owners saw to the Christianization of the slaves. Instead of the doctrines which produced the rugged aggressively independent and justice-seeking spirit that we associate with Colonial America as the New England Conscience, the slaves were indoctrinated in the most submissive "trust-your-master" pie-in-the-sky after-you-die form of Christianity. . . .

The tactics of nonviolence will continue and should continue. We too believed in nonviolent tactics in Monroe. We've used these tactics; we've used all tactics. But we also believe that any struggle for liberation should be a flexible struggle. We shouldn't take the attitude that one method alone is the way to liberation. This is to become dogmatic. This is to fall into the same sort of dogmatism practiced by some of the religious fanatics. We can't afford to develop this type of attitude.

We must use nonviolence as a means as long as this is feasible, but the day will come when conditions become so pronounced that nonviolence will be suicidal in itself. The day is surely coming when we will see more violence on the same American scene. The day is surely coming when some of the same Negroes who have denounced our using weapons for self-defense will be arming themselves. There are those who pretend to be horrified by the idea that a black veteran who shouldered arms for the United States would willingly take up weapons to defend his wife, his children, his home, and his life. These same people will one day be the loud advocates of self-defense. When violent racism and fascism strike at their families and their homes, not in a token way but in an all-out bloody campaign, then they will be among the first to advocate self-defense. They will justify their position as a question of survival. When it is no longer some distant Negro who's no more than a statistic, no more than an article in a newspaper; when it is no longer their neighbors, but it means them and it becomes a matter of personal salvation, then will their attitude change.

As a tactic, we use and approve nonviolent resistance. But we also believe that a man cannot have human dignity if he allows himself to be abused; to be kicked and beaten to the ground, to allow his wife and children to be attacked, refusing to defend them and himself on the basis that he's so pious, so self-righteous, that it would demean his personality if he fought back.

We know that the average Afro-American is not a pacifist. He's not a pacifist and he has never been a pacifist and he's not made of the type of material that would make a good pacifist. Those who doubt that the great majority of Negroes are not pacifists, just let them slap one. Pick any Negro on any street corner in the U.S.A. and they'll find out how much he believes in turning the other cheek.

All those who dare to attack are going to learn the hard way that the Afro-American is not a pacifist; that he cannot forever be counted on not to defend himself. Those who attack him brutally and ruthlessly can no longer expect to attack him with impunity.

The Afro-American cannot forget that his enslavement in this country did not pass because of pacifist moral force or noble appeals to the Christian conscience of the slave-holders. . . .

(25)

Rap Brown: Poem*

> H. Rap Brown succeeded Stoke!y
> Carmichael as chairman of SNCC
> in 1967. A brilliant speaker who
> was able to integrate the language
> of the black ghetto into a revolu-
> tionary appeal, he became the
> foremost advocate of militant black
> power. In his book, *Die, Nigger,
> Die,* he recalls some of the adoles-
> cent games which were practiced in
> the ghetto as a way of keeping
> sharp.

That's why they call me Rap, 'cause I could rap. (The
name stuck because Ed would always say, "That my nigger
Rap," "Rap my nigger.") But for dudes who couldn't, it
was like they were humiliated because they were born Black
and then they turned around and got humiliated by their
own people, which was really all they had left. But that's
the way it is. Those that feel most humiliated humiliate
others. The real aim of the Dozens was to get a dude so mad
that he'd cry or get mad enough to fight. You'd say shit
like, "Man, tell your mama to stop coming around my house
all the time. I'm tired of fucking her and I think you should
know that it ain't no accident you look like me." And it
could go on for hours sometimes. Some of the best Dozens
players were girls.

Signifying is more humane. Instead of coming down on
somebody's mother, you come down on them. But, before
you can signify you got to be able to rap. A session would
start maybe by a brother saying, "Man, before you mess
with me you'd rather run rabbits, eat shit, and bark at the
moon." Then, if he was talking to me, I'd tell him:

---

* "Poem," by H. Rap Brown in *Good Times* (San Francisco: Vol. 2,
No. 17, April 30, 1969).

Man, you must don't know who I am.
I'm sweet peeter jeeter the womb beater
The baby maker the cradle shaker
The deerslayer the buckbinder the women finder
Known from the Gold Coast to the rocky shores of Maine
Rap is my name and love is my game.
I'm the bed tucker the cock plucker the motherfucker
The milkshaker the record breaker the population maker
The gun slinger the baby bringer
The hum-dinger the pussy ringer
The man with the terrible middle finger.
The hard hitter the bullshitter the polynussy getter
The beast from the East the Judge the sludge
The women's pet the men's fret and the punks' pin-up boy.
They call me Rap the dicker the ass kicker
The cherry picker the city slicker the titty licker
And I ain't giving nothing but bubble gum and hard times and
   I'm fresh out of bubble gum.
I'm giving up wooden nickels 'cause I know they won't spend
And I got a pocketful of splinter change.
I'm a member of the bathtub club; I'm seeing a whole lot of ass
   but I ain't taking no shit.
I'm the man who walked the water and tied the whale's tail in a
   knot
Taught the little fishes how to swim
Crossed the burning sands and shook the devil's hand
Rode round the world on the back of a snail carrying a sack say-
   ing AIR MAIL.
Walked 49 miles of barbwire and used a Cobra snake for a neck-
   tie
And got a brand new chimney setting on top made from the
   cracker's skull
Took a hammer and nail and built the world and called it "THE
   BUCKET OF BLOOD"
Yes, I'm hemp the demp the women's pimp
Women fight for my delight.
I'm a bad motherfucker. Rap the rip-saw the devil's brother 'n
   law.
I roam the world I'm known to wander and this .45 is where I
   get my thunder.
I'm the only man in the world who knows why white milk makes
   yellow butter.
I know where the lights go when you cut the switch off.

I might not be the best in the world, but I'm in the top two and
my brother's getting old.
And ain't nothing bad 'bout you but your breath.

Now, if the brother couldn't come back behind that, I
usually cut him some slack (depending on time, place, and
his attitude). We learned what the white folks call verbal
skills. We learned how to throw them words together.

(26)

Malcolm X Speaks*

Malcolm X was the most important
black American revolutionary of
the twentieth century. Beginning as
a criminal and serving long jail
sentences, Malcolm converted to
Islam in prison. For years he was
Elijah Muhammad's chief spokesman, but after he became more
militant, he was ejected from the
Muslims by Elijah. At that point,
Malcolm's thinking and activity
turned toward socialist revolutionary solutions, and before he
was assassinated, in 1965, he had
become the black leader whose influence on current white and black
radical thinking is most crucial.

If violence is wrong in America, violence is wrong
abroad. If it is wrong to be violent defending black women
and black children and black babies and black men, then it
is wrong for America to draft us and make us violent
abroad in defense of her. And if it is right for America to
draft us, and teach us how to be violent in defense of her,
then it is right for you and me to do whatever is necessary
to defend our own people right here in this country. . . .

. . . There's been a revolution, a black revolution,
going on in Africa. In Kenya, the Mau Mau were revolutionary; they were the ones who brought the word "Uhuru"

* *Malcolm X Speaks,* ed. George Breitman (New York: Grove Press,
1965).

to the fore . . . they believed in scorched earth, they
knocked everything aside that got in their way, and their
revolution also was based on land, a desire for land. In
Algeria, the northern part of Africa, a revolution took
place. The Algerians were revolutionists, they wanted land.
France offered to let them be integrated into France. They
told France, to hell with France, they wanted some land,
not some France. And they engaged in a bloody battle.

So I cite these various revolutions, brothers and sisters, to
show you that you don't have a peaceful revolution. You
don't have a turn-the-other-cheek revolution. There's no
such thing as a nonviolent revolution. The only kind of
revolution that is nonviolent is the Negro revolution. The
only revolution in which the goal is loving your enemy is
the Negro revolution. It's the only revolution in which the
goal is a desegregated lunch counter, a desegregated theater, a desegregated park, and a desegregated public toilet;
you can sit down next to white folks on the toilet. That's
no revolution. Revolution is based on land. Land is the
basis of all independence. Land is the basis of freedom,
justice, and equality. . . .

Revolution is bloody, revolution is hostile, revolution
knows no compromise, revolution overturns and destroys
everything that gets in its way. And you, sitting around here
like a knot on the wall, saying, "I'm going to love these
folks no matter how much they hate me." No, you need a
revolution. Whoever heard of a revolution where they lock
arms . . . singing "We Shall Overcome"? You don't do
that in a revolution. You don't do any singing, you're too
busy swinging. It's based on land. A revolutionary wants
land so he can set up his own nation, an independent
nation. These Negroes aren't asking for any nation—
they're trying to crawl back on the plantation.

When you want a nation, that's called nationalism. When
the white man became involved in a revolution in this
country against England, what was it for? He wanted this
land so he could set up another white nation. That's white
nationalism. The American Revolution was white national-

ism. The French Revolution was white nationalism. The Russian Revolution, too—yes, it was—white nationalism. You don't think so? Why do you think Khrushchev and Mao can't get their heads together? White nationalism. All the revolutions that are going on in Asia and Africa today are based on what?—black nationalism. A revolutionary is a black nationalist. He wants a nation. . . . If you're afraid of black nationalism, you're afraid of revolution. And if you love revolution, you love black nationalism. . . .

I am going to organize and head a new mosque in New York City, known as the Muslim Mosque, Inc. This gives us a religious base, and the spiritual force necessary to rid our people of the vices that destroy the moral fiber of our community.

Our political philosophy will be black nationalism. Our economic and social philosophy will be black nationalism. Our cultural emphasis will be black nationalism. . . .

The political philosophy of black nationalism means: we must control the politics and the politicians of our community. They must no longer take orders from outside forces. We will organize, and sweep out of office all Negro politicians who are puppets for the outside forces.

Our accent will be upon youth: we need new ideas, new methods, new approaches. We will call upon young students of political science throughout the nation to help us. We will encourage these young students to launch their own independent study, and then give us their analysis and their suggestions. We are completely disenchanted with the old, adult, established politicians. We want to see some new faces—more militant faces. . . .

Concerning nonviolence: it is criminal to teach a man not to defend himself when he is the constant victim of brutal attacks. It is legal and lawful to own a shotgun or a rifle. We believe in obeying the law.

In areas where our people are the constant victims of brutality, and the government seems unable or unwilling to protect them, we should form rifle clubs that can be used to defend our lives and our property in times of emergency, such as happened last year in Birmingham; Plaquemine, Louisiana; Cambridge, Maryland; and Danville, Virginia. When our people are being bitten by dogs, they are within their rights to kill those dogs.

We should be peaceful, law-abiding—but the time has come for the American Negro to fight back in self-defense whenever and wherever he is being unjustly and unlawfully attacked.

If the government thinks I am wrong for saying this, then let the government start doing its job.

I'm not a politician, not even a student of politics; in fact, I'm not a student of much of anything. I'm not a Democrat, I'm not a Republican, and I don't even consider myself an American. If you and I were Americans, there'd be no problem. Those Hunkies that just got off the boat, they're already Americans; Polacks are already Americans; the Italian refugees are already Americans. Everything that came out of Europe, every blue-eyed thing, is already an American. And as long as you and I have been over here, we aren't Americans yet.

Well, I am one who doesn't believe in deluding myself. I'm not going to sit at your table and watch you eat, with nothing on my plate, and call myself a diner. Sitting at the table doesn't make you a diner, unless you eat some of what's on that plate. Being here in America doesn't make you an American. Being born here in America doesn't make you an American. Why, if birth made you American, you wouldn't need any legislation, you wouldn't need any amendments to the Constitution, you wouldn't be faced with civil-rights filibustering in Washington, D.C., right now. They don't have to pass civil-rights legislation to make a Polack an American.

No, I'm not an American. I'm one of the 22 million black people who are the victims of Americanism. One of the 22 million black people who are the victims of democracy, nothing but disguised hypocrisy. So, I'm not standing here speaking to you as an American, or a patriot, or a flagsaluter, or a flag-waver—no, not I. I'm speaking as a victim of this American system. And I see America through the eyes of the victim. I don't see any American dream; I see an American nightmare.

These 22 million victims are waking up. Their eyes are coming open. They're beginning to see what they used to only look at. . . .

If you don't take this kind of stand, your little children will grow up and look at you and think "shame." If you don't take an uncompromising stand—I don't mean go out and get violent; but at the same time you should never be nonviolent unless you run into some nonviolence. I'm nonviolent with those who are nonviolent with me. But when you drop that violence on me, then you've made me go insane, and I'm not responsible for what I do. And that's the way every Negro should get. Any time you know you're within the law, within your legal rights, within your moral rights, in accord with justice, then die for what you believe in. But don't die alone. Let your dying be reciprocal. This is what is meant by equality. What's good for the goose is good for the gander. . . .

A CON MAN?

If I wanted to be just a con man, I wouldn't be fool enough to try it on these streets where people are looking for my life, where I can't walk around after dark. If I wanted power, I could have gone anywhere in the world. They offered me jobs in all the African countries.

Muhammad is the man, with his house in Phoenix, his $200 suits, and his harem. He didn't believe in the black state or in getting anything for the people. That's why I got out. . . .

ON RACISM

Usually the black racist has been produced by the white racist. In most cases where you see it, it is the reaction to white racism, and if you analyze it closely, it's not really black racism. I think black poeple have shown less racist tendencies than any people since the beginning of history. . . .

If we react to white racism with a violent reaction, to me that's not black racism. If you come to put a rope around my neck and I hang you for it, to me that's not racism. Yours is racism, but my reaction has nothing to do with racism. My reaction is the reaction of a human being, reacting to defend himself and protect himself. This is what our people haven't done, and some of them, at least at the high academic level, don't want to. But most of us aren't at that level. . . .

INTERMARRIAGE*

I believe in recognizing every human being as a human being—neither white, black, brown, or red; and when you are dealing with humanity as a family there's no question of integration or intermarriage. It's just one human being marrying another human being, or one human being living around and with another human being.

I may say, though, that I don't think it should ever be put upon a black man, I don't think the burden to defend any position should ever be put upon the black man, because it is the white man collectively who has shown that he is hostile toward integration and toward intermarriage and toward these other strides toward oneness.

So as a black man and especially as a black American, any stand that I formerly took, I don't think that I would have to defend it, because it's still a reaction to the society, and it's a reaction that was produced by the society; and I think that it is the society that produced this that should be attacked, not the reaction that develops among the people who are the victims of that negative society.

BERTON: But you no longer believe in a black state?

MALCOLM: No.

BERTON: In North America?

---

* This excerpt is from an interview taped on the Pierre Berton Show, taped at Station CFTO-TV in Toronto, January 19, 1965.—Editors' note.

MALCOLM: No, I believe in a society in which people can live like human beings on the basis of equality.

(27)
Eldridge Cleaver's Farewell Address*

> Eldridge Cleaver, like Malcolm X, was schooled in the American ghettos and prisons. After being paroled in 1967, Cleaver became a member and then an officer of the Black Panther Party, and in 1968, ran for President in 1968 on the Peace and Freedom Party ticket in California. Like other Panther leaders, Cleaver was continually harassed by police and rearrested after being wounded in a shoot-out provoked by Oakland police in 1968. Rather than return to prison, he chose exile. The following excerpts from Cleaver's farewell speech in November, 1968, indicate his talents both as a speaker and as a revolutionary.

Now, when I went into the penitentiary I made a decision. I took a long hard look at myself and I said, well, you've been walking this trip for a little too long, you're tired of it. It's very clear that what you had going for yourself before you came in was not adequate. While you're here you're going to have to work with yourself, deal with yourself, so that when you get out of here you're going to stay out. Because it was pretty clear to me that that was my last go-round, that I could not relate to prison any more. So I guess I developed something of a social conscience. I decided to come out here and work with social problems, get involved with the Movement and make whatever contribution I possibly could. When I made that decision, I thought that the parole authorities would be tickled pink with me, because they were always telling me to do exactly

* "Farewell Address," in *Eldridge Cleaver, Post-Prison Writings and Speeches,* ed. Robert Scheer (New York: Random House, 1969).

that. They would tell me I was selfish. They would ask me why I didn't start relating to other people, and looking beyond the horizons of myself.

So I did that, you know. And I just want to tell you this. I've had more trouble out of parole officers and the Department of Corrections simply because I've been relating to the Movement than I had when I was committing robberies, rapes, and other things that I didn't get caught for. . . . There's something more dangerous about attacking the pigs of the power structure verbally than there is in walking into the Bank of America with a gun and attacking it forthrightly. Bankers hate armed robbery, but someone who stands up and directly challenges their racist system, that drives them crazy. . . . I didn't leave anything in that penitentiary except half of my mind and half of my soul, and that's dead there. I have no use for it. It's theirs. They can have that. That's my debt to them. That's my debt to society, and I don't owe them a motherfucking thing! They don't have anything coming. Everything they get from now on, they have to take! I believe that our time has come. A point has been reached where a line just has to be drawn, because the power structure of this country has been thoroughly exposed. There is no right on their side. . . .

. . . there is a point where caution ends and cowardice begins . . . all I see is a very critical situation, a chaotic situation where there's pain, there's suffering, there's death, and I see no justification for waiting until tomorrow to say what you could say tonight. I see no justification for waiting until other people get ready. . . . I've watched them shove shit down people's throats. I knew there was something wrong with the way that they were treating people. I knew that by no stretch of the imagination could that be right. It took me a long time to put my finger on it, at least to my own satisfaction. And after seeing that they were the opposite of what they were supposed to be, I got extremely angry at them. I don't want to see them get away with anything. I want to see them in the penitentiary. They belong in there because they've committed so many crimes against the human rights of the people. They belong in the penitentiary! . . . if you really want to understand and see what's behind the prison system, you have to look at Juvenile Hall. You have to go down to Juvenile Hall. That's where I started my career, at about the age of twelve, for some charge. I don't know what it was—vandalism. I think I ripped off a bicycle, maybe two or three bicycles. . . . They took me to Juvenile Hall, and it took me about six months to get out again. . . . Then I moved up the ladder from Juvenile Hall to Whittier Reform School for youngsters. I graduated from there with honors and went to another one a little higher, Preston School of Industries. I graduated from that one and they jumped me up to the big leagues, to the adult penitentiary system.

I noticed that every time I went back to jail, the same guys who were in Juvenile Hall with me were also there again. . . . In the California prison system, they carry you from Juvenile Hall to the old folks' colony, down in San Luis Obispo, and wait for you to die. . . . Not by any stretch of the imagination can the children in the Juvenile Halls be condemned, because they're innocent, and they're processed by an environment that they have no control over.

. . . You have to ask yourself, why is there not in this country a program for young people that will interest them? That will actively involve them and will process them to be healthy individuals leading healthy lives. Until someone answers that question for me, the only attitude I can have toward the prison system, including Juvenile Hall, is tear those walls down and let those people out of there. That's the only question. How do we tear those walls down and let those people *out* of there?

People look at the point in the Black Panther Party program that calls for freedom for all black men and women held in federal, state, county, and municipal jails. They find it hard to accept that particular point. They can relate to running the police out of the community, but they say, "Those people in those prisons committed crimes. They're convicted of crimes. How can you even talk about bringing them out? If you did get them out, would you, in the black community, take them and put them on trial and send them back again?" I don't know how to deal with that. It's just no. NO! Let them out and leave them alone! Let them out because they're hip to all of us out here now. Turn them over to the Black Panther Party. Give them to us. We will redeem them from the promises of the Statue of Liberty that were never fulfilled. We have a program for them that will keep them active—twenty-four hours a day. And I don't mean eight big strong men in a big conspicuous truck robbing a jive gas station for seventy-five dollars.[1] When I sit down to conspire to commit a robbery, it's going to be the Bank of America, or Chase Manhattan Bank, or Brinks.

I've been working with Bobby Seale on the biography of Huey P. Newton. . . . One of the things that just blew my mind was when he mentioned that prior to organizing the Black Panther Party, he and Huey had been planning a gigantic bank robbery. They put their minds to work on that because they recognized that they needed money for the Movement. . . . But as they thought about it, they thought about the implications. Bobby tells how one day while they were discussing this, Huey jumped up and said, "Later for a bank. What we're talking about is politics. What we're talking about essentially is the liberation of our people. So later for one jive bank. Let's organize the brothers and put this together. Let's arm them for defense of the black community, and it will be like walking up to the White House and saying, "Stick 'em up, motherfucker. We want what's ours." . . .

This piggish, criminal system. This system that is the enemy of people. This very system that we live in and function in every day. This system that we are in and under at this very moment. *Our* system! Each and every one of your systems. If you happen to be from another country, it's still

[1] Two days before this speech, eight Panthers had been arrested following a gas station robbery in San Francisco. Charges against five of them have since been dropped.

your system, because the system in your country is part of
this. This system is *evil*. It is criminal; it is murderous. And
it is in control. It is in power. It is arrogant. It is crazy. And
it looks upon the people as its property. So much so that
cops, who are public servants, feel justified in going onto a
campus, a college campus or high school campus, and
spraying mace in the faces of the people. They beat people
with those clubs, and even shoot people. . . .

. . . I call for the freedom of even those who are so
alienated from society that they hate everybody. Cats who
tattoo on their chest, "Born to Hate," "Born to Lose." I
know a cat who tattooed across his forehead, "Born to
Kill." He needs to be released also. Because whereas Lyn-
don B. Johnson doesn't have any tattoos on his head, he
has blood dripping from his fingers. LBJ has killed more
people than any man who has ever been in any prison in the
United States of America from the beginning of it to the
end. He has murdered. And people like prison officials,
policemen, mayors, chiefs of police—they endorse it. They
even call for escalation, meaning: kill more people. I don't
want it. The people who are here tonight, because I see so
many faces that I recognize, I could say that I know you
don't want it either. There's only one way that we're going
to get rid of it. That's by standing up and drawing a firm
line, a distinct and firm line, and standing on our side of the
line, and defending that line by whatever means necessary,
including laying down our lives. Not in sacrifice, but by
taking pigs with us. . . .

I cannot relate to spending the next four years in the
penitentiary, not with madmen with supreme power in their
hands. . . . While they have sadistic fiends, mean men,
cruel men, in control of that apparatus, I say that my
interest is elsewhere. My heart is out here with the people
who are trying to improve our environment. . . .

. . . Talk all this shit that you want to, issue all the
orders that you want to issue. I'm charged with a crime in
Alameda County and I'm anxious to go to trial because we

can deal with it. . . . But don't you come up to me telling me that you're going to revoke my parole on a charge for which I put in nine years behind the walls, and for which I was supposed to receive my discharge next month. Don't you come up to me talking that shit because I don't want to hear it.

(28)

Dialogue Between Julius Lester and Kathleen Cleaver*

The seriousness of the black revolutionary movement in 1969 is evidenced by the bitterness of the ideological struggles being waged not only against white America and its institutions, but between black revolutionaries. The exchange between Julius Lester, an ex-Student Non-Violent Coordinating Committee member and writer, and Kathleen Cleaver, Secretary of Communications for the Black Panther party, despite the venomous language, must be seen as part of this struggle for ideological clarity, especially on the crucial issues of the nature and role of black nationalism and the proper relationship of black revolutionary organizations to white groups like SDS. Both Kathleen Cleaver and Julius Lester derive much of their political radicalism from their years spent working with SNCC.

The fact that the exchange was printed in the *Guardian* (April 19, May 3, May 10, 1969) indicates that the questions being debated among the blacks are vitally important to the entire radical movement.

* "Dialogue Between Julius Lester and Kathleen Cleaver" in *National Guardian* (April 19, May 3, May 10, 1969).

JULIUS LESTER

With the articulation of Black power, and its tenets of the unassailable right of blacks to define for themselves, we hoped that a new day had arrived. Whites would attempt to organize whites, remaining aware of what was happening within the black movement, supporting that movement and joining in actions whenever the black movement desired such.

If white radicals were able to abide by this, it would serve to build trust between black and white radicals and bury that history of white supremacist attitudes eventually overriding white radical pretensions, with the subsequent betrayal of blacks.

The recent SDS statement on the Black Panther party shows that history has repeated itself. The intent of the SDS statement was to show support for the Black Panther party, an aim with which no one has any disagreement. . . .

SDS goes even further, saying that revolutionary nationalism is correct and cultural nationalism is incorrect. On what basis does SDS presume to know anything about nationalism? The correct and incorrect aspects and uses of nationalism is the most difficult of problems for nationalists; and no one in SDS can ever be a nationalist. If SDS were going to enter into this ideological debate, as it did, then it has a responsibility to define and discuss cultural nationalism and revolutionary nationalism before reaching its conclusions. SDS simply states its conclusions, which are nothing more than a parroting of the Panther position.

Categorically to state that cultural nationalism is "reactionary" is to falsify irresponsibly the history of the black movement. It is cultural nationalism that has laid the foundation for revolutionary nationalism. It is cultural nationalism that has, more than any other ideology, brought a common consciousness to blacks. . . .

The job is to criticize cultural nationalism in such a way as to aid the growth to revolutionary nationalism. To con-

demn cultural nationalism outright is to divide the movement and create conditions for warring factions. . . .
Also, it is necessary to distinguish between cultural
nationalism and the establishment's attempts to exploit
nationalism.

One of the most difficult of ideological battles is going to
be moving cultural nationalists to a position of revolutionary nationalism. That battle cannot be won by the
outright condemnation of cultural nationalism at this stage.
For SDS to inject itself into this ideological struggle is
arrogant beyond all imagining, for it is not a struggle in
which SDS has to involve itself. No white organization has
the right to condemn cultural nationalism, because no white
person can be a cultural nationalist. No white organization
has the right to support revolutionary nationalism, because
no white can be a revolutionary nationalist. SDS, however,
arrogated unto itself these rights.

When SDS characterizes cultural nationalism as "pork-
chop nationalism," it is guilty of a racism which blacks have
had to endure for much too long. SDS should have enough
respect for blacks to use its own language, and not to
appropriate the language of another people. One of the
hardest and most bitter struggles blacks have waged has
been against cultural imperialism. Now it seems that a fight
must also be waged against SDS, a group from which one
would have expected a little more understanding and sensi-
tivity. . . .

SDS should have accorded the black movement and the
black community a modicum of respect by not making this
statement public, whatever its private opinions may be. By
the open attacks which the Black Panther party has been
making on cultural nationalism, it should be apparent that
there is an intense ideological struggle taking place within
the black movement. . . . What is at issue here is the
correct relationship a white radical organization should
have to the black radical movement. By presuming to know
what program, ideology, military strategy, and what particular organization best serve the interests of the black

community, SDS has served to set us back. Those blacks who are suspicious of working with whites will have their suspicions confirmed by this statement. Those blacks who maintain that whites cannot be revolutionary will have this statement to offer as proof. . . .

KATHLEEN CLEAVER

The entire apparatus of U.S. pig law enforcement, co-ordinated out of Washington by the FBI, CIA, Department of Justice and Department of Defense, is waging a full-scale campaign to destroy the leadership and organization of the Black Panther party across the country, and radical white groups along with black people all over the country are moving to defend the Black Panther party. Now Julius Lester raises his whine in chorus with the opposition. . . .

The thrust of Lester's argument against the resolution is that SDS, being a white organization, has no right to evaluate or criticize or form an opinion regarding any black organization, [and] specifically, to insist that any black organization is in the vanguard of the black liberation struggle. Lester states, "That right belongs to the black community and the black community alone." For him these are mere words. For the Black Panther party, this is practice. For without the sustained support of the black people in black communities across the country, the Black Panther party could not have grown into a national organization of 45 chapters in the two short years following the attempted murder and jailing of Huey P. Newton by the Oakland police force in October, 1967.

SDS did not designate the Black Panther party by fiat as the vanguard party, but merely recognized the objective reality of the black colony. That same reality is recognized by J. Edgar Hoover and his pigs across the country, state legislatures and local police forces, and is viciously attacked by them. If Julius Lester is somehow antagonized by the vanguard position of the Panthers, he cannot blame SDS for recognizing it, nor can he bring back to life the 15 members of the Black Panther party who have died at the hands of pig violence, whose blood placed the party in the vanguard of the people's liberation struggle. For SDS to recognize the true role the Panthers play in the black movement is no "insult" to black people. . . .

For SDS to agree with Huey P. Newton and the Black Panther party does not seem to be any abrogation of black people's rights. It is a necessary step in breaking down the prison of racism that keeps both black and white people fighting separately against capitalist exploitation and perpetuates the very capitalist-imperialist-neocolonialist empire that has black people as its foremost victims. Ideas are not the property of a racial group, but belong instead in the realm of the true or false.

Finally, Lester commits the very crime for which he attacks SDS—not defining either cultural or revolutionary nationalism (after an involved defense of cultural nationalism)—but merely taking a position on their value and relationship to the struggle. Lester comes to the crux of his argument; he states, "No white organization has the right to condemn cultural nationalism, because no white person can be a cultural nationalist. No white organization has the right to support revolutionary nationalism because no white person can be a revolutionary nationalist." . . .

According to this line of thinking, when black cultural nationalists murdered Bunchy Carter and John Huggins on the UCLA campus, no white person could support or condemn this atrocity because they could not be members of US [a Los Angeles black cultural nationalist group, members of which have been accused of killing Carter and Huggins] or the Panthers, cultural nationalists or revolutionary nationalists. We don't have to be Chinese to decide whether Mao Tse-tung or Chiang Kai-shek is a better leader of the Chinese people, to support one or condemn the other. But this is the stagnation that Julius Lester's thinking would lead us to.

With his adept use of words, Lester tries to confuse the classic distinctions between different ideological principles represented by the terms of cultural nationalism and revolutionary nationalism. Fanon put an end to that debate with his statement. "The only culture worth holding onto is revolutionary culture." But for those who don't relate to this terminology, there will always be distinctions between those who move to serve the needs of the people (revolutionaries) and those who move to manipulate the people (cultural or *reactionary* nationalists—like Papa Doc Duvalier and Tubman), and to replace the white oppressor with a black one. . . .

Neither SDS, the FBI, CIA, US, ABM, or any other force will set black people back: the inevitable birth of the black revolution is in the stages of labor now and the child is going to be delivered shortly. . . .

Perhaps if Lester would come out of his act for a day, come across to our side of the tracks and help us run a breakfast program for the children, or a political education class, or a day-care center, or a mimeograph machine to put out leaflets for the May 1 demonstration for bail for Huey Newton, he might learn something about serving the needs of the people and might put that paper column to some worthwhile use.

Until he does that, he will find his time consumed with contriving arguments against white organizations which support revolutionary nationalism and all other sorts of trivia which don't relate to the needs of black people or of radical journalism, and he might as well go print his shit in some reactionary rag which would delight in his mentality —because black people don't have time for his bullshit. He is even too cowardly to attack the Black Panther party directly, but has to hide behind a white organization to deal his dirt. And if he feels we have no right to attack cultural nationalism while cultural nationalists are killing and starving black people, if he feels no one outside of the black community has the right to support revolutionary nationalism as exhibited in the daily work of the Black Panther party, not only is he counterrevolutionary, he is a fool, and a disservice to the people and needs to peddle his madness

to people who will buy it, because we don't want to hear it
again. . . .
   All power to the people!

JULIUS LESTER

   In the history of radical movements, a point is reached
when organizations and individuals in the movement begin
arguing with one another. This is inevitable, because within
a radical movement there are conflicts on strategy, tactics,
and politics.
   For a while, it is possible to hide these conflicts for the
sake of unity and solidarity. When these conflicts come into
the open, however, the splits within the movement can
become so great that organizations sometimes spend as
much time fighting each other as they do in organizing.
Sometimes the conflicts lead to one organization splintering
into many smaller organizations which then proceed to fight
each other. At other times it has led to a severe weakening
of the radical movement. It has also led to violence within
the movement. . . .
   White America has always told itself who and what black
America was and what was best for it. It has always looked
at black America and said, this one or that one is the
leader, the representative, and he is the one to whom whites
should listen and give support if they wish to encourage
"responsible" leadership among blacks. . . .
   Every white radical in the country seems to have
"Panther fever," another manifestation of the "Oh I wish I
were black" syndrome, which is merely whites once again
side-stepping the difficult work of organizing the white
community. To give the BPP political support is one thing.
To regard it as the *sine qua non* of revolution is another.
Many feel that the BPP is above criticism and look critically on any black they even suspect of looking critically at
BPP. Others feel that the BPP should not be criticized while
it is under attack from the government. . . .
   In an industrial society, the vanguard is the most politi-

cally conscious sector of the working class. Thus it would seem that black workers would eventually be the vanguard party. And by far the most important single development of the past year in the black movement has been the formation of radical black labor groups in auto factories. It is a very young movement, but it might be suggested that it is they and the politically conscious workers to come who will be the vanguard, because it is they who know the system at its industrial heart, who are the very power source of the system.

The Black Panther party maintains, however, that it is the vanguard, and he who does not recognize them as such is their enemy, if not the enemy. Thus they attack cultural nationalism as reactionary and cultural nationalists become the enemy. They have equated cultural nationalism with reactionary nationalism, and unless one correctly identifies the enemy, he might be fighting a potential comrade.

Reactionary nationalism is very evident now under the guise of black capitalism in magazine ads, and on television. Blackness is used as a smokescreen for the same ideology and program which has been responsible for the oppression of the people. But because it is packaged in blackness it has a new look.

Cultural nationalism, on the other hand, is an act of identification with black culture whose manifestations have been Afros, daishikis, black studies, etc. Reactionary nationalism wraps itself in the clothes of cultural nationalism. Sometimes it wraps itself in the rhetoric of cultural nationalism, e.g., a person taking an African name and still talking the same old stuff. Sometimes it might even wrap itself in the rhetoric of revolutionary nationalism.

Cultural nationalism can come in a daishiki, a suit or in quoting Fidel, Che or Mao. In and of itself, cultural nationalism is apolitical, and is, therefore, easily coopted by reactionary forces, e.g., the Ford Foundation. At the same time, however, cultural nationalism represents the first stirrings of self-recognition, and it has been the beginning of political involvement for thousands.

Cultural nationalism was a significant part of the teachings of Malcolm X and Stokely Carmichael. Cultural nationalism is a significant part of the thought of LeRoi Jones and, in his quiet way, Jones is one of the most influential people among black youth. It was on the base of cultural nationalism (black consciousness, black pride, black awareness, and a simplistic articulation of black power) provided by these men and others that the BPP was able to build and articulate its ideas of revolutionary nationalism.

The creation of the BPP was part of the logical historical progression, and black history is falsified if this is not recognized. The BPP itself is part of an historical progression growing from Robert Williams, Elijah Muhammad, Malcolm X, SNCC, Stokely, Rap; and they in turn have helped to create a consciousness around the necessity for armed struggle, program, organizational discipline, as well as helped to create the conditions necessary for DRUM and the other new black labor organizations.

Cultural nationalism is not the enemy of revolutionary nationalism. Reactionary nationalism is, and to confuse it with cultural nationalism is to leave the cultural nationalists at the mercy of reactionary forces. . . .

. . . Black revolutionaries, as do all revolutionaries, have the most awesome of responsibilities; criticism is one means by which we can assure ourselves that we fulfill those responsibilities.

(29)

"Dick Gregory Is Alive and Well"*

Dick Gregory grew up in the Chicago ghetto, made it to college on an athletic scholarship, and was then "discovered" as a performer. Gregory used race as his comedy

* From a speech televised for NET television for a program called "Dick Gregory Is Alive and Well."

theme, and won fame as a civil
rights comedian. But as the civil
rights movement developed Gregory became a participant. Arrested many times in northern and
southern civil rights marches, he
devoted most of his time to movement work. In the late 1960s he
combined his political education
with his comic talents and gave
lectures throughout the country,
mostly on college campuses. The
following excerpts are from a
speech-performance at the University of Alabama in Tuscaloosa
before a racially mixed audience.

About a year ago in Chicago I was walking down the
street, downtown in the Loop, about ten o'clock in the
evening. A white cat walking down the sidewalk, he see me
coming, he jump all the way off the sidewalk and get in the
gutter. Scared to death. He say, "Mister, you're not going to
bother me, are you?"

I said, "No, my man, I'm Dick Gregory, I'm dedicated
and committed to non-violence." "You mean you are *the*
Dick Gregory? You don't carry no gun or no knife?" I said,
"No." He said, "You don't do no shooting or cutting?" I
said, "No." He said, "Well stick 'em up, nigger." . . .

I grew up seeing things in the ghetto that most white
Americans don't even know exists. And then they scream
about black folks should respect the police. And we have to
laugh at that, because if they was in the black ghetto and
was seeing the things that happen to us in that black ghetto,
and the things that we have to see, they couldn't have respect for their policemen.

And also there seems to be something that a lot of people
fail to understand, that when the civil rights movement
started there was a passionate resentment for the police, not
because he was any worse, not because—as a matter of fact
there's less police brutality now since the civil rights movement than it was before. But the problem is to grow up in
the black community in America, and all your life see the

whore, the prostitute, the pimp, and the dope pusher, and the cop—and this dope pusher that's really a detriment to not only the black community, but to any community, and not being molested by the police. And then I look at a black civil rights worker come in my community to uplift me, and he gets all this static from the police. You know, the cops is watching him, they knocking him down, they making arrests. . . .

We came here, we had natural kinky hair, right? Then we started combing our hair so we could look like the slave master, right? My woman went to the beauty parlor and got a hot comb on her hair to straighten it out so it could look like the master's wife, right? Now we're in trouble, right? Because any time I want to emulate and look like the people who have misused me, then we're in trouble.

So what happened, young black folks like Stokely and Rap, that was hip enough to know that we needed an identity, that identity was not with the man up on the hill; that identity was not with a Cadillac; that identity was not with how far you could hit a baseball; that identity was not where you live; that identity was not how many A's you made in school, but identity was with self. Right here, with self.

I got to have a black cat to give me my ghetto news. Because I don't want to hear nothing about no humidity, you understand? I don't want to hear nothing about no barometer; I don't want to hear nothing about no wind velocity. Because I get that through the hole in the back window, I know about the wind velocity. Understand? . . .

We'd appreciate it if you'd get that white boy history book out of my community. That book that everybody wants to talk about a nigger is a hoodlum and a criminal. And I read your white history, it tells me you came to these shores and discovered a country that was already occupied. Now who's a criminal? How you going to discover something that's not only occupied, but being used at the time. That's like me and my old lady walking out of here today and you and your lady sitting in your brand new auto-mobile, and my lady says, "Gee, honey, that's a beautiful automobile, I sure wish it was ours." And I say, "Well, let's discover it."

So we wish you to get that white history out of our community, and maybe we could behave. And when you take it out, read it. Sometime we going to believe you read your history. "Give me liberty or give me death." Who said that? Rap Brown, didn't he? What did Stokely Carmichael say? It's in your history book. "Don't shoot till you see the whites of their eyes." You see, maybe if you read your history you'd understand me.

People run around saying, "Black folks ought to have respect for the police." We can't have respect for the police after reading your white history, because we see where you didn't have respect for the police. It's in your history book. It says in the early days when the British was the police, a white boy by the name of Paul Revere rode through the white community and said, "Get a gun, white folks, the police is coming."

You all do understand them "White Panthers," don't you? And then the riots start out, the niggers get to break-ing windows and stealing television sets, taking them home, and everybody says we're hoodlums because we steal tele-vision sets during the riot. I don't know how you can accuse me. When I read your history it say not only did you get on that stranger's ship, you dumped all his tea in the water. What the hell you mad about? The niggers got the sense to take it home with him. . . .

Five years ago four white boys burned up their draft cards and within two weeks time the Senate and Congress had passed an anti-draft card burning bill. We haven't been able to get them to pass an anti-lynching bill in a hundred years. This country just told me she thinks more of a piece of cardboard than she thinks of my black mammy. I'll bring her to her knees for that.

I
wants
<u>YOU</u>
nigger

Become a member of the world's highest paid black mercenary army!

Support White Power — travel to Viet Nam, you might get a medal!

Fight for Freedom . . . (in Viet Nam)

Receive valuable training in the skills of killing off other oppressed people!

(Die Nigger Die — you can't die fast enough in the ghettos.)

So run to your nearest recruiting chamber!

W H Y ? Black people fighting Yellow people for White People . . .

(30)

"I Wants You, Nigger"

The anti-Vietnam War movement
in the ghettos had many levels, including religious and pacifist approaches. But the most direct anti-
war approach was taken by SNCC
and the Black Panthers. This poster
was hung on telephone poles and
pasted in many ghetto store windows.

THE CHICANOS

*T*he horde of banditti, of drunkards, of fornicators . . .
*vandals vomited from Hell, monsters who did defiance
to the Laws of Nature . . . shameless, daring, ignorant,
ragged, bad-smelling, long-bearded men with hats turned
up at the brim, thirsty with the desire to appropriate our
riches and our beautiful damsels."*

A Mexican newspaper describing
the American volunteer army in
the Mexican-American War.

*"Texans could not get it out of their heads that their
manifest destiny was to kill Mexicans and take over
Mexico."*

Erna Fergusson,
Our Southwest.

*"It is clear that the danger is not that Mexico may return to
primitivism: the Indian does not have the strength for that.
The danger and the scheme are that a Spanish Mexico
should give place to a Texan Mexico with the Anglo-Saxon
acting as owner and builder, and the Indian as roadmender,
peasant and fellah in 'Mexican towns' such as you see from
Chicago to New Mexico, more miserable than the medieval
ghetto, but without the genius which suddenly blossoms and
lifts the Jew above his oppressors."*

José Vasconcelos,
*The Autobiography of
a Mexican Ulysses.*

VIVA OUR "MESCANS"

Like most of American history, the story of the Spanish-speaking people of the Southwest falls into two categories. One is myth. The other is the unwritten history of continual subjugation and oppression. The myth is well known. It tells of kindly Spanish padres working together with gentle Indians to plant seeds in the fertile soil, white-clad peons taking siestas to the strum of Spanish guitars, and black-haired *señoritas* with long lashes and curvy bosoms dancing with castanets and listening to love songs crooned to them from under their balconies at night. Only occasionally are regrets expressed over the cruelties and excesses that characterized the conquest of the west.

Our Spanish past is celebrated in many towns in California and the Southwest. The celebrations are of a romantic past that never existed. The *Los Angeles Times* enthusiastically describes a celebration of Mexican independence: "Vivas and olés filled the air. . . . Los Angeles yesterday donned the festive regalia of her Mexican heritage . . . Cinco de Mayo Festival On, Si, Si." Then it reports that two Southern California towns with large Mexican populations chose Miss Frances Anderson and Miss Virginia Thomas as their reigning *señoritas*. The Anglo's patronizing view of his "Mexican heritage" is clear when in 1944 the *Times* commended a program for teaching Spanish in the lower grades with "We . . . have missed learning the homey, friendly gossip of the little people who have big hearts even if lean purses. We have missed much señores. . . . Viva Mexico! Viva el Español." The disparity between real Mexican-American history and the comfortable myth of our Spanish past is vast. The truth is that Spanish-speaking people have always been victims of Anglo brutality, both physical and psychic.

The Anglo view grew out of open racism that began with
the conquest of New Mexican and Spanish-American civilization. The conquerors did not look kindly on "the little
people," who were seen as obstacles in the path of American destiny to be eliminated or at least reduced to
weakness.

American history books call what happened The Settlement of the West or The Great Race West; the *corridos* (folk
ballads—see glossary) of New Mexico and Texas call it
The Conquest. The American dream, which grew out of the
American myth, expresses a desire for a happy merging of
cultures. But the most astute Spanish-speaking people and
perceptive Anglos know it was a case of gradual genocide.

The Aztecs had conquered some Mayan civilizations by
destroying them; they merged with others. Slavery, and
human sacrifices to the sun god, were common in the Aztec
world. The Spaniards arrived as the Aztec empire was
crumbling. They set Indian against Indian, destroyed Aztec
rulers, enslaved many people, and began a widespread
search for gold and other wealth. Their search brought
them—by then they were *mestizos* (of mixed Indian-
Spanish blood) after two generations—to the western part
of what is today the United States at the beginning of the
sixteenth century.

The Spaniards did not discover the great sources of
wealth they had expected to find. They encountered, instead, a rugged country and hostile Indians, who within a
few short years became masters of guerrilla warfare, especially with the aid of horses which the Spaniards had given
them. In some sections some Spaniards made peace with the
Indians, or married them with a dispensation from the
Pope; in others they enslaved them. Their settlements spread
and had little communication with each other.

A life style emerged from the geography and economy,
from California to Texas and New Mexico. The Spaniards
developed agrarian communities that were poor, relatively
egalitarian, and spiced with Indian ways. After a century

the Spaniards became Indo-Hispanic people in culture and blood. They were Western in religion and technology, but had no ambition to save the world or make it over in their own image.

Anglo invaders came two centuries later as pioneer farmers, cowboys, drifters, gold-hungry miners, merchants, hunters, and finally as soldiers opening the West to the world market system. Each group claimed to stand for progress, Christianity (which did not include Catholicism), and peace. Each group fought, and imposed its ways and religion. Despite the fighting, economic progress came to the frontier. The Indo-Hispanic people were then confronted by the peculiar laws of American expansionism, which combined democracy with racism, ambition with greed, the gun with the Bible, often creating a nightmare instead of the dream.

Most Mexicans had little chance to think or argue about their positions; the conquest happened too quickly and violently. However, from the beginning of the conquest, Mexican community leaders have divided into assimilationists, who thought it possible to peacefully coexist, and those who foresaw the Yankee juggernaut and called for resistance. The inheritors of the 350-year-old tradition of resistance have only just begun to organize. They are trying, under the leadership of men like Cesar Chavez and Reies Tijerina, to stop anti-Mexican racism, alleviate the extreme poverty of Mexican-Americans in the Southwest, and revive their old culture. Like some of the other nonwhite minority groups, the new *chicanos* no longer believe that integration into white society is possible or even desirable.

It is possible, of course, as in other minority groups, for some individuals to "make it" by becoming wealthy and losing their ethnic characteristics. But a growing number of Mexicans talk about those who have "made it" as *vendidos* or *malinches*. Like the blacks and Indians, the Mexicans of the Southwest have waited long enough for the promises of security and opportunity in white America to come true. Zapata posters now adorn walls that once displayed

F.D.R.'s smiling photo. *La Raza** extends from Texas to California. The Chicano Press Association has offices not only in Texas, New Mexico, Colorado, and California—the states with the largest Mexican populations—but also in Chicago and towns like Wautoma, Wisconsin, where permanent Mexican communities grew out of migrant-labor groups over the years.

The newly awakened Mexican-Americans now know that the conflict between Anglos and the Mexicans goes back to their earliest encounters. The result was that the Spanish-speaking people became victims of a kind of cultural imperialism that promised them equality but practiced a form of genocide.

THE BEGINNINGS

Thirty-three years after Ponce de León founded St. Augustine, Florida, in 1565, Spanish explorers established Santa Fe in New Mexico. In the late seventeenth century, Texas settlements were founded by the Spaniards; a century later, in the 1770s, the chain of Spanish missions was created in California. These settlements had little in common except that the inhabitants spoke Spanish and were legally part of Mexico after its independence was declared.

Until the middle of the nineteenth century, the *Californios,* the *Nuevo Mexicanos,* and the *Tejanos* each went their own separate ways. The cement of their old Spanish culture had cracked, and not even the struggle for Mexican independence had provided strong enough ties for those north of the border to feel a kinship with Mexico. Each Southwest community developed more or less uninfluenced by the Yankees to the east or the Mexicans to the south. Their language, religion, foods, and skills came from

---

* Literally translated, *La Raza* means race or people. However, it also means the concept of a whole culture which must be defended. Now used by Spanish-speaking people in the U.S. to differentiate themselves from the Anglo culture.

Spanish-and-Indian Mexico, and were augmented by those of northern Indian cultures. Peace was established with some Indian tribes, and often intermarriage took place.

Other Indian tribes, such as the Apaches, refused to make peace or assimilate. The Apaches wiped out some early Spanish settlements and made communication and transportation between the remaining ones difficult or impossible. The Spaniards made a serious error by allowing all captive Indians to be herders and teaching them to ride horses. The nomadic Apaches, for example, began to steal the Spaniards' horses and barter them for captives. They became a constant menace to the Spanish settlers. For more than two hundred years, the Apaches, like their Yaqui cousins in Sonora, militantly defended their land and civilization against intruders, both Spanish and Anglo. Their armed struggle continued into the early twentieth century; then an old and tired Geronimo finally fell to Arizona rangers.

By the time of the Anglo-American conquest in the middle of the nineteenth century, the guerrilla tactics of nomadic Indians had put the Spanish-speaking settlements on the defensive. To travel from San Antonio to Santa Fe in 1848, the voyager had first to go south to Durango, Mexico, then back up to El Paso, and from there to Sante Fe—an extra two hundred miles.

The Indians kept the Spaniards isolated in missions and forts, but they also held back the Anglos, thus serving inadvertently as a temporary shield for the Spanish settlements. The Indian problem, plus the rugged terrain and the Civil War, kept the Americans from exploiting the lands and minerals in the Southwest until the late nineteenth century, thus preventing, for a while, any conflict with the Spanish settlements.

In Texas, New Mexico, and California, the Spanish-Indian-Mexican settlements had established stable and often comfortable ways of life before any significant contact with the Anglos came about. When it did, bitter conflicts arose over cultural differences, land, and the wealth on the land. The Spanish-speaking settlements had merged in relative harmony with some of the Indian tribes in the Southwest, but expanding Anglo America had no desire to do likewise. "Remember the Alamo," had become a battle cry; it also implied a race war. An American major once described the white race as exterminating or crushing the inferior race in attempting to realize its "manifest destiny." An American soldier wrote in a letter that "The Mexican, like the poor Indian, is doomed to retire before the more enterprising Anglo-Americans."[2] Most of the Spanish-speaking people accepted the inevitable. Some understood, accepted, even cooperated in the giant frauds and political deals which turned over their lands to the invaders. Others fought in the old Spanish *macho* tradition, but the Colt 45s and shotguns of the Anglos made their defeat inevitable.

TEXAS

"All truce between them and us is at an end. . . ."

J. N. Cortina, September 30, 1859.[3]

The history of Texas from the nineteenth century to the present comes in two versions: the Anglo-Texan and the Mexican. The Texans' folklore history glorifies the conquest and reduces the Mexicans to stereotypes. It is perpetuated by "reputable" historians as well as ethnocentric Texans. Stereotypes are found in attitudes and anecdotes passed down since the 1830s when Mexican "atrocities" against the white Texas settlers became popular story-telling material. Later this material was absorbed into speeches for the political campaign to annex Texas by declaring war against Mexico in 1846–1848.

[2] Carey McWilliams, *North from Mexico*. Philadelphia and New York: J. B. Lippincott Co., 1949, p. 125.

[3] J. N. Cortina, "Proclamation," in *Difficulties on Southwestern Frontier*, 36th Cong., 1st Sess., 1859–60. Washington: Thomas H. Ford, printer, No. 52, Vol. VIII, p. 71.

The Mexican-American war, called "Mr. Polk's War," is one of the central events in Spanish-American history in the United States. It was fought, according to historians David S. Muzzey and John A. Kraus, in order "that we should carry our boundary to the Rio Grande, that we should extend our protection over our 'fellow-citizens' in Texas, that we should rebuke Mexico for her impudent and impotent defiance." It gained territory for the U.S. greater than that of Germany and France combined. "Ho, for the halls of the Montezumas!" was the cry, as Americans marched off to conquer in 1846.

Some Americans then, as with the Vietnam war today, protested their country's policy with regard to Mexico. The Reverend William Jay, son of the first Chief Justice John Jay, documented the fraudulent means used by the United States to bring about the War. Daniel Webster called it "a war of pretext, a war in which the true motive is not distinctly avowed, but in which pretenses, afterthoughts, evasions and other methods are employed to put a case before the community which is not a true case." The U.S. Government was not above using subversive methods, as Webster pointed out. With the hope of setting up a puppet government in Mexico, the government issued orders to its naval forces blockading Mexico to allow Santa Anna, the Mexican military leader (who had been in exile) to slip through the lines into Mexico on the very day Polk sent his war message to Congress. "How came it into Mr. Polk's head that Mr. Santa Anna was likely to come that way?" asked Webster, who then proceeded to reveal that secret agents of the U.S. had arranged the illegal border crossing. But the U.S. had outsmarted itself, for Santa Anna proved to be unreliable puppet material. Frederick Douglass demanded "instant recall of our forces from Mexico." He spoke out against the "disgraceful, cruel, and iniquitous war" in which Mexico was the "victim to Anglo-Saxon cupidity and love of dominion." Abraham Lincoln, then a freshman congressman, suggested that there be an investigation of the precise location of the first clash between U.S. and Mexican forces.

He felt certain (it turned out he was correct) that it was on Mexican territory.

A group of enlisted men, predominantly Irish Catholic immigrants who had joined the Army because it was a refuge from the discrimination they encountered in civilian life, were shocked by the behavior of the Americans, particularly Texans, toward the Mexican peasantry. Furthermore, the anti-Catholic attitudes of their officers contributed to their growing disenchantment with the United States Army. Finally, the desecration of Catholic churches in Mexico by U.S. soldiers (closely paralleling the burning of Catholic churches in New England and other parts of the nation) turned the tide for them. Following the lead of Sgt. John Riley of the 5th U.S. Infantry, many enlisted men joined the Mexican Army and formed a battalion called *Los Patricios* (for Saint Patrick). After fighting heroically in several engagements, most of the members of the battalion were killed or captured at the Battle of Churubusco after their ammunition ran out. Almost all of those captured were hanged by their former comrades in arms.

The Mexicans, in gratitude, erected a plaque at San Jacinto Church in Mexico City, inscribed "In Memory of The Heroic San Patricio Battalion/Martyrs Who Gave Their Lives For Mexico During The Unjust American Invasion of 1847."

Mexicans were thought of as bestial, treacherous, cowardly, natural-born thieves, sexual fiends, and perverts. In this view a Mexican would stab you in the back, and he comes from inferior races: the Spanish, who are the lowest of Europeans (along with the Italians), and the cowardly southern Indians (Mexican and American), who are not like the superior northern tribes.

Scholars also helped create the stereotype of the Mexican. *The* historian of the West, Walter Prescott Webb, wrote:

Without disparagement it may be said that there is a cruel streak in the Mexican nature, or so the history of Texas would lead us to believe. The cruelty may be attributed partly to the Indian

blood. . . . The Mexican warrior . . . was, on the whole, inferior to the Comanche and wholly unequal to the Texan. The
whine of the leaden slugs stirred in him an irresistible impulse
to travel with rather than against the music. He won more victories over the Texans by parley than by force of arms. For making promises—and for breaking them—he had no peer.[4]

Historic battles, such as The Alamo, Mier, and Goliad
(where some Mexican officers did commit atrocities), became part of Texas and later national popular history.
Stories about them fed the spirit of conquest. They proved
the valor of the Yankee pioneer and the evil of the red,
brown, and dark-eyed people. For example, Anglos held
the entire Mexican population responsible for the execu-
tions of captives carried out by General Santa Anna who
was acting on his own authority. The Mexican general was
enraged at the audacity of the foreigner's attempt to conquer Mexico and decided to teach the Anglos a lesson. (His
officers had tried to stop him.) A century after The Alamo,
Mexican atrocities were used as one of the excuses to "re-
patriate" (deport) hundreds of thousands of Mexicans.

Historian J. Frank Dobie wrote in *The Flavor of Texas:*
"I should name the experiences of Texans as prisoners to
the Mexicans" as the "most movingly and dramatically
recorded."[5] Historian Webb, on the other hand, calls the
terror methods used by the group that became known as the
Texas Rangers, "revenge by proxy."[6] Also cited are members of voluntary brigades, such as Hay's Rangers, who
fought in the Mexican War and made daring raids at Mier
and Goliad, who murdered any Mexicans who crossed them
to avenge the brutal imprisonment their mercenary army
had suffered at the hands of Santa Anna. Some Texas
Rangers, like Bigfoot Wallace, a Mexican War veteran who
had fought at Mier, might have been motivated by personal
revenge. But the Rangers as a group wreaked the kind of

[4] Walter Prescott Webb, *The Texas Rangers.* Boston and New York:
Houghton Mifflin Co., 1935, p. 14.
[5] J. Frank Dobie, *The Flavor of Texas.* Dallas: Dealey and Lowe,
1936, p. 125.
[6] Webb, *op. cit.,* p. 87.

terror which historian Américo Paredes says "makes an occupied country submissive, something the Germans knew when they executed hostages in the occupied countries of Europe during World War II."[7] The histories of men like Webb and Dobie refined the Ranger myth and the Mexican stereotype and made them acceptable to educated Americans. Paredes suggests that had The Alamo not existed, it would have been invented.

"Cruelty" and "inferiority" were central to the Texas stereotype of Mexicans. The stereotype was justified for Texans; most Mexicans behaved submissively toward Anglos, thus proving their inferiority, and those who resisted were *supermachos,* thus proving their cruelty.

(The role of the resisters in the white American conquest may become more important in the present than it was in the past. Just as Nat Turner has regained an important place in the history of black liberation, so may men like Cortina play an increasingly important role as *La Raza Unida* revives its past heroes.)

One of the resisters was Juan Nepomucena Cortina, known as "The Red Robber of the Rio Grande." In 1859 Cortina, a well-to-do landowner in Cameron County, Texas, began his political career by shooting a deputy who was trying to arrest one of his servants. For Cortina, the Yankee arrogance displayed in that incident was unbearable. Two months later, Cortina gathered an army and rode into Brownsville (where he had been born when it was still in Mexican territory). Five shots found their *gringo* marks. They looted Anglo stores and released their *gente* (people) from the jail. Cortina understood very well how the *gringo* had conquered by the gun and was well on the road to legally, or illegally, robbing from Mexicans anything worth possessing. He also knew there was only one way to prevent that and live like a man: use the gun on the *gringos.* For Cortina, it was a war of liberation, and armed struggle was the only way. *Gringo* elections were phony, just as their

[7] Américo Paredes, *With His Pistol in His Hand.* Austin: University of Texas Press, 1958, p. 26.

laws and treaties were. They were meant for the conqueror, not the conquered.

Retaliation against Cortina's raids and those of other resisters proved to be a self-fulfilling prophecy. The adjutant general of the U.S. reported in 1875:

Soon after the raid of Mexicans . . . some raids occurred of a different character. Bands of Americans went to a place called La Para, where a store was burned and several persons killed. This was incited partly for revenge on Mexicans, and partly to suppress the killing of cattle for their hides.

There is a considerable element in the country bordering on the Nueces and west, that think the killing of a Mexican no crime, and the effect has been to stop, to a considerable extent, the trade between Laredo and Corpus Christi.[8]

Cortina was an upper-class Mexican of the group "protected by their position from the kind of petty persecution that fell to the lot of their more unfortunate countrymen not so well situated economically."[9] Actually most upper-class Mexicans cooperated with the conquerors, hoping to maintain their wealth and position which the *gringos* assured them would be protected. As biographer Goldfinch concludes, ". . . those among them whose lot was at all tolerable were unwilling to start any disturbance in defense of their rights."[10] If a lower-class Mexican, who was a peon even before the Americans took over, asserted his rights under the law or the Treaty of Guadalupe-Hidalgo, he was dealt with by the Texas Rangers who were available to back up their countrymen if a "greaser" started any trouble.

Cortina, educated and free all his life, could not tolerate the abuse of his people. He embodied the heroic tradition of the Spanish gentleman with an educated mind and voice, as well as *machismo*. He had learned the ways of the *gringos* as an official in the Quartermaster Corps of the United

[8] "Report Of The Adjutant General For The Year 1875," House Executive Documents, Frontier Troubles, U.S. Congress, p. 121.

[9] Charles W. Goldfinch, *Juan N. Cortina, A Re-Appraisal*. Brownsville, Texas: Bishop's Print Shop, 1949, p. 40.

[10] *Ibid.*

States Army. When he returned to his large estate he had already made up his mind that no matter what it cost him, he would not permit more abuses. After the Brownsville affair, he became Public Enemy Number One, and war was declared between the Texans and Cortina's band.

Cortina rallied his people for guerrilla warfare. Texans identified all Mexicans as Cortina men and burned Mexican homes indiscriminately.

Cortina also appealed to border Mexicans, who were willing to help because they had all had bitter experiences with the laws of the Anglos. Generally what happened was that an alliance of Anglo lawyers and deputy sheriffs would threaten to burn the Mexicans' homes and lynch them if they refused to abandon their homes and lands.

Some members of the patron class opposed Cortina because their commercial interests required peace with the Americans; others feared that the United States would not be satisfied with Texas, New Mexico, Arizona, and California, and would use Cortina's war as a pretext to "liberate" all of Mexico. It was admitted, however, by Major Heintzleman that "The marauders have active sympathy of the lower classes of the Mexican population."[11]

Cortina was hunted on both sides of the border as a cattle thief rather than as a political rebel. He has been described in American history books as a colorful, though bloodthirsty, bandit. However, his own statements make clear that he thought of himself as the leader of a conquered people: "Mexicans! My part is taken; the voice of revelation whispers to me that to me is entrusted the work of breaking the chains of your slavery, and that the Lord will enable me, with powerful arms, to fight against our enemies, in compliance with the requirements of that Sovereign Majesty, who from this day forward, will hold us under His protection!"[12]

Cortina's manifestoes charged that the *gringos* had tried

[11] Lyman L. Woodman, *Cortina, Rogue of the Rio Grande.* San Antonio: The Naylor Co., 1950, p. 49.
[12] Cortina, *op. cit.,* p. 81.

to "blacken, deprecate and load with insults" the Mexican
residents of Texas and he promised that "our personal
enemies shall not possess our lands until they have fattened
it with their own gore."

An Army officer stationed at the border described Cortina's exploits: "He had defeated the Gringo and his position was impregnable. He had the Mexican flag flying in his
camp and numbers were flocking to his standards. He was
the champion of his race. . . ."[13] But his success was
short-lived. The Texans hired some Mexicans to capture
and kill him. In 1873 the Mexican authorities captured
Cortina. But instead of putting him in prison they made him
a General-in-Chief of the Mexican Army.

Cortina's quarrel had started with some deputy sheriffs,
lawyers, and speculators. It spread until it included the
entire *gringo* population. Cortina's hatred of the *gringos*
grew from his observations of their behavior. "Our object
. . . has been to chastise the villainy of our enemies . . ."
he said in a proclamation to the people of Brownsville. He
claimed that the Anglos had formed "a perfidious inquisitorial lodge to persecute and rob us, without any cause, and
for no other crime on our part than that of being of
Mexican origin, considering us, doubtless, destitute of those
gifts which they themselves do not possess."[14] Americans,
on the other hand, felt that the Cortina War, as it had
become known, was primarily a race war. A United States
major reported from the border in February, 1860: "The
industrious, enterprising, active race on one side cannot
exist in such close proximity with the idle and vicious on the
other without frequent collisions."[15]

Other "bandits" like Cortina believed that the conflict
between Anglos and Mexicans could be resolved in only
two ways: either submission of Mexicans and strangulation
of their culture or death by violence, a man's way of dying.
The Cortina War was followed by general race wars in

[13] McWilliams, *op. cit.*, p. 107.
[14] *Ibid.*, p. 70.
[15] Woodman, *op. cit.*, pp. 57–58.

other sections of Texas. Using Cortina tactics, although perhaps with less ideology, Mexican bandits and guerrillas made the border areas a battleground for several decades, with rustling and lynching as common as rolling sagebrush. Texans brought Mexican-branded cows to the slaughter-houses, and Mexicans crossed the Rio to bring home what they called *las vacas de tata,* "grandfather's cattle."

In the nineteenth century, Mexican-Americans were still very much Mexicans, although with a strong border flavor. Cortina's followers, and those enlisted with other bandits, demonstrated that armed revolt was a popular response to *gringo* conquest. However, none of these movements suc-ceeded in establishing their counterparts in Mexico or the organization of anything more than heroic but foredoomed efforts along the border. The American dynamo could not have been stopped, even if Mexico had offered her re-sources; such an offer might have led to a conquest of all of Mexico—something Sam Houston proposed in 1858.

Despite the recognized impossibility of stopping the con-queror, some Mexicans along the Texas border fought on. The hopelessness of winning back their territory, however, forced many of them to move from militant aggression into banditry. But it was not simple looting; it was looting directed against the *gringos* and, therefore, produced a satisfaction that went beyond the lust for wealth. Their pillaging was often accompanied by cries of "Death to the Americans!" and "Long Live the Mexican Republic!"

At the same time, no force in the white community ex-isted that was capable of organizing behind the principles of American equality. The strong racial hatred lurking behind the flimsy rhetoric of tolerance burst out in the open at the first sign of racial strife, and the Anglo community leaped to the racist cause.

Mexicans quickly became the Negroes of the Southwest. Although not slaves, they remained in a state of peonage to a white American master who was not interested in just keeping his local rancho going, but in rapidly increasing his profits. The limited local market gave way to the world market. Americans had the capital and Mexicans provided the labor. The Mexicans were taken out of their old settlements and the rural ranchos to work for new bosses. Their culture was diluted. The stereotype of the lowly Mexicans, which originated with the Texan influx into Mexican territory, grew; in the minds of whites, Mexicans, like Negroes, acquired characteristics of the savage, the child, and the animal. Many Mexicans were part Indian, which put them even lower in the esteem of whites. However, an important distinction was made by whites between the blood of northern Indians, who were considered handsome and brave, and that of Mexican Indians to the south, who were considered ugly and degenerate. The term "greaser"[16] was born around this time.

All Mexicans, no matter how light-skinned or refined, were "greasers"; all Anglos were *gringos*. The origins of both words had little to do with their later use as derogatory racial expressions. *Gringo* was a corruption of *griego,* meaning Greek, and was applied to all foreigners. To *hablar en gringo* meant to talk gibberish. In later years Mexicans found other derivations. General Green led an assault into Mexico during the Mexican-American War, and supposedly the populace began shouting, "Green, Go Home!" Another possible origin was a popular song the Yankee troops sang as they marched through Mexico, "Green Grow the Rushes." "Greaser" had an equally uncertain origin. It may have referred to the Mexicans who greased the carts and wagons on the trails or perhaps to the Mexicans and Indians in California who loaded greasy hides onto ships. Whatever its origin, its meaning is clear: an inferior person.

The white stereotype of the Mexicans included rich and poor. Yet each characteristic attributed to Mexicans was also a characteristic of the Anglos themselves. A stereotyped Mexican was by his nature a thief, particularly prone to stealing livestock; yet cattle barons stole stock from border Mexicans and then shot anyone who complained. The

16 McWilliams, *op. cit.,* p. 115.

Mexican was supremely passionate, went the stereotype, and had no hesitation about killing: but the record of the Texas Rangers in savage and indiscriminate killing of Mexicans is horrible to contemplate; also, lynch mobs, the United States Army, local sheriffs, any drunken cowhand, could kill innocent Mexicans without fear of punishment. Of course many Mexicans killed Anglos, but the balance sheet was overwhelmingly against the Mexicans. Anglos projected onto Mexicans the very traits they had used to conquer the Mexican, his land, and when they wished, his women.

After creating the Mexicans as they wanted them to be—treacherous, childlike, primitive, lazy, and irresponsible—the Anglos went on to treat them accordingly in law and life. For example, the conquest of the Southwest was followed by the Treaty of Guadalupe-Hidalgo in 1848. The treaty guaranteed Mexicans the right of full citizenship, but their land and cattle were stolen or taken by fraud, they almost never received fair trial, and they were manipulated by politicians, lawyers, and land grabbers. Historians tend to gloss over this aspect of United States history and write it off to unfortunate growing pains. However, Walter Prescott Webb was one historian who correctly summed up the plight of the Mexicans:

Not only were the Mexicans bamboozled by the political factions, but they were victimized by the law. One law applied to them, and another, far less rigorous, to the political leaders and to the prominent Americans. The old landowning Mexican families found their titles in jeopardy and if they did not lose in the courts, they lost to their American lawyers. The humble Mexicans doubted a government that would not protect their person and the higher classes distrusted one that would not safeguard their property.[17]

Through the nineteenth century, outbreaks between Anglos and Mexicans occurred constantly in Texas. One incident occurred when an American took over a salt mine near El Paso. It had been communal property for hundreds of years, but he began to operate it for his sole profit. A

[17] Webb, *op. cit.*, pp. 175–76.

priest, Padre Borajo, led his flock in a fight in which several Anglos were killed. In retaliation, Texas Rangers slaughtered many Mexicans. To them, no Mexican was too important or too wealthy to escape whipping or shooting.

The Texas Rangers are an important part of American myth, and are portrayed as the most courageous of white men. "Shoot first and ask questions later," was the Ranger motto. By the 1880s the Ranger was "the man to deal with the Mexicans." The Plains Indians had been pacified or wiped out, but the Mexicans were still a problem. The border, no matter how well guarded, could easily be violated; rustling was still carried on from both sides. The *corridos* sung along the border portray the Rangers as *rinches* (derogatory Mexican word for rangers) rather than John Waynes or Gary Coopers. One ballad goes, "They kill three fine cocks, those miserable rinches."[18]

Another one says:

> The "rinches" are very brave,
> that cannot be denied;
> they hunt us like deer
> in order to kill us.[19]

Anglo legends were countered by Mexican folk poets in Texas who created their own superheroes. Most of these folk heroes, immortalized in the *corridos,* defended the dignity of *La Raza y nuestra gente* (our people). In the *corridos* the Mexicans fight it out with the sheriffs or *rinches*. After killing many *gringos* without ever shooting them in the back, they succumb to overwhelming numbers and weapons. They are doing it for Mexico and *La Raza*.

The "Corrido of Gregorio Cortez," based on an incident that took place in 1901, is a good example of the genre. (The entire *corrido* is printed in the Documents section.) In the *corrido* Cortez killed a sheriff in self-defense, after the sheriff had murdered his brother. Cortez killed several more Texas lawmen and outrode and outsmarted hundreds of pursuers. Cortez was so brave and skillful with his gun,

---

18 Paredes, *op. cit.,* p. 145.
19 *Ibid.,* p. 146.

says one version of the ballad, that the *rinches* could take him only if he were willing:

Then the Americans said,

> "If we catch up with him, what shall we do?
> If we fight him man to man,
> Very few of us will return". . . .
> When the sheriffs arrived,
> Gregorio gave himself up,
> "You take me because I'm willing,
> but not any other way". . . .
> Then said Gregorio Cortez
> With his pistol in his hand,
> "Ah, so many mounted Rangers?
> Just to take one Mexican."[20]

The spirit of resistance expressed in the *corridos* was not lost on the Texans; despite the official peace of the late nineteenth century, racial tension still existed. When the Mexican Revolution broke out in 1910, some Mexican border residents feared that the flames of the revolution would spread to Texas. That fear became a reality in 1916 when Pancho Villa crossed the border and hit Columbus, New Mexico. General Pershing pursued General Villa back into Mexico, just as the Rangers of old had chased Cortina; the spirit of the 1840s had never really died out. Pershing's men sang a song expressing the prevailing sentiment:

> It's a long way to capture Villa,
> It's a long way to go;
> It's a long way across the border
> Where the dirty greasers grow.

For their part, the Mexican-Americans on the border cheered the daring Mexican general.

Stories of atrocities spread on both sides. It was "stored away in the back of the El Pasoan mind that these Mexicans will take it into their heads to have an especially-appointed uprising at the expense of the Americans."[21] Ernest

20 *Ibid.*, pp. 3, 159.
21 Tracy Hammond Lewis, *Along the Rio Grande*. New York: Lewis Publishing Co., 1916, p. 7.

Gruening, the former senator from Alaska, wrote that "Americans continued to be killed by vengeful Villistas, at times for no other reason than they were 'gringos.' Mexicans likewise were killed in Texas chiefly because they were 'greasers.' "[22]

Throughout the Southwest the Mexican Revolution and Anglo fears that Mexico would become a staging ground for a German invasion of America fanned the old fires of race hatred. In 1917 in Bisbee, Arizona, many Mexicans were among the Wobblies who participated in a copper strike. They were all rounded up by more than 2,000 vigilantes in a secret predawn raid and deported from the state or forced to flee across the border into Mexico.

Eighty years after the Guadalupe-Hidalgo treaty, which guaranteed protection for all Mexicans, no Mexican living in the Southwest could feel secure at any time or any place. They continued to suffer from the often sadistic whims of the Texas Rangers and gun-happy cowhands. In Texas, open season on Mexicans reached new peaks. No jury would convict any white man accused of killing a Mexican. Mexican President Carranza reported 114 known murders of Mexicans, a figure acknowledged by United States officials. To this day old Mexicans in the border towns tell stories of the terror during the rustling days and the revolutionary war years. Américo Paredes dedicated his 1958 book on Gregorio Cortez to "My father, who rode a raid or two with Catarino Garza [also listed as a cattle thief in the Texas histories, but who was a Raza man like Cortina] and to all those old men who sat around on summer nights, in the days when there was a chaparral, smoking their cornhusk cigarettes and talking in low, gentle voices about violent things, while I listened."[23]

Many of the *corridos* and folk tales exaggerate, but they do tell the history of a people who suffered much violence to their persons and to their culture. The *corridos* also

[22] Ernest Gruening, *Mexico and Its Heritage*. New York and London: The Century Co., 1928, p. 529.
[23] Paredes, *op. cit.*, Frontispiece.

express a fear of *gringo* power. In the end, however, they accept the Mexican plight as inevitable. Today, when the children and grandchildren of the border Mexicans hear the old stories, they begin to hate anew and to think about retribution and justice for current abuses.

IN THE MOUNTAINS
OF NEW MEXICO

"The sun has exploded, señor," cried the shepherd to his patron. "We saw it. It was so bright that we fell on our knees and our sheep stampeded. Take us back to our families and let us go to church. It is the end of the world." This was July 16, 1945, near Alamogordo, New Mexico. For the isolated New Mexico communities it was indeed the end of the world as they had known it.

Settled in 1598—years before the founding of Jamestown—by Juan de Oñate and about five hundred men, New Mexico was supposed to have been the source of incredible gold and jeweled wealth. The Spanish monarchy had been encouraging explorers since 1539 and even though they found little wealth, belief in the gold story persisted. Onate and his successors came in the tradition of the *conquistadores*. Their treatment of even the most cooperative Indians was so intolerable that the Pueblos revolted in 1680, destroying most of the Spanish settlements and forcing the Spaniards to flee to Texas. In 1693, having learned from experience and recognizing that the Apache threat was the most dangerous, the Spaniards reconquered their old territory and began to intermarry with the Pueblos and other Indian tribes offering no resistance to them. Spanish culture and language prevailed, but they were mixed with a strong Indian flavor.

Of all the Spanish settlements, New Mexico remained

closest to the old culture, partly because of its geographic barriers to Anglo invasion. Even up to the present, parts of New Mexico are "in many respects extensions of Latin America into United States territory."[24] In January, 1966, the *Albuquerque Journal* reported that "Sen. Tibo Chavez (D., Valencia) inquired Tuesday during a Senate session what the Senate rules had to say about a member eating tortillas in the chamber. He referred to Sen. Mathias Chacon (D., Rio Arriba), who was taking a quick lunch during the discussion on Senate Reapportionment." The presiding officer ruled that the only prohibition "required that eating of tortillas be done quietly."[25]

The Spanish conquerors, after succeeding in subduing or assimilating most of the Indians, lost their ambition for gold and became farmers. The population was small, relatively egalitarian, sharing a life of poverty. Through the end of the eighteenth century, New Mexico was peaceful and unchanging.

Even after the Santa Fe Trail was opened in 1822 and Anglo businessmen came into New Mexico, most of their trade was with Mexico, reinforcing the cultural ties and similarities between the New and Old Mexico.

Then, in 1841 a group of Texans, under the Republic of Texas flag, set forth with much bravado to invade and seize the New Mexico territory. The expedition was intercepted and soundly defeated by the New Mexicans; its leaders were sent to Mexico City as war prisoners. The Texans, never ones to take affront from Mexicans, retaliated with raids on commercial caravans bound for Santa Fe. The atrocities committed by Texans against New Mexicans produced such hatred on the part of the New Mexicans that many, according to Carey McWilliams, "were inclined to look upon the arrival of American troops as a measure of protection

[24] John A. Burma, *Spanish Speaking Groups in the United States*. Chapel Hill: Duke University Press, 1954, p. 4.
[25] Nancie L. Gonzalez, "The Spanish Americans of New Mexico, A Distinctive Heritage," in *Mexican-American Study Project, Advance Report 9*. University of California at Los Angeles, 1967, p. 3.

against further encroachments on the part of the Texans."[26]

By 1846, the year of the conquest by Americans, New Mexico had undergone a change from an agricultural to a sheep-herding economy. The egalitarian social structure had been broken up by the granting of large estates, especially after Mexican independence. A class of *ricos* (rich) was created, some of whom rented land and sheep to tenants. Before 1846 no more than a few hundred Anglos had settled in New Mexico; many of them had married into Spanish families and accepted the old culture.

The conquest of New Mexico by the Anglos in 1846 was relatively bloodless. The majority of the poor Mexicans and the Indians felt no deep commitment to Mexico and those who tried to resist were betrayed by their own leader, Governor Manuel Armijo, who literally sold the territory for a large bribe to American officials. In addition, many of the *ricos* saw the conquest as a chance to increase their wealth through expanded trade. Under the Treaty of Guadalupe-Hidalgo, any Mexican citizen could return to Mexico in the course of one year; those who remained automatically gained United States citizenship. Slightly more than 1,000, out of an estimated 60,000, returned to Mexico.

General Kearny's U.S. troops moved into Santa Fe shortly after the Mexican resistance group was betrayed by Armijo. The *ricos* claimed they wished to resist, but factionalism prevented them from organizing after their leader betrayed them. Revolt came the next year, 1847; it was carried out by a combination of *campesinos* (peasants), some pure Indian *ricos* (rich), and clergymen. The leader of the revolt was Padre José Antonio Martinez, a priest-rancher and the first newspaper publisher in New Mexico. He joined forces with the charismatic peon, Pablo Montoya. Centering around the city of Taos, their revolutionary activity included the assassination of the American civil governor, many exhortations to freedom, and a kind of free

26 McWilliams, *op. cit.*, p. 117.

thinking that was deemed very dangerous by many *ricos,* and by the Americans and the Catholic Church as well. (Padre Martinez not only thought freely, but acted upon his beliefs, denouncing various Church practices, especially tithes and fees. He educated peons at a school which he founded, and had several wives and many children. He was later excommunicated for his unorthodox beliefs and practices.)

The revolt itself was put down in a massacre by American troops. The rebels became the victims of an orgy of killing that included firing squads and mutilations. Word of these cruelties spread quickly and formed the foundation for a militant hatred of *gringos* in New Mexico.

Had it been the first and last incident, it might have been forgotten. But further conflicts ensued between sheep and cattle ranchers, and later between railroad interests and railroad workers and the local population. The anti-Mexican feelings of newcomers, many of them from Texas, were easily set aflame. The continual incursions on Mexican liberty and property by cattlemen and lawyers, who stole much land, produced a resistance similar to the one which developed in Texas. Lone gunfighters began to take on the grievances of their people.

One such folk hero was Elfego Baca of western New Mexico. In 1884 he appointed himself a deputy, arrested an unruly Texas cowhand, locked him up, and barricaded himself in an adobe house with guns and ammunition. He proceeded to demonstrate his courage and his marksmanship over a period of thirty-six hours during which he was surrounded by scores of Texans. After the gunfight, the Texans gathered their dead and wounded, and for a time their encroachments stopped. The fact that Baca was then tried for murder and acquitted was an interesting reversal of the usual course of events.

Another gunman, Sostenes L'Archeveque, killed twenty-three *gringos* in eastern New Mexico in the 1880s. Sostenes' father had been one of the Texans' victims, and he took his revenge during a one-man campaign of robbing and killing.

Finally, his own people, afraid of the reprisals that had resulted from other armed resistances, trapped and killed this "Mexican Billy the Kid." Reprisals came anyway. The Texans lynched and murdered any dark-skinned New Mexican they thought was in league with Sostenes. The reprisals drove the Mexicans from the New Mexico panhandle. Another bitter lesson was learned.

New Mexico continued as an Indo-Hispanic land for many years, despite the chicanery and manipulations of the Anglo minority and their *rico* allies; the old culture hung on. But because the Anglos remained a minority, New Mexican statehood was delayed until 1912, when Anglo political control was finally established. Not until then, sixty-six years after it had become part of the United States as a result of the Mexican-American War, was New Mexico allowed into the union.

After statehood, the mass of people were led to believe that they would be represented in politics by their own race. But the *ricos* and the Anglo politicians had common interests in maintaining the old class structure. The *ricos,* using their economic power and appealing to ethnic ties, usually controlled enough votes to sustain themselves as a multifamily ruling group. Statehood changed nothing. The Anglos and *ricos* transferred their old social and economic alliance into political control of the state through control of the state courts, key state appointments, and various bureaus, such as the Indian Bureau.

The alliance between the Anglos and *ricos* had developed out of abortive, grass-roots politics begun in the 1870s. At the end of the century, lower-class Mexicans, under the direction of Francisco Chavez, himself a *rico,* began to organize against the corrupt gang of *ricos* and Anglos. Some reforms came about when Chavez was elected to the territorial senate and served twelve years as its presiding officer. He was murdered in 1904, many thought by the *rico-gringo* gang known as the Santa Fe Ring. The Ring later convinced Congress they could control the territory, thus making it acceptable for statehood.

Spanish surname candidates continued to win elections (and still do), but as New Mexico entered the modern period, the race and class lines coincided more and more. The *ricos* became whiter and acquired Anglo surnames, while the poor became darker and acquired Spanish names.

In the late nineteenth century, another type of resistance group evolved in New Mexico—to fight for the land which the natives had lost through swindles or threats against their lives. Such groups still exist. Professor Clark Knowlton of the University of Texas at El Paso wrote about one such organization in a letter to the authors dated February 23, 1968:

The Black Hand came into existence about ten or fifteen years ago in response to a drive by Anglo-American owned land and cattle companies to force Spanish-Americans to leave the land on which they and their ancestors have been living for around two hundred and fifty years. The title to this land was lost to the Spanish-Americans by legal trickery.

This land was later sold to these large land and cattle companies. The Spanish-Americans have responded by organizing very informal, loosely-structured underground organizations to burn homes and barns, cut fences and kill livestock belonging to Anglo-American ranchers who have bought title from these large land and cattle companies. These groupings . . . are in considerable danger from law enforcement agencies.

The Black Hand is merely a name. It is not one that is used by the local Spanish-Americans. It is a name that was created by Anglo-Americans. For over one hundred years there has been a sequence of such organizations in various parts of New Mexico. The so-called Black Hand is but one, as is [Reies Tijerina's] Alianza. There have been others and there will be more until the land, water, and grazing issues are settled to the satisfaction of the Spanish-American people.

So it was not surprising to *chicanos* when on June 5, 1967, Reies Lopez Tijerina, whose family had come to what is now United States territory in the sixteenth century, led a band of his people, known as *La Alianza,* to the Court House at Tierra Amarilla and took it over. One deputy sheriff died. Local, state, and national officials expressed shock; the National Guard was called in to put down the insurrectionists, who had come to claim the land they felt was theirs. The incident was blamed on "communists" and "outside agitators." The formation of *La Alianza* to reclaim *chicano* territory was an authentic response to the conquest of New Mexico, which humiliated the Indo-Hispanic natives, destroyed their culture, and deprived them of their land.

CALIFORNIA

"The early Californians, having lived a life of indolence without any aspiration beyond the immediate requirement of the day, naturally fell behind their more energetic successors, and became impoverished and gradually dispossessed of their fortunes as they idly stood by, lookers-on upon the bustle and enterprise of the new world before them, with its go-aheadtiveness and push-on keep-moving celerity."[27]

In 1769, seven years before Thomas Jefferson drafted the Declaration of Independence and more than two hundred years after Juan Rodriguez Cabrillo had landed on California soil, Father Junipero Serra arrived in San Diego. Padres like Serra were often accompanied by soldiers and adventurers from many cultures, and within two years the local Indians had received their first taste of Christianity and "civilization." By 1771 it had already become a custom for soldiers to ride into the neighboring Indian village, lasso the females, and drag them back to camp. Such men were among the founding fathers of the state of California.

California was a savage area for most of the early Spanish gentlemen who colonized it. These men became extremely chauvinistic about their new land, and although it was legally a part of Mexico, it became more and more

[27] Alfred Robinson, *Life in California During a Residence of Several Years in That Territory*. San Francisco: W. Doxey Co., 1891, p. 254.

like an independent duchy. The state founders and their ancestors called themselves *Californios,* while those who came later to do the labor were Mexicans. The Spanish origin of California is today a source of pride to many of the Anglo families who "married into the Spanish aristocracy." But actually the men who founded the territory were neither gentlemen nor Spaniards. The original settlers of Los Angeles, for instance, included two Indians from Mexico, a mulatto, two Spaniards married to Indians, two Negroes, an Indian married to a mulatto, a *mestizo* married to a mulatto, and an Oriental, probably Chinese.

Through the late seventeenth and early eighteenth centuries, California was, in historian Josiah Royce's words, "an outlying and neglected Mexican province."[28] The power of the padres and the missions waned in the process of secularization, and the mission Indians disappeared with them. By the 1830s California was all but nominally independent of Mexico.

Californios were usually whiter and more overtly Spanish, and made up the upper class. Indians, *mestizos,* and the generally darker people did the labor, while the *Californios* lived a relatively carefree life. Political battles were *Californio* feuds, since one group of families controlled northern California and another controlled southern California. In 1842, when Mexico made one last effort to reassert her control by sending up a Mexican governor and army, the *Californios* temporarily ceased their feuding and united against the governor and his convict army. Josiah Royce's description of the battle is illuminating: "The battle itself was as bloodless as most California encounters. Tremendous cannonading is sometimes said, in the accounts, to have taken place. Two or three horses and mules were hurt; but the armies on both sides kept well out of range. . . . Civilized warfare was, in fact, introduced into California through the undertakings of our own gallant [John C.]

[28] Josiah Royce, *California, A Study of American Character.* New York: Alfred A. Knopf and Co., 1948, p. 25.

Fremont.[29] For in civilized warfare, as is well known, somebody always gets badly hurt."[30]

Then came the Mexican War and the arrival of Anglos in large numbers. The Anglos arrived first as fighters in the Bear Flag Rebellion and other minor wars. For the first time *Californios* died in battle. At the same time, racism and the world market system were introduced in California. With the discovery of gold, hundreds of thousands of Anglos flocked to the new territory, and the *Californios,* who had ruled the area so casually and had owned most of its wealth, were swiftly disgraced and displaced within fifteen years. Despite their wealth, the *Californios* were still "greasers" to the newcomers. The *Californios'* refusal to identify with the lower classes of Mexicans, plus their north-south family tiffs, prevented them from unifying against the *gringo* assault.

With the wars and annexation (1846–48) came "rain on the sheepfold," as one sad *Californio* put it.

CALIFORNIA RESPONDS
TO CONQUEST

"When I see a Mexican approaching, I cock my rifle and cover him with it. At the same time calling to him to raise his hand away from his lasso which hangs at his saddle bow. In this way I keep my rifle on him until he has passed and gone beyond lasso distance."[31]

The Spaniards and Mexicans originally came to Cali-

[29] Fremont led five exploratory expeditions across the Great Basin to the Pacific Coast under the aegis of the United States Congress. Three of these followed the outbreak of the Mexican War. The first was in 1843–44 when he commanded an expedition authorized by the War Department.

[30] Royce, *op. cit.,* pp. 24–25.

[31] William Ingraham Kip, *The Early Days of My Episcopate* [1892]. As cited in Leonard Pitt, *The Decline of the Californios.* Berkeley and Los Angeles: The University of California Press, 1966, p. 82.

fornia for gold, but, ironically, it was the Anglos who
discovered it and who, in pursuit of it, trampled Mexican
and Indian culture during the 1850s, a decade unmatched
in lust and cruelty. The reasons why the *Californios* had
failed to find the gold point up the differences between their
culture and that of the invaders. The Mexicans did not lack
the necessary adventurousness of spirit or skills as miners,
but they were inhibited by their fear of Indian attacks in the
Sierra. The significant factor, however, was their content-
ment with the tempo of rancho life, which stood in sharp
contrast to the violence of the Gold Rush:

"Vagabonds from every quarter of the globe. Scoundrels from
nowhere, rascals from Oregon, pickpockets from New York, accomplished gentlemen from Europe . . . and assassins manufactured in Hell for the expressed purpose of converting high-
ways and biways into theaters of blood; then, last but not least,
Judge Lynch [who lent his name to lynching] with his thousand
arms, sightless eyes, and five hundred lying tongues."[32]

The old way of life was destroyed by the *gringos*. Once
infrequent incidents quickly became common occurrences;
lynching Mexicans was one of them. The *Californios* came
down from the Sierra into the cities and valleys; some
Mexicans remained to teach the newcomers how to mine.
At the same time, the Anglo newcomers began a campaign
against any "foreigners" they thought were going to
"plunder" California's gold. General Persifer F. Smith, soon
to be in charge of the United States Army in Monterey,
declared in 1849 that he would "consider everyone who is
not a citizen of the United States, who enters upon public
land and digs for gold, as a trespasser."[33] General Smith
included in his declaration Mexicans who had been born in
California!

The racism of the Anglos, who came to claim California
as their own, had an important economic factor. Many of
the newcomers lured to California by gold failed to make

[32] Description by Hugo Reid, *gringo* member of the California Constitutional Convention. As cited in Pitt, *ibid.*, p. 52.
[33] Gen. Persifer F. Smith, quoted in Pitt, *ibid.*, pp. 55–56.

their big strike in the fields and were forced to seek other work in order to get another grubstake that would enable them to return to the mines. Competition for jobs outside the fields became intense, and unemployed Anglos encountered additional difficulties because nonwhites were willing to work for lower wages than whites. Typically, when a group of Chileans was chased from the Sierra gold fields by Anglos, they were viciously harassed after they arrived in San Francisco by the Hounds, a gang made up of ex-volunteers from the Mexican War and stray Australians.

When California finally became a free state, some Anglos demanded that the peons be eliminated. An early California legislator described the peons as "the refuse population from Chile, Peru and Mexico . . . as bad as any of the free Negroes of the North or the worst slaves of the South."[34] But smart white businessmen considered cheap Mexican labor a godsend. The same Mexicans who were forced out of the northern placer mines in 1849 were then hired by shrewd Yankee patrons who spoke no Spanish and kept their guns loaded to protect their Mexican laborers. These laborers worked for $1.00 a day, one-fourth of what the Anglo was paid.

The *Stockton Times* described the Mexican laborer, as opposed to the Anglo, as "milder in spirit, more contented to endure, more willing to suffer, more weak spirited." The Spanish-speaking worker was not a latent capitalist who carefully invested his earnings. He worked hard and when he was done he went home with his hard-earned wages to spend them on himself and his family. "Americans," wrote an American general, "by their superior intelligence and shrewdness in business, generally contrived to turn to their own benefit the earnings of Mexicans. . . ."[35]

A Foreign Miners Tax Law and other measures to make mining prohibitive or very expensive for all except United States citizens were enacted in some counties. In others vigilantes routed out a few Mexicans and lynched them to

[34] *Ibid.*, p. 58.
[35] *Ibid.*, p. 59.

set an example. But the shrewder and more farsighted businessmen, who needed their cheap labor, tried to protect the Mexicans. Nevertheless profits dropped as the Mexicans left the mining areas. The Mexicans found new protectors among those businessmen who could not afford to lose so many laborers and customers. Both those who advocated the removal of the "foreigners" and the "protectors" acted out of their own special brand of racism.

The Mexicans crossed and recrossed the border. A few, who could avoid the vigilantes hunting gold-bearing Mexicans, were able to carry the precious ore out with them. Those who remained in California blended in with the *Californios.* The native-born *Californios,* on the other hand, could not go to Mexico without sacrificing all they owned. Most of them stayed and submitted to the conquerors. They were abused and lynched, had their property stolen, and their women raped. Still, the property owners and middle-class patrons among them continued to argue that reason and law would solve their problems and that there were reasonable *gringos* who would protect all law-abiding citizens. A few *Californios* decided that armed struggle was the only way to preserve their dignity; these people are now described in history books as bandits. Their real role is obscured, just as Cortina's is.

The decision that no alternative existed but armed struggle was a direct response to the racism written into the Anglos' laws and practiced in their social life. The historian H. H. Bancroft lists a fantastic number of Mexicans who were whipped and lynched during the 1850s. No Mexican could get a fair trial. Lynching was a common practice. If a Mexican was suspected of a crime and could not be found, another Mexican was often substituted in the jail or even on the gallows.

Part of the Anglo fear of Mexicans, as with Negroes, was based on the alleged sexual superiority of the darker-skinned people. The "greaser" women were supposedly corrupting the white men. In 1851, in the mining country, a prostitute named Juanita was hanged by an angry mob after a passion death occurred in which she was involved. The miners assumed that Juanita's supersexuality was responsible for the murder and punished her. Here was the myth of the passionate, flaming Mexican woman come to life.

To realize the fears of the bigots, many Mexicans, out of bitterness, new feelings of rootlessness, and uncertain identities, decided to play it the Yankees' way. The *bandidos* and mining camp whores played their roles well. With their families broken up, their village culture infested with the poison of cold Yankee business morality, Mexicans faded into the newly created urban *barrios* or emerged as free souls, patriots, rebels, killers, or plunderers. They became pirates who sought, not Spanish galleons, but Anglo gold. They sought a renewal of their pride and manhood, which the whites had stripped away. Yankee governors and legislators had little concern for the domestic "greasers"; they were looking across the Pacific, following the course of the war against the brown men in the Philippines.

The legends of Mexican badmen so widely believed today are best exemplified in the tales about Joaquin Murieta. Murieta was the story-book figure both the Anglos and the Mexicans wanted and needed. His cry was, *"Maten los gringos!"* He was wild, carefree, heroic. Latin in looks and behavior, he was the man all Mexicans wanted to be, the man all Yankees saw in every Mexican. He was blamed for almost every daring and cruel crime committed over almost a decade—sometimes simultaneously in northern California and Los Angeles. His pickled head, or sometimes a fake head, was exhibited at county fairs after his death. Who he was is still not clear. A *Californio* whose land was stolen, whose wife was defiled, who watched his men being abused and lynched—any or all of these? He may never have existed, except in the imaginations of those who needed such a man to exist.

Joaquin was called "The Native," also "The Bandit." To the Mexicans he was a hero, for his crimes, like all crimes by Mexicans, were transformed into patriotic acts. When a hanging took place, it was always for more than stealing—

it was for resisting. Joaquin was the excuse for miners to hunt Mexicans and for Mexicans to rob and kill *gringos*.

By the time armed resistance came to an end in the late nineteenth century, dozens of Joaquins had been hanged and shot down. The conquest of California had been completed, and the Anglo victors could revive Spanish culture in the church bazaars they called "fiestas" and in annual celebrations of "mescans" and Spaniards. "Californios did not 'disappear, ignored of the world,' however, as Mariano Vallejo had feared—far from it. No sooner had they died than the *gringo* practically immolated himself upon their graves. The 'Spaniards' went into apotheosis; 'Spanish California' had become a cult."[36] The Anglos dressed up in the costumes they imagined the old *patrones* would have worn on party days. The language, the old culture, the old easy way of life became fond, sad memories to the *Californios* who were now absorbed into the Yankee world market system.

THE MODERN ERA: DEPRESSION, DEPORTATION, WELFARE AND REVIVAL

Like the rest of the nation's poor, the Mexican-Americans have gradually shifted from rural to urban life, from subsistence farming to the welfare doles. Those in the past who crossed the Rio Grande from Mexico as wetbacks (illegal immigrants) and remained in the United States lost some of their Mexican identity in the crossing. In the *barrios* Mexicans grew up in an emasculated culture. Legends of Cortina and Murieta, of Villa and Zapata, provided a heroic past with which they could identify. But most young *barrio* residents grew up knowing little of their past. The memory of their cultural heroes had dimmed under the strain of

[36] *Ibid.*, p. 284.

daily life in the mines, new cotton fields, fruit valleys and sheep pastures, brick factories, and on the railroads.

Rural life in the Southwest changed with the coming of large-scale farming, made possible by the availability of cheap Mexican labor. White tenant farmers were slowly pushed aside as white corporate farmers took over, bringing with them hordes of Mexican laborers. The Mexicans worked for lower pay and under more adverse conditions than any Anglo worker would stand for. The native Mexican population merged with hundreds of thousands of imported hands to build the Southwest. The fabric of white, small-farm culture was torn apart. The Mexican laborers remained illiterate generation after generation. Since the children were needed as fieldhands if the family was to survive, they were not sent to school. (The schools taught only in English anyway.)

From the late nineteenth century through the 1920s, Mexicans moved in and out of the Southwest. The new immigrants migrated to conquered territory as peons. They lived in poor *barrios,* in an increasingly bastardized culture that was more Anglo than Mexican. Native Mexicans who adjusted to the conquest, however, became *petit bourgeois* who offered professional services to Mexican immigrants.

A conquered people who became a racial minority in a new culture, the Mexican-American lived a semipeasant existence, just as he would have back in Mexico. By the 1920s, the shift from rural and semirural shanty towns into urban slums was well under way.

The *Saturday Evening Post* described the Mexican section of East Los Angeles in 1928: ". . . In no part of Poland or of southeastern Europe have I seen a more ignorant or more destitute class of people than the Mexican peons who were packed into the shacks that have flowed over this former truck garden district and in a few years time have buried it in slums."[37]

During the 1920s racial feelings in middle-class and

[37] *Saturday Evening Post,* March 10, 1928, p. 41.

lower-middle-class America returned to post–Civil War intensity. The Klan was strong not only in the South, but in Indiana, Ohio, and New Jersey as well. The Southwest was less organized in its racism, but its racial feelings toward Indians and Mexicans were just as strong. The racists sought restrictions against Mexican immigrants on the basis that "greasers" were really only 1/16th to 1/64th white. In other words, they were considered primarily Indian or Negro or both. Their legal status as full-fledged whites was totally ignored. Furthermore, the African features of some of the *Veracruzanos* (descendants of runaway slaves who settled in Vera Cruz) provided ample foundation, for some Anglos, for the notion that many Mexicans were descendants of runaway slaves.

More common, though, among both Anglos and Mexicans during the 1920s and early 1930s, was the idea that the Mexicans were a third race—the bronze people, not quite Negro and not quite white. A Mexican consul general stationed in Texas commented that ". . . . future generations of Mexicans, living in the United States, will live apart from the larger society, which is basically white and Nordic. . . . Mexicans will never be an integral part of the spiritual life of the American people." Then the learned consul general said: "Consequently, the United States will never be a harmonious social unit as it was when it was founded. Instead the United States will be a society divided into three parts: white, bronze and black."[38]

By the era of large-scale unemployment during the 1930s, the same Mexican nationals who had been imported as cheap labor were seen as potential trouble makers. Militant attempts by the Mexicans to form unions, from 1900 through the 1930s, had been met with extreme brutality. They were deported *en masse,* and with them went some of their native American brethren; to the immigration officials one "spic" or "greaser" looked like any other, and their names were all the same anyway. No distinction was made

[38] José Vasconcelos, *Mexican Ulysses.* Translated and abridged by W. R. Crawford. Bloomington, Ind.: Indiana University Press, 1963.

between Mexican nationals and United States citizens with Mexican names. Deportation, or repatriation as it was called, was also a means of breaking strikes and of reducing the relief load. Union leaders, organizers, and "agitators" were often singled out for deportation. It was also assumed that Mexicans were highly susceptible to communism,[39] another good reason for getting rid of them.

Those who escaped the mass deportations to Mexico found homes in the already congested *barrios* of southwestern cities. There, together with their large families, the survivors began life in the immigrant half-world, as Ruth Tuck called it.[40] It was a half-world for the Mexicans because they were treated differently from other immigrant groups who could assimilate by fighting for a place in the American mainstream in the schools, on the job, and finally by entering politics and government. The individual European immigrant, for example, gained strength from his ghetto culture. Even after he had moved from the ghetto, he continued to gain strength from it; he stood as a symbol of mobility to the ghetto dwellers left behind. For the Mexican, this happy mixture of support from the Old and the New Worlds did not exist. Ruth Tuck described a Mexican from the half-world:

There was one thing which impressed Juan and his *compadres* as they talked, in bunk houses, around picking fires, or in cheap cafes of El Paso's poor districts. The life they had led before was valueless to them here. No American was interested in it; no one considered it anything but "low" or "savage" or "funny"; manifestations of another culture were likely to be met with reactions ranging from aversion to ridicule to incarceration. Juan had not enjoyed high status in his own country; he had known both exploitation and injustice; but he had been able to feel a certain sureness in his way of life. The little pattern of Los Conejos was part of the big pattern of Mexico; it had its place, its validity, and its worth. But in the United States it had no worth; he began to feel powerful pressures on him to make him into something

[39] See Document 6, "Deporting Jesus."
[40] Ruth Tuck, *Not With the Fist*. New York: Harcourt, Brace, 1946, pp. 89–90.

he was not prepared to be, a person he hardly understood—the man who was "just like everyone else." He could refuse, he could hang back, or he could fail. The penalties would be obvious. He would not be sent to prison or deprived, openly, of his few possessions. He would just be pushed into a half-world, a place reserved for the "foreigner" and the half-assimilated, where advantage, opportunity, and recognition were sharply limited. He would be hung between his old world and the new, with no place except among other dwellers of the half-world.[41]

Juan was first generation and suffered the shock of shifting from one culture to another, like the shock of a cold shower after a warm bed. The second-generation Mexican-American went through life under the cold shower, so to speak.

In Texas, in 1943, there were almost 300,000 Mexican-American children of school age, including those who went to Catholic schools. One is stunned by the statistics: 42 percent of those children received no education that year; of those who were in school, 92.8 percent were in the elementary grades!

In the 1940s, approximately 200 Mexican-American youngsters at Los Angeles' Central Junior High School regularly dropped out from March to May to work the crops; in Texas, the season is September to January. If they returned in September or as late as November, their attitude was summed up by the following quote from a Mexican dropout in a book by Beatrice Griffith: "Lots of kids that go to pick the fruits get behind from school, or sometimes you wait until the next term comes. But then you forget how to talk good English cause you only talk Mexican at home. Or maybe you don't go back cause the teacher calls you dumb Mex—cause nobody's got time to help you, there's too many kids late from the crops. So a lot of kids quit and start hunting jobs."[42]

Miss Griffith also reported of an adolescent who went to one of the field or crop schools: "You sat there in that little room in the fields, not caring for anything or any part of it.

---

[41] Ibid., pp. 89–90.
[42] Beatrice Griffith, America Me. New York: Houghton Mifflin Co., 1948, p. 119.

The teachers hated it, and the kids hated the teachers—cause we knew we couldn't finish the school, or any other. So you remain the dumb jerk that you are."[43]

Mexican-American politics have always stressed the importance of *La Raza,* at least rhetorically, and "race leaders" have had to convince the *barrio* people that service is the aim of political office. Often rhetoric has camouflaged the failure of Mexican-American politicians to achieve any significant gains, as well as to mask corruption and betrayal to Anglo bosses. But while the *raza* politico must always pretend militancy in speech, in order to win election, another type of leader has lived as a direct parasite off the ignorance of the migrant worker.

The *coyote,* which refers to a sneak, or a wolf disguised as a sheep, convinces the gullible that he has invaluable services, whereas in reality his sole aim is to fleece the poor. His type is familiar to all poverty cultures, whether he be called a hustler, a shark, or any other colloquialism. In the *barrio,* the *coyote* usually operated in and around the employment services. He charged workers fees for job placement, transportation, and food in transit, usually at considerably marked-up prices. A San Antonio *coyote*'s operation was to "load the poor devils like sardines in the old trucks and hand them a few loaves of bread. When they reached the beet fields he'd collect for the transportation both ways, but when the beet season was over, the Mexicans would find themselves stranded up north [Colorado]."[44]

Coyotes are usually exposed after short periods and they move to other communities to set up their hustle. Some move directly into politics, identifying themselves as superrace men. One such leader was described by a *chicano* attorney: "He can't read or write or understand a word of English. He has no scruples. Give him money and he will have meetings. There will be a band and he distributes

[43] *Ibid.,* p. 119.
[44] Sister Frances Jerome Woods, *Mexican-American Ethnic Leadership in San Antonio, Texas.* Washington, D.C.: Catholic University of America Press, 1949, pp. 70–71.

pamphlets and the politicians can talk over the microphone.
. . . He makes no demands for better streets, sewage disposal, etc. He simply organizes meetings for politicians and gets paid."

Most *chicano* politicians were publicly indignant in the *barrios* when individuals or the *barrio* were subjected to abuses by Anglos, but as politicians they accepted the system of institutionalized racism and chose to remain inside of it, some working to change it, others merely playing an empty role of "representing" the Mexican-American. The majority in the *barrios* came to react to the very word "politics" as if it were a disease. But no political career was possible for the man who did not publicly proclaim loyalty to *La Raza*.

The radical politician in the past has screamed about injustice and discrimination, but often also quietly counsels youth who take him seriously "to go to school and learn. This country has wonderful opportunities." This same politician, who might belong to a group like the Mexican American Political Association, which usually ended up endorsing Democrats who promised small favors to the *barrios,* and especially to its middle class members, spoke with a fiery tongue against the injustice of the *gringo,* but lived by the very value system that the *gringo* offered to all immigrants as the success formula.

Few Mexican-Americans escaped their heritage since few were accepted into Anglo society. The educated and successful often had to turn back to the *barrio,* from where they won their prestige and status. Mexican-American politics was confusing to the *barrio* people since it did not have a line, or ideology, but rather spoke in terms of justice and freedom.

THE ZOOT SUIT RIOTS

"Everybody was against us—the police most of all. So what could we do but fight?"

A nineteen-year-old Mexican boy
after fracturing the skull of
a sailor in Los Angeles in 1943.

"For a long time I've worried about the attitude toward Mexicans in California and states along the border. These zoot suit riots have roots in things which happened long before."

Mrs. Eleanor Roosevelt.

"This isn't a Mexican problem, this is an American problem. It is one of juvenile delinquency. . . ."

Governor Earl Warren, after being
informed that 98 percent of
the Mexicans involved were American born.

By the early 1940s, the image of the Mexican in the Southwest had grown more fearsome as he congregated in larger and larger slums. Juvenile crime, vice, and violence plagued these areas. In Los Angeles or San Antonio, high rent and low income were the rule. This meant roomers and overcrowding. Father's claims to *machismo* were weakened by the overwhelming difficulties of trying to be a provider and by his lack of prestige in the eyes of society. The oldest boy often filled the father role; at the same time, he fought to regain the *machismo* his father had lost. Often he failed in school and was then rejected by employers for being a drop-out. Sometimes employers rejected him just for being Mexican. His bitterness, like that of most American poor, was often acted out by beating the younger children; he also turned to the *pachucos* (Mexican urban gang members), who shared the same experiences. In East Los Angeles, Mexican crime was so widespread that a police officer was assigned to "make a study of the Mexican people" and report on the reasons for the violence.

Lieutenant Ayres of the Los Angeles County Sheriff's Department gave his analysis of the problem:

. . . to get a true perspective of this condition we must look for a basic cause that is . . . fundamental. . . . Let us view it from the biological basis—in fact, as the main basis to work from. Although a wild cat and a domestic cat are of the same family they have certain biological characteristics so different that while one may be domesticated, the other would have to be caged to be kept in captivity; and there is practically as much difference between the races of man as so aptly recognized by Rudyard Kipling when he said when writing of the Oriental, "East is East and West is West, and never the twain shall meet."[45]

Ayres, who believed in the treacherous and superpassionate Mexican, went on to explain Mexican behavior as contrasted with the "fair fight" attitude of Americans:

The Caucasian, especially the Anglo-Saxon, when engaged in fighting, particularly among youths, resort to fisticuffs and may at times kick each other, which is considered unsportive, but this Mexican element considers all that to be a sign of weakness, and all he knows and feels is a desire to use a knife or some lethal weapon. In other words, his desire is to kill, or at least let blood. That is why it is difficult for the Anglo-Saxon to understand the phsychology [sic] of the Indian or even the Latin, and it is just as difficult for the Indian or the Latin to understand the phsychology [sic] of the Anglo-Saxon or those from Northern Europe.[46]

Ayres's report, made during World War II when Nazi racism was the official ideology of Germany, was accepted not only by the majority of American whites, but by government officials as well. Los Angeles police chief, C. B. Horrall, endorsed Lt. Ayres's report as "an intelligent state-

---

[45] Ralph Guzman, *The Function of Ideology in the Process of Political Socialization: An Example in Terms of the Mexican-American People Living in the Southwest*. Unpublished manuscript, 1966.
[46] *Ibid.*, pp. 35–36.

ment of the psychology of the Mexican people, particularly the youths."[47]

The Zoot Suit Riots of June, 1943, proved to be a self-fulfilling prophecy for the police. Gangs of Mexican teenagers, *pachucos,* wearing the then stylish long-draped suits with baggy, narrow-bottomed trousers and striped T-sweaters, and sporting ducktail haircuts, became involved in gang fights with service men who had come to their *barrios* in search of bars, whores, and donnybrooks. For the Anglos the zoot suits worn by many Mexican and Negro teenagers and young adults had become symbolic of the enemy. The fights erupted into open warfare on the streets of Los Angeles and other southern California communities. Groups of service men waited in ambush for lone or small groups of Mexicans, and then beat and stripped them. The *San Francisco Examiner* of June 9, 1943, described one fight as follows: "Last night's rioting alone left scores of the grotesquely clothed youths injured, more than 60 in jail and [a] half dozen in hospitals. . . . this correspondent rode with a flying squadron of police as they raced from scene to scene to sporadic outbursts of violence. We usually arrived only in time to find perspiring service men striding away from nearly nude zoot suiters, their clothing ripped or slashed to shreds."[48] The *New York Times* described a 1943 fight in San Diego: ". . . twelve zoot suiters filed into court shorn of their 'ducktail' hair. Police explained that 'by coincidence' there happened to be a barber in the jail; he had a workout during the night after their arrest. The prisoners, according to police, were mobbed by 50 soldiers, sailors, and marines, who were released to military authorities after 'cooling off' in jail."[49]

The old white racism clashed with the Mexicans' deep resentment of their present and past treatment. The explosion that ensued cut deep into the World War II ideology of racial harmony and tolerance, and once again exposed the

[47] *Ibid.,* p. 36.
[48] *San Francisco Examiner,* June 9, 1943, p. B.
[49] *New York Times,* June 12, 1943.

emptiness of the American Dream to whites and Mexicans alike. Official ideology, as expressed by the Citizens Committee of California's then governor, Earl Warren, denied any racial overtones in the riots, despite the fact that only Mexican and Negro teenagers were beaten and arrested. Warren's committee concluded "that the problem is one of American youth, not confined to any racial group. The wearers of zoot suits are not necessarily persons of Mexican descent, criminals, or juveniles. Many young people today wear zoot suits."[50]

The ultimate apologia came from the president of the California State Chamber of Commerce, Preston Hotchkiss. After Mrs. Roosevelt expressed concern over race riots, and specifically over the treatment of Mexican-Americans as a cause for the riots, Hotchkiss declared:

These so-called zoot-suit riots have never been and are not now in the nature of race riots. The trouble commenced several months ago as sporadic clashes between juvenile gangs in various parts of Los Angeles and environs, without regard to race or color. In fact, most of the clashes were between youths of Mexican origin, but they also included some whites and Negroes.

The statement that citizens of California have discriminated against persons of Mexican origin is untrue, unjust, and provocative of disunion among people who have lived for years in harmony.[51]

(Race riots also occurred in Detroit and Harlem at the same time as the California zoot suit explosion. There had been previous riots in Beaumont, Texas, in 1942.)

The truth was that the Mexican-American populations of Los Angeles and every other city or town in the Southwest had never lived in harmony with the Anglos or their institutions. Lieutenant Ayres's report backed up by police chief Horrall, made clear the official police attitudes toward Mexicans—attitudes also shared by most Anglos.

Today the economic standing and social status of Mexican-Americans have changed only a little from what they

[50] California Citizens Committee on Civil Disturbances in Los Angeles, *Report and Recommendations,* June 12, 1943, p. 7.
[51] *Los Angeles Examiner,* June 18, 1943, p. 15.

were in the 1930s. The 1960 census shows that Mexican-Americans have moved out of agricultural into urban employment. An authoritative 1968 Labor Department study, however, points out that "the relative employment of Mexican-American men was still very slight in the high earnings professional and managerial occupations and very great in the low wage classifications."[52] So despite today's affluence, Mexican-Americans in states like New Mexico and Texas are roughly in the same position—or worse off—than they were thirty years ago. In Texas, "Mexican-Americans have not been able to improve their relative occupational position," according to the Labor Department study. In New Mexico, "during the 1940s, Mexican-Americans lost ground to Anglos. It was only in California and Colorado, where a small number of Mexican-Americans reside, that any degree of improvement can be found."[53] The study also states: "While the general population was shifting from agricultural to non-agricultural employment, Mexican-Americans were not able to make comparative occupational gains. Mexican-American movement out of agriculture lagged behind the general population movement. The reasons for this are no doubt complex but involve, among other factors, comparative occupational preferences and qualifications and discrimination by the majority population."[54]

Translated, the phrase "discrimination by the majority population" means that the Mexican-American population has the highest drop-out and illiteracy rate of all the minority groups, except perhaps for some Indians. It means they have the lowest income level, the highest disease rate, and the highest infant-mortality rate. It means that in Los Angeles, the majority of Mexican-American children have no private medical care, only that of doctors in the county hospital where they were born. It means that 30 percent of

[52] Walter Fogel, "Job Gains of Mexican-American Men," *The Monthly Labor Review,* U.S. Department of Labor, October, 1968, pp. 22ff.
[53] *Ibid.,* pp. 26–27.
[54] *Ibid.,* p. 27.

all the visits to the pediatric clinics are made by Mexican-Americans, although they represent only 8½ percent of the city's population. Almost any southwestern city with a Mexican population could supply similar—or worse—statistics.

In the city of Lubbock, Texas, the most recent census (1960) reveals that almost 70 percent of Mexican-Americans received less than four years of schooling, while less than 5 percent completed high school. In all of Texas, over 51 percent of those with Spanish surnames completed only four years of grade school. 13.6 percent of Mexican families in Texas earn less than $1,000 a year! And only 2.7 percent earn over $10,000, as compared to the 13.1 percent of white families in the over-$10,000-a-year bracket.

Most Mexicans reside in "deteriorating" or "dilapidated" housing, as defined by the U.S. Census Bureau in 1960.[55]

". . . the housing dollar of Spanish-speaking buys less than the housing dollar of other whites. . . . In Texas and California these families occupy worse housing than any other ethnic group, and the housing situation of the Spanish-speaking population of Texas is the worst in the Southwest. In 1950, more than four-fifths of the Spanish-speaking families of Texas were housed in substandard dwellings. . . . In other southwestern cities . . . deterioration, dilapidation, and overcrowding are common characteristics of the homes of Spanish-speaking."[56]

[55] Deteriorating housing needs more repair than would be provided in the course of regular maintenance. It has one or more defects of an intermediate nature that must be corrected if the unit is to continue to provide safe and adequate shelter.

Dilapidated housing does not provide safe and adequate shelter. It has one or more critical defects, or has a combination of intermediate defects in sufficient number to require extensive repair or rebuilding, or is of inadequate original construction. Critical defects result from continued neglect or lack of repair or indicate serious damage to the structure.

[56] Lawrence B. Glick, "The Right to Equal Opportunity," in *La Raza, Forgotten Americans*, edited by Julian Samora. Notre Dame: University of Notre Dame Press, 1966, p. 107.

THE *CHICANOS:* MEMBERS OF THE THIRD WORLD

In the early 1960s, Cesar Chavez organized successful strikes in California's Central Valley, using the concept of *La Raza* as an organizing tool. He stressed the Spanish language, Indo-Hispanic culture, and religion (Catholicism, as well as the protective *Virgen de Guadalupe* inherited from the Aztecs) when talking with workers from the Texas cotton fields or the grape valleys of California. His style captured the imagination of the field workers, and the new Mexican-American was born, the *chicano* who could feel proud to be a Mexican and who could also feel that his *raza* brother, Fidel Castro, was in some way fighting the same battles he was.

In northern New Mexico, Reies Lopez Tijerina touched the same sensitive chord as did Cesar Chavez. By reviving old traditions and laws, Tijerina rallied the *chicano* residents of isolated Rio Arriba County to claim what he felt was rightfully theirs—namely, land which had been made into a United States national forest. In the ensuing action, violence and death brought the *Alianza* (the organization created to reclaim *chicano* territory) of New Mexico to national attention, and especially to the attention of the young *chicanos* in the *barrios* throughout the Southwest. Tijerina, Chavez, and younger militants with brown berets and brown satin jackets were responding not only to the needs of their own people, but to the consciousness of blacks and student activists as well.

The grape strikes, the *Alianza,* the rebirth of the *chicano* press in the format of an underground press, and the growing self-awareness of the younger Mexicans, has been occurring all during the 1960s. Their heroes are not only Juarez, Zapata, and Villa, but Joaquin Murieta, Cortina, and other heroes of Mexican resistance to Anglo conquest. With this new self-awareness there has come a shift away from the older political tradition of reward your friends and punish your enemies. Such older organizations as the Mexican-American Political Association have not always been able to deliver votes and other political support, a fact well known to both their friends and their enemies. As a result, the Mexican-Americans have little political strength. A few older politicians with Spanish surnames have been able to capitalize on their ancestry to get themselves elected. They have also combined militant talk and accommodationist action for the same purpose. The older political organizations tend to reject activism or any form of direct confrontation.

Inevitably conflict has developed between the old and new politics. The new *Raza* politicians, angry young men in brown berets, call the old politicians *malinches* and try to force the older politicos to change their politics; failing that, they denounce them as puppets.

The *chicanos'* demands for an equal share in American life, like those of the blacks and Indians, came with the rise of modern liberal rhetoric. The American Dream and the centuries-old ideals of equality and justice were rediscovered during the Kennedy era. But public admission of racism and promises to meet the problem head-on have only brought out more clearly than ever the deeply rooted contradictions in American life and history.

Mexican-Americans have come alive as a racial minority, and in their new consciousness have begun to probe the old injustices suffered by their ancestors at the hands of the *gringos*. In the *barrios,* mothers and fathers are now taking an active interest in their children's schools. And the teenagers have begun to demand their rights as *chicanos,* closing down schools if necessary, as they did in East Los Angeles in 1968. They discovered that the Constitution of California provided for two official languages and so they are beginning to demand that Spanish be taught, along with English, in their schools. The young *chicanos* had to prove to themselves, as well as to the *gabachos* (Anglos), that Spanish is just as good as English.

But the new consciousness and the new militancy should not be mistaken for revolutionary behavior. The grape pickers and the members of *La Alianza* in New Mexico want what they feel they have a right to: decent wages and living conditions, equal treatment on all levels, and their own union. They also want the land that rightfully—by treaty—belongs to them. The *barrio chicanos,* like ghetto blacks, want more humane and ample welfare, better treatment from public agencies, and a myriad of reforms the U.S. Government has officially stated they are entitled to receive.

These demands fall within the possibility of fulfillment; at the same time a revolution—in alliance with other racial groups—is also possible. Some of the revolutionary exhortations, however, like those of the Mexican ruling party before elections, are only rhetoric. Nevertheless, unlike the hollow speeches of older Mexican politicians, the revolutionary talk is truly angry. It is the language of newly freed men who realize they have been had. The revolutionaries want revenge and justice; but they have no specific solutions. All they can cry is "Down with the bad, up with the good!"

Examples of the new militancy are expressed in any of the newly founded *chicano* papers. For example, *El Gallo,* in Denver, ran a column headed "La Raza Youth 50% of Vietnam Casualties." The headline actually referred to a casualty report for one day in which three out of six Americans from Colorado killed had Spanish surnames. This kind of sensationalism, however, should not obscure the extent to which *chicanos* understand the meaning of the failure of liberalism and the American Dream. *El Gallo* concludes the same article as follows:

The cream of the Raza youth and the blackman take the brunt of the suffering. The school counselors, employment counselors, Juvenile Court and Probation Officers tell our boys to join the service. Meanwhile Politicians and rich Industrialists and war profiteers line their pockets while our people give their bodies for purple hearts. The latest killed in action reports show that one out of three killed in action are chicanos. Fight the war at home against brainwashing, Unemployment, Lily white anglo produced education, Discrimination, Bigots, one sided Court systems, Police Brutality, the rape of your culture, destruction of your manhood. Fight here at home. Fight the real enemy. Join the Revolution. ¡Viva la Revolución!"[57]

Throughout the Southwest, posters of Zapata, Villa, and Huey P. Newton appeared on the walls of thousands of young *chicanos*. A *chicano* cooperative in northern New Mexico harvested its first and second crops and attempted to rebuild a medical clinic that had been bombed by Minutemen. Reies Tijerina began to serve a long prison sentence after being convicted on charges stemming from his raid on the Tierra Amarilla courthouse. *Chicano* studies programs appeared in colleges and junior colleges and Brown Beret chapters spread throughout southwest cities.

At the same time as radical *chicano* activity spread among youth, the farmworkers union grew closer to the AFL–CIO and the liberal wing of the Catholic Church. While varieties of brown capitalism were offered by government agencies, radical brown poets began meeting regularly, and published *El Pocho Che,* a *chicano* memorial to Ernesto "Che" Guevara.

Conflicts between *chicanos* and blacks erupted over how the small rewards in the poverty programs were to be divided and quarrels broke out inside some of the radical organizations. The struggles emerged from competing nationalisms and although both militant blacks and militant *chicanos* recognized the dangers of division, the disagreements could not always be submerged. Among radical *chicanos,* the word revolution is frequently used, militancy is very high, but beneath the rhetoric lies little content. But some of the young *chicanos* who associate themselves with the third-world movement no longer think of their position in American society as only "their" problem. They have

[57] *El Gallo,* Denver, Colorado, March, 1968, p. 3.

come to define American society as a world empire and to identify their struggle with blacks, Vietnamese, Cubans, women, and all oppressed people.

Some of these *chicano* youth have rejected the authority of the white rulers. The system of thought that has told them to wait, to be patient, to have faith in gradual evolution, no longer holds their mind. But the radical *chicanos,* like the Black Panthers, do not know yet exactly what they want and in which direction their movement ought to go. They are dissatisfied with nationalism, but beyond identifying themselves rhetorically with blacks and Indians they have not been able to forge a new strategy. So they remain still defined by the ideology of America: another minority fighting to melt into the pot while they insist they fight for their historic identity.

Inside the *chicano* communities a struggle has begun to develop a new political and cultural style; it is a struggle between the old-timers, the accommodationists with loud but empty rhetoric and the young and angry men in brown berets, who have learned not only of Juarez, Zapata, and Villa but of Joaquin Murieta and Cortina and the other heroes of Mexican Resistance to the Anglo conquest. Their style is best presented by the Teatro Campesino, an agit-prop type theater, founded in response to the grape strike. Teatro has performed all over the country, bringing the new idea of *La Raza* into all *barrios*.

PANCHO VILLA RIDES AGAIN

At the door, and along the aisles, are young men in brown berets and brown belted gentleman hunters' coats. The young men and women are dressed in working-class mod style, with beehived hairdos and smoky glasses. They have a trace of Old World accent, but it could as easily be Italian as

Mexican. Their vocabularies are small in both languages, but they are still loud and emotive. The play by Teatro Campesino begins with a *corrido* about Pancho Villa's horse and the Brown Berets assert themselves, and force the talking and standing part of the audience to hush and sit in a dilapidated *barrio* auditorium.

The play attacks *gringos,* welfare workers, contractors, the American way of life and calls for revolution. Part of the audience shouts, "¡Viva la Revolución!" When Zapata's picture is projected onto a lowered screen, near bedlam breaks loose. The juvenile hero of the play is a hoodlum who is free, a thief with healthy instincts and emotions, partly a Mexican stereotype of a *machista,* a gallant and twinkling-eyed rascal who loves frijoles and tortillas and likes them even better when they are stolen. He defines his revolution late in the play: get rid of stores, cops, contractors, etc. His brother is a "good boy," who repudiates his Mexican heritage and strives to be "an American."

During intermission, the Brown Beret spokesman says, "¡Viva la Revolución!" and "We are the Revolution," and "We must pull together," and asks for money. His Spanish is poor, as is his English. He makes the *chicano* sign, crossing arms, and the audience shouts again. A man then announces a picket line in the morning, but neglects to explain what it is for. Perhaps the audience knows it is connected with the grape boycott. It doesn't matter. It is a neighborhood, ethnic theater, and no one in the audience has to be told that Teatro is their theater, whether it is in San Francisco's Mission or the *barrios* of San Jose, Los Angeles, or Albuquerque.

Among the youth, the style of the Black Panthers and SNCC, in dress and in cool, has come together with the *machista* tradition as it has mutated in the *barrios.* It is a mocking Mexican *macho* who can laugh at his own outbursts of sincere passion. Like a man who has almost matured enough to fit into the cultural suit of his forefathers, the young Mexicans lay the problem out. The shrunken head of Pancho Villa, played by an actor whose body is hidden behind a TV set, but whose head rests on top of the set, a symbol throughout the play of revolution and of all the characteristics that disgust the Anglo, begins to argue with the young *chicano* who wants to "make it" in the Anglo world. The hideous, mustachioed head who eats cockroaches and frijoles and makes loud and disgusting noises, screams at the youth in Spanish: "I am who I am!" The youth replies: "Speak English!" The youth leaves, confused, but still determined to "make it" as the Anglo consumer, the faceless, identityless imitator of the WASP. The shrunken head of Pancho Villa turns to the audience and exhorts them in Spanish, English, and both languages mixed together not to forget who they are. He is with them and once more he shall ride amongst his people on a white horse or a souped-up Chevy, and the revolutionary sparks that flicker amongst the *barrio* people shall combine to ignite a raging fire.

Fires broke out in Southern California in August, 1970, after a *chicano* anti-war demonstration was broken up by the police and a well-known Mexican-American writer was killed. To the *chicanos* the lesson was clear: they were still victims.

GLOSSARY

La Alianza (La Alianza Federal de las Mercedes)
organization formed in New Mexico and led by Reies Lopez Tijerina, to reclaim Mexican land taken over by the U.S., especially national forest land in Rio Arriba County. It is the descendant of similar organizations that date back to the nineteenth century.

Anglo
Mexican-American word for a white American.

barrio
Mexican-American neighborhood.

Californio
word early Spanish settlers of California used to describe themselves.

cantina
bar.

chicano	a term used by some Mexican-Americans to describe themselves.
corrido	Mexican ballad.
gabacho	Mexican word for an Anglo.
gente	people.
gringo	derogatory Mexican jargon for a Yankee.
machismo	masculinity associated with Latin American culture.
malinche	Mexican-American equivalent for an Uncle Tom.
"*mescan*"	Anglo mispronunciation of "Mexican," especially in the Southwest.
mestizo	a person of mixed Spanish and Indian blood.
pachuco	member of a Mexican-American urban gang, usually in his teens or twenties.
La Raza	literally translated, race or people. Now used by Mexican-Americans who describe themselves as being in opposition to anything Anglo; they are *La Raza,* people in resistance. The word is also used to mean the concept of resistance.
La Raza Unida	Mexican-American political organization of resistance.
rico	a rich person.
rinches	derogatory Mexican word for Rangers.
vendido	sellout.

(1)
"Revolt of the Pueblo Indians"*

> Spanish abuse of Indians in the
> seventeenth century brought about
> a major revolt by Indians who had
> already been Christianized. The
> following accounts present the
> *conquistador* and the Indian ver-
> sion of the same events.

. . . With regard to the general uprising of the Christian Indians and the propositions of your lordship's *auto,* this cabildo, with zeal for the service of both Majesties and for the public welfare, in protecting and safeguarding his Majesty's vassals, regarding the matter with due attention and replying to all the proposals, says: First, that the convocation and plot of the said Indians seems to have been so secret that they perpetrated their treason generally in all the jurisdictions of the kingdom, as was seen, beginning on the night of August 9, when the said Indians took up their arms and, carried away by their indignation, killed religious [sic], priests, Spaniards, and women, not sparing even innocent babes in arms; and as blind fiends of the devil, they set fire to the holy temples and images, mocking them with their dances and making trophies of the priestly vestments and other things belonging to divine worship. Their hatred and barbarous ferocity went to such extremes that in the pueblo of Sandia images of saints were found among excrement, two chalices were found concealed in a basket of manure, and there was a carved crucifix with the paint and varnish taken off by lashes. There was also excrement at the place of the holy communion table at the main altar, and a sculptured image of Saint Francis with the arms

* Charles William Hackett, *Revolt of the Pueblo Indians of New Mexico and Oterman's Attempted Reconquest, 1680–1682* (Albuquerque: University of New Mexico Press, 1942).

hacked off; and all this was seen in one temple only, as we were marching out. The church of the villa was entirely consumed by fire before your lordship's eyes and those of this cabildo and of the people who were present in the siege to which the enemy subjected us. When they had us surrounded in the said casas reales, and fighting with them, because the said temple was not defended it caught fire and burned until it was consumed and entirely demolished, only the walls remaining. All this was in addition to the ravages and sacrileges that they committed in the other jurisdictions of thirty-four pueblos, and in the estancias and houses of the Spaniards of which the said New Mexico is composed, its settlements being so scattered and undefended that the people who are now in this army have escaped by a miracle. Here we have found that the prelate and the head of this church has lost eighteen clerical ministers and two lay religious, which make twenty-one. There have died besides more than three hundred and eighty Spaniards—men, women, and children—with some servants, among whom are seventy-three Spaniards of military age, all of whom have perished at the hands of the rebellious enemy, having been robbed of arms, haciendas, and everything they possessed. The same was done before your lordship's eyes, alike in the said villa, where they sacked our houses and set fire to them, and in the convents and estancias, for the truth of this is proved by what we saw for ourselves on the march which was made to leave the kingdom. We found the pueblos deserted, the convents and estancias sacked, and the horses, cattle, and other articles of our household goods on the mesas and in the roughest parts of the sierras, with the said enemy guarding all of it and verbally mocking and insulting us . . . Our return to the kingdom must be in the form of a conquest with men, arms, and supplies to safeguard and garrison it as it is reduced to the yoke of the holy gospel and obedience to the Catholic Majesty, so that they [the Indians] may be subjected and their allies intimidated by the authority and arms of his Majesty. . . .

DECLARATION OF AN INDIAN REBEL [*Place of the Arroyo de San Marcos, August 23, 1680*]

. . . Having been asked where he was going and why he left the casas reales and joined with the Indian rebels, he said that Ambrosio de Carbajal caught him in a cornfield where he was attempting to hide, and that his reason for leaving the casas reales was that he believed that the Spaniards must perish, along with the señor governor and captain-general, and that in case they should happen not to be defeated, they would probably take him to some other country, and he did not wish to leave this one. He stated that he did not find any of the rebels that night, and the following day he went toward the villa because of having learned that the señor governor and all the people who were with him were marching out. On reaching the villa he found inside and out of the casas reales a large number of the rebellious Indians who were sacking the place, taking out a large amount of property belonging to the señor governor, which he had left behind. He recognized among the pillagers Indians of all nations, and a number of Taos and Pecuríes, and he heard an Indian of Tesuque named Poquete tell of having seen the great number of Indians who were dead in the plaza of the villa, and in the houses, streets, and environs. The said rebels had told him, "We are at quits with the Spaniards and the persons whom we have killed; those of us whom they have killed do not matter, for they are going, and now we shall live as we like and settle in this villa and wherever we see fit." . . . He did not know his age or how to sign. Apparently he is more than sixty years old. . . .

DECLARATION OF PEDRO NARANJO OF THE QUERES NATION [*Place of the Rio del Norte, December 19, 1681*]

In the said plaza de armas on the said day, month, and year, for the prosecution of the judicial proceedings of this case his lordship caused to appear before him an Indian prisoner named Pedro Naranjo, a native of the pueblo of San Felipe, of the Queres nation, who was captured in the advance and attack upon the pueblo of La Isleta. He makes himself understood very well in the Castilian language and speaks his mother tongue and the Tegua.

Asked whether he knows the reason or motives which the Indians of this kingdom had for rebelling, forsaking the law of God and obedience to his Majesty, and committing such grave and atrocious crimes, and who were the leaders and principal movers, and by whom and how it was ordered; and why they burned the images, temples, crosses, rosaries, and things of divine worship, committing such atrocities as killing priests, Spaniards, women, and children, and the rest that he might know touching the question, he said that since the government of Señor General Hernando Ugarte y la Concha they have planned to rebel on various occasions through conspiracies of the Indian sorcerers, and that although in some pueblos the messages were accepted, in other parts they would not agree to it; and that it is true that during the government of the said señor general seven or eight Indians were hanged for this same cause, whereupon the unrest subsided. . . . Finally, in the past years, at the summons of an Indian named Popé who is said to have communication with the devil, it happened that in an estufa* of the pueblo of Los Taos there appeared to the said Popé three figures of Indians who never came out of the estufa . . . and these three beings spoke to the said Popé, . . . They told him to make a cord of maguey fiber and tie some knots in it which would signify the number of days that they must wait before the rebellion. . . . The said cord was taken from pueblo to pueblo by the swiftest youths under the penalty of death if they revealed the secret. Everything being thus arranged, two days before the time set for its execution, because his lordship had learned of it and had imprisoned two Indian accomplices from the pueblo of Tesuque, it was carried out prematurely that night, because it seemed to them that they were now discovered; and they killed religious [sic], Spaniards, women, and children . . . Finally the señor governor and those who were with

* An Indian house of religion.—Editor's Note.

him escaped from the siege, and later this declarant saw
that as soon as the Spaniards had left the kingdom an order
came from the said Indian, Popé, in which he commanded
all the Indians to break the lands and enlarge their cultivated fields, saying that now they were as they had been in
ancient times, free from the labor they had performed for
the religious and the Spaniards, who could not now be
alive. He said that this is the legitimate cause and the reason
they had for rebelling, because they had always desired to
live as they had when they came out of the lake of Copala.
Thus he replies to the question. . . .

. . . Asked what arrangements and plans they had made
for the contingency of the Spaniards' return, he said that
what he knows concerning the question is that they were
always saying they would have to fight to the death, for they
do not wish to live in any other way than they are living at
present; and the demons in the estufa of Taos had given
them to understand that as soon as the Spaniards began to
move toward this kingdom they would warn them so that
they might unite, and none of them would be caught. He
having been questioned further and repeatedly touching the
case, he said that he has nothing more to say except that
they should be always on the alert, because the said Indians
were continually planning to follow the Spaniards and fight
with them by night, in order to drive off the horses and
catch them afoot, although they might have to follow them
for many leagues. What he has said is the truth, and what
happened, on the word of a Christian who confesses his
guilt. He said that he has come to the pueblos through fear
to lead in idolatrous dances, in which he greatly fears in his
heart that he may have offended God, and that now having
been absolved and returned to the fold of the church, he has
spoken the truth in everything he has been asked. His declaration being read to him, he affirmed and ratified all of it.
He declared himself to be eighty years of age, and he signed
it with his lordship and the interpreters and assisting witnesses, before me, the secretary. . . . Before me, Francisco Xavier, secretary of government and war.

(2)

Resistance and Accommodation*

Juan Cortina's armed resistance to the white Texans stands in contrast to the approach taken by the conservative editor of the Spanish-language newspaper *El Clamor Público* in Los Angeles. Both were responses to the treatment of Mexicans by whites, in the 1850's, especially to the wanton murder of Mexicans by police or other whites. The *El Clamor Público* story refers to an armed uprising by some angry Mexicans after a deputy policeman had murdered, in cold blood, a popular member of the *barrio*.

JUAN CORTINA PROCLAMATION

An event of grave importance, in which it has fallen to my lot to figure as the principal actor since the morning of the twenty-eighth instant, doubtless keeps you in suspense with regard to the progress of its consequences. There is no need of fear. Orderly people and honest citizens are inviolable to us in their persons and interests. Our object, as you have seen, has been to chastise the villainy of our enemies, which heretofore has gone unpunished. These have connived with each other, and form, so to speak, a perfidious inquisitorial lodge to persecute and rob us, without any cause, and for no other crime on our part than that of being of Mexican origin, considering us, doubtless, destitute of those gifts which they themselves do not possess.

To defend ourselves, and making use of the sacred right of self-preservation, we have assembled in a popular meeting with a view of discussing a means by which to put an end to our misfortunes.

* "Juan Cortina Proclamation," in *House Executive Documents,* 36th Congress, 1st Sess. (Washington: Thomas H. Ford, Printer, 1860).

El Clamor Público (Los Angeles: July 26, 1856 and August 2, 1856).

Our identity of origin, our relationship, and the community of our sufferings, has been, as it appears, the cause of our embracing, directly, the proposed object which led us to enter your beautiful city, clothed with the imposing aspect of our exasperation. . . .

The unfortunate Viviano Garcia fell a victim to his generous behavior; and with such a lamentable occurrence before us on our very outset, we abstained from our purpose, horrified at the thought of having to shed innocent blood without even the assurance that the vile men whom we sought would put aside their cowardice to accept our defiance.

These, as we have said, form, with a multitude of lawyers, a secret conclave, with all its ramifications, for the sole purpose of despoiling the Mexicans of their lands and usurp them afterwards. This is clearly proven by the conduct of one Adolph Glavecke, who, invested with the character of deputy sheriff, and in collusion with the said lawyers, has spread terror among the unwary, making them believe that he will hang the Mexicans and burn their ranches, etc., that by this means he might compel them to abandon the country, and thus accomplish their object. This is not a supposition—it is a reality; and notwithstanding the want of better proof, if this threat were not publicly known, all would feel persuaded that of this, and even more, are capable such criminal men as the one last mentioned, the marshal, the jailer, Morris, Neal, etc. . . .

. . . All truce between them and us is at an end, from the fact alone of our holding upon this soil our interests and property. And how can it be otherwise, when the ills that weigh upon the unfortunate republic of Mexico have obliged us for many heart-touching causes to abandon it and our possessions in it, or else become the victims of our principles or of the indigence to which its internal disturbances had reduced us since the treaty of Guadalupe? when, ever diligent and industrious, and desirous of enjoying the longed-for boon of liberty within the classic country of its origin, we were induced to naturalize ourselves in it and form a part of the confederacy, flattered by the bright and peaceful prospect of living therein and inculcating in the bosoms of our children a feeling of gratitude towards a country beneath whose aegis we would have wrought their felicity and contributed with our conduct to give evidence to the whole world that all the aspirations of the Mexicans are confined to one only, *that of being freemen;* and that having secured this ourselves, those of the old country, notwithstanding their misfortunes, might have nothing to regret save the loss of a section of territory, but with the sweet satisfaction that their old fellow-citizens lived therein, enjoying tranquillity, as if Providence had so ordained to set them an example of the advantages to be derived from public peace and quietude; when, in fine, all has been but the baseless fabric of a dream, and our hopes having been defrauded in the most cruel manner in which disappointment can strike, there can be found no other solution to our problem than to make one effort, and at one blow destroy the obstacles to our prosperity.

It is necessary. The hour has arrived. Our oppressors number but six or eight. Hospitality and other noble sentiments shield them at present from our wrath, and such, as you have seen, are inviolable to us.

Innocent persons shall not suffer—no. But, if necessary, we will lead a wandering life, awaiting our opportunity to purge society of men so base that they degrade it with their opprobrium. Our families have returned as strangers to their old country to beg for an asylum. Our lands, if they are to be sacrificed to the avaricious covetousness of our enemies, will be rather so on account of our own vicissitudes. As to land, Nature will always grant us sufficient to support our frames, and we accept the consequences that may arise. Further, *our personal enemies shall not possess our lands until they have fattened it with their own gore.*

We cherish the hope, however, that the government, for the sake of its own dignity, and in obsequiousness to justice, will accede to our demand, by prosecuting those men and bringing them to trial, or leave them to become subject to the consequences of our immutable resolve.

It remains for me to say that, separated, as we are, by accident alone, from the other citizens of the city, and not having renounced our rights as North American citizens, we disapprove and energetically protest against the act of having caused a force of the national guards from Mexico to cross unto this side to ingraft themselves in a question so foreign to their country that there is no excusing such weakness on the part of those who implored their aid.

Rancho Del Carmen,
County of Cameron, September 30, 1859

There are, doubtless, persons so overcome by strange prejudices, men without confidence or courage to face danger in an undertaking in sisterhood with the love of liberty, who, examining the merit of acts by a false light, and preferring that of the same opinion contrary to their own, prepare no other reward than that pronounced for the "bandit," for him who, with complete abnegation of self, dedicates himself to constant labor for the happiness of those who, suffering under the weight of misfortunes, eat their bread, mingled with tears, on the earth which they rated.

If, my dear compatriots, I am honored with that name, I am ready for the combat. . . .

Mexicans! When the State of Texas began to receive the new organization which its sovereignty required as an integrant part of the Union, flocks of vampires, in the guise of men, came and scattered themselves in the settlements, without any capital except the corrupt heart and the most perverse intentions. Some, brimful of laws, pledged to us their protection against the attacks of the rest; others assembled in shadowy councils, attempted and excited the robbery and burning of the houses of our relatives on the other side of the river Bravo; while others, to the abusing of our unlimited confidence, when we intrusted them with our titles, which secured the future of our families, refused to return them under false and frivolous pretexts; all, in short, with a smile on their faces, giving the lie to that which their black entrails were meditating. Many of you have been robbed of your property, incarcerated, chased, murdered, and hunted like wild beasts, because your labor was fruitful, and because your industry excited the vile avarice which led them. A voice infernal said, from the bottom of their soul, "kill them; the greater will be our gain!" Ah! this does not finish the sketch of your situation. It would appear that justice had fled from this world, leaving you to the caprice of your oppressors, who become each day more furious toward you; that, through witnesses and false charges, although the grounds may be insufficient, you may be interred in the penitentiaries, if you are not previously deprived of life by some keeper who covers himself from responsibility by the pretence of your flight. There are to be found criminals covered with frightful crimes, but they appear to have impunity until opportunity furnish them a victim; to these monsters indulgence is shown, because they are not of our race, which is unworthy, as they say, to belong to the human species. . . .

Mexicans! Is there no remedy for you? Inviolable laws, yet useless, serve, it is true, certain judges and hypocritical authorities, cemented in evil and injustice, to do whatever suits them, and to satisfy their vile avarice at the cost of your patience and suffering; rising in their frenzy, even to the taking of life, through the treacherous hands of their bailiffs. The wicked way in which many of you have been oftentimes involved in persecution, accompanied by circumstances making it the more bitter, is now well known; these crimes being hid from society under the shadow of a horrid night, those implacable people, with the haughty spirit which suggests impunity for a life of criminality, have pronounced, doubt ye not, your sentence, which is, with accustomed insensibility, as you have seen, on the point of execution.

Mexicans! My part is taken; the voice of revelation whispers to me that to me is entrusted the work of breaking the chains of your slavery, and that the Lord will enable me, with powerful arm, to fight against our enemies, in compliance with the requirements of that Sovereign Majesty, who, from this day forward, will hold us under His protection. On my part, I am ready to offer myself as a sacrifice for your happiness; and counting upon the means necessary for the discharge of my ministry, you may count upon my cooperation, should no cowardly attempt put an end to my days. This undertaking will be sustained on the following bases:

First: A society is organized in the State of Texas, which devotes itself sleeplessly until the work is crowned with success, to the improvement of the unhappy condition of those Mexicans resident therein; exterminating their tyrants, to which end those which compose it are ready to shed their blood and suffer the death of martyrs.

Second: As this society contains within itself the elements necessary to accomplish the great end of its labors, the veil of impenetrable secrecy covers "The Great Book" in which the articles of its constitution are written; while so delicate are the difficulties which must be overcome that no honorable man can have cause for alarm, if imperious exigencies require them to act without reserve.

Third: The Mexicans of Texas repose their lot under the good sentiments of the governor elect of the state, General Houston, and trust that upon his elevation to power he will begin with care to give us legal protection within the limits of his powers.

Mexicans! Peace be with you! Good inhabitants of the State of Texas, look on them as brothers, and keep in mind that which the Holy Spirit saith: "Thou shalt not be the friend of the passionate man; nor join thyself to the madman, lest thou learn his mode of work and scandalize thy soul."

El Clamor Público, JULY 26, 1856

. . . We do not wish to excuse or justify the disorders that occurred on the unforgettable night of Tuesday. The behavior of the people that fomented that meeting is quite mistaken. Their thinking is bad—if they wanted to attack the Americans who have entrenched themselves in the walls of the city. They can never accomplish this with security, because at the same time they take on grave responsibilities, endangering the life of their families and causing hardships to their properties. The death of Don Antonio Ruiz has exasperated the feelings of all Mexicans. It is becoming a very common custom to murder and abuse the Mexicans with impunity. And the Mexicans are growing tired of being run over and having injustices committed against them: but to take up arms to redress their grievances, this is an act without reason. We desire to re-establish peace: those misguided Mexicans should return as before to their homes and we hope for an immediate reform to take place.

El Clamor Público, AUGUST 2, 1856

The first occupants of this sort were of Spanish descent and when California came to be an integral part of the Northern Republic, many citizens remained to enjoy their properties that they had just obtained from Mexico via cession, sale, etc. These people from the mere fact of having remained obtained the same rights and privileges of American citizens. But no sooner had order been re-established when the National Congress dictated a law that established a commission to revise land titles. This measure cost uncountable expenses for the property owners and many had spent all their fortune to defend their property. Before their titles were approved, they had to make two or three trips to Washington and finally their labors and watchfulness yielded them nothing. After three years of continuous litigation most of the landowners are ruined. At the end, not satisfied with having uprooted from the hands of the Californians and Mexicans their possessions, the last session of the Legislature passed a law whose object was to declare as public property all California land, except that which had a government title.

This latest blow has extinguished forever the hopes that

they had in the new government that had just been inaugu-
rated on the Pacific beaches. But this isn't all, for not content with having plundered their properties under the
shadow of the law, they have subjected all Hispano-Ameri-
cans to a treatment that has no model in the history of any
nation conquered by savages or by civilized peoples.

All are convinced that California is lost for all Hispano-
Americans and here in Los Angeles because of the latest
revolution if before they asked for favors, now they will ask
for justice on their knees and for freedom to pursue their
jobs.

Almost all of the newspapers of the North are continually full of lynchings that happened in the mines. And, oh
fate! Mexicans alone have been victims of the insane furor
of the people! Mexicans alone have been sacrificed on
ignominious gallows which are erected to hurl their poor
souls to eternity. Is this the freedom and equality of the
country that we have adopted?

(3)

It Is Time to Unite*

> Organized resistance in the Cali-
> fornia mine fields during the 1850s
> was rare among Spanish-speaking
> workers, but some evidence exists
> of attempts at unified resistance to
> American abuse. One of the bills
> posted on the trees in the diggings
> near Columbia carried the follow-
> ing:

NOTICE: It is time to unite: Frenchmen, Chileans, Peru-
vians, and Mexicans, there is the highest necessity of
putting an end to the vexations of the Americans in California. If you do not intend to allow yourselves to be
fleeced by a band of miserable fellows who are repudiated
by their own country, then unite and go to the camp of

* Ira B. Cross, *A History of the Labor Movement in California*
(Berkeley: University of California Press, 1935).

Sonora next Sunday: there will we try to guarantee security for us all, and put a bridle in the mouths of that horde who call themselves citizens of the United States, thereby profaning that country.

(4)

Murieta, Vasquez and Cortez: Legends, Bandits, or Revolutionaries?

> Joaquin Murieta, Tiburcio Vasquez, and Gregorio Cortez were both real people and legends, bandits and revolutionaries. The roles were inseparable given the nature of the times in the West. Political activity was meaningless to Mexicans and outside of the mild, reasoned protest of *El Clamor Público* the only other road to resistance was with gun in hand. The tradition of Mexican gunfighters who fought for the dignity of the race is well expressed in the lyrics of "El Corrido de Gregorio Cortez."

JOAQUIN MURIETA*

He had been brought in contact with many of the natives of the United States during the war between that nation and his own, and had become favorably impressed with the American character, and thoroughly disgusted with the imbecility of his own countrymen; so much so that he often wished he had been born on the soil of freedom. The sluggishness and cowardice of the Mexicans he compared with the energy, activity, and bravery of the Americans, and their undying love of liberty; and were it not for that happy and peaceful little home in one of the most charming valleys of Sonora, he would have relinquished at once all

* *Life of Joaquin Murieta, The Brigand Chief of California* (San Francisco: Butler & Co., 1859).

claim to nativity, and have become, what he already was at heart, an American.

His meditations were suddenly cut short by the wild shouting and yelling of hundreds of miners in the streets, intermixed with cries of "hang 'em!" "hang 'em!" "string 'em up and try 'em afterwards!" "the infernal Mexican thieves!" Joaquin rushed out, and was just in time to see his brother and Flores hauled up by their necks to the limb of a tree. They had been accused of horse-stealing by the two Americans from San Francisco, who claimed the animals as their own, and had succeeded in exciting the fury of the crowd to such an extent that the doomed men were allowed no opportunity to justify themselves, and all their attempts to explain the matter and to prove that the horses were honestly obtained, were drowned by the fierce hooting and screaming of the mob. Struck dumb with surprise and horror, Joaquin could at first only gaze upon the swinging corpse of Carlos, and the crowds of demoniac wretches around him, and wonder if the scene were real; but tears at length came to his relief and saved his brain from madness, and then with a heart full of desire for revenge, he obtained a mule and returned with all speed to Sacramento. Here he took the boat for San Francisco, from whence he proceeded to the Mission, sought the house of Sepulveda and acquainted his wife with the murder of his brother. Although Carmela shuddered with horror at the recital of the facts by Joaquin, yet with true womanly feeling, she begged him to seek not for revenge and thus endanger his own life, but to leave the perpetrators to that punishment which their guilty conscience would mete out to them sooner or later. She assured him that all Americans were not as depraved and bloodthirsty as those who composed that mob of murderers, and with all the strength of a loving heart, implored him to yield to no criminal temptation.

With tears and entreaties, and words of love and consolation, a change was wrought in the heart of Joaquin, and his spirit imbued with a feeling of forgiveness.

"Well," said he, rising from the feet of his beloved part-

ner, where he had been reclining, and listening with deep
devotion, "Well, it is all past; let us be cheerful and happy,
and when I have collected some of this golden sand, we will
return." A few days afterwards, Joaquin, accompanied by
his wife, reached the mines on the Stanislaus River, where he
built a comfortable cabin, and commenced washing the glit-
tering particles from the earth. The country was then full of
lawless and desperate men, calling themselves Americans,
who looked with hatred upon all Mexicans, and considered
them as a conquered race, without rights or privileges, and
only fitted for serfdom or slavery. The prejudice of color,
the antipathy of races, which are always stronger and bit-
terer with the ignorant, they could not overcome, or would
not, because it afforded them an excuse for their unmanly
oppression. A band of these men, possessing the brute
power to do as they pleased, went to Joaquin's cabin and
ordered him to leave his claim, as they would not permit
any of his kind to dig gold in that region. Upon his refusing
to leave a place where he was amassing a fortune, they
knocked him senseless with the butts of their pistols, and
while he was in that condition, ravished and murdered his
faithful bosom-friend, his wife.

The soul of Joaquin now became shadowed with despair
and deadly passion; but still, although he thirsted for revenge, he felt himself as yet unable to accomplish anything,
and would not endanger his freedom and his life in attempting to destroy single-handed, the fiendish murderers of his
wife and brother. He determined to wait and suffer in
silence, until a fitting opportunity occurred for the carrying
out of his plans. Accordingly he went (in April, 1850) to
mining at "Murphy's Diggings" in Calaveras County; but
meeting with very little success, he abandoned the business,
and sought to improve his fortune by dealing "monte," a
game very common in Mexico, and considered by all
classes in that country as an honorable occupation. For a
time, fortune smiled upon him and furnished him with a
golden evidence of her good will; but then came a change,
suddenly and heavily, and Joaquin was at once hurled into

the deep and dark abyss of crime. He had gone a short distance from camp to see a friend by the name of Valenzuelo, and returned to Murphy's with a horse which his friend had lent him. The animal, it was proved by certain individuals in town, had been stolen some time previously, and a great excitement was immediately raised. Joaquin found himself surrounded by a furious mob and charged with the theft. He informed them when and where he had borrowed the horse, and endeavored to convince them of Valenzuelo's honesty. They would hear no explanation, but tied him to a tree and disgraced him publicly with the lash. They then went to the residence of Valenzuelo and hung him without allowing him a moment to speak. Immediately there came a terrible change in Joaquin's character, suddenly and irrevocably. His soul swelled beyond its former boundaries, and the barriers of honor, rocked into atoms by the strong passion which shook his heart like an earthquake, crumbled and fell. Then it was that he resolved to live henceforth only for revenge, and that his path should be marked with blood.

On a pleasant evening, not long after this unfortunate occurrence, an American was wending his way along a trail at a short distance from the town. Upon descending into a ravine, through which ran the narrow pathway, he was suddenly confronted by Joaquin, whose eyes glared with the fury of an enraged tiger, and whose whole form seemed to quiver with excitement. For an instant each gazed upon the other, and then with a fierce yell Joaquin sprang upon the traveler and buried in his breast a long two-edged dagger.

"What—what means this?" gasped the victim as he sank to the ground, "why do you murder me? oh! mercy—spare my life."

"You showed no mercy to me," replied Joaquin, "when you assisted in tying and lashing me in the presence of a multitude of people. When, in the proud consciousness of your strength, and supported by the brute force of some of your own countrymen, you seized upon an innocent man— a *man*—with heart and soul, and with all the noble attributes received from his Maker—a man possessed of more truth and honor than could have been found among those who helped to torture him; when you seized him and bound him, and scored his back with the ignominious lash, you did not then think of *mercy*. When your countrymen hung my brother by the neck like a dog, was there any mercy shown him? When they cruelly murdered my heart's dearest treasure, in my own presence and almost before my eyes; and when she must, with her silvery voice, have faintly appealed for mercy, was that appeal heeded by the inhuman wretches? Ah! my brain is on fire!" he added, pressing his left hand to his forehead, while with the other he inflicted another wound.

"Murder?" muttered the damned man, raising himself upon his elbow and staring with wild, glassy eyes upon the savage features of the desperado. "The mercy—mer—," but the steel had now entered his heart—and he fell back a corpse . . .

Fear and consternation spread among the individuals who had been leaders in that mob and they were afraid to go as far as the outskirt of the town. Whenever any of them strolled out of sight of the camp, or ventured to travel on the highway, they were suddenly and mysteriously killed. Reports came in from time to time that the dead bodies of Americans had been found on the roads and trails, and it was always discovered that the murdered men belonged to the mob who had whipped Joaquin. He had now made himself amenable to the law by the commission of these bloody deeds, and his only safety lay in a continuance of the unlawful course which he had begun. For the furtherance of his plans he found it necessary to have horses and money, which he could not obtain except by adding robbery to murder, and thus he became a bandit and an outlaw before his twentieth year.

It became generally known, in 1851, that an organized banditti was ranging the country, and that Joaquin was the leader. Travelers were stopped on the roads and invited to "stand and deliver"; men riding alone in wild and lonesome regions, were dragged from their saddles by means of the lasso, and murdered in the adjacent chaparral. Horses were stolen from the ranches, and depredations were being committed in all parts of the State, almost at the same time.

Joaquin's superior intelligence and education gave him the respect of his comrades, and appealing to the prejudice against the "Yankees," which the disastrous results of the Mexican war had not tended to lessen in their minds, he soon assembled around him a powerful band of his countrymen, who daily increased, as he ran his career of almost magical success. . . .

TIBURCIO VASQUEZ

Born in Monterey in 1835, [Tiburcio] Vasquez suffered at the hands of the whites who moved into California. He came from a family of means, knew how to read and write, and had opportunities to pursue other careers. However, at the age of seventeen, he fell in with a group of outlaws of Mexican descent, and from that time on led a life of crime. He was very brave, had the sympathy of the Mexican elements of the population, and was able to elude the various lawmen who chased him for many years. Not always, however; he was imprisoned three times. He escaped and was captured a few times. Part of a transcript of his prison record of his third term reads:

"On June 25, 1859, on opening the lower prison wall gates at 4 o'clock, P.M., forty-two Mexican prisoners made a break. They were employed in the brick yard. After passing the gate they took the gate keeper and overseer, bound them and took them toward San Rafael."*

Later, he was implicated in inciting another break.

Nothing seems to have begun to convince him to change his ways, and as soon as he was released he began again to rob. He seems to have been responsible for several murders as well as innumerable thefts, though he did deny taking life. He was captured at last in 1874, tried and hung for murder.

* Robert Greenwood, *The California Outlaw, Tiburcio Vasquez* (Los Gatos: The Talisman Press, 1960).

While awaiting trial in jail, he was interviewed by several people. According to Greenwood he said,

My career grew out of the circumstances by which I was surrounded. As I grew to manhood I was in the habit of attending balls and parties given by the native Californians, into which the Americans, then beginning to become numerous, would force themselves and shove the native-born men aside, monopolizing the dance and the women. This was about 1852. A spirit of hatred and revenge took possession of me. I had numerous fights in defense of what I believe my rights and those of my countrymen. The officers were continually in pursuit of me. I believed we were unjustly and wrongfully deprived of the social rights that belonged to us.

At about the same time he told the same person that "Given $60,000 I would be able to recruit enough arms and men to revolutionize Southern California."

EL CORRIDO DE GREGORIO CORTEZ*

In the county of El Carmen
A great misfortune befell;
The Major Sheriff is dead;
Who killed him no one can tell.

At two in the afternoon,
In half an hour or less,
They knew that the man who killed him
Had been Gregorio Cortez.

They let loose the bloodhound dogs;
They followed him from afar.
But trying to catch Cortez
Was like following a star.

All the rangers of the county
Were flying, they rode so hard;
What they wanted was to get
The thousand-dollar reward.

And in the county of Kiansis
They cornered him after all;
Though they were more than three hundred
He leaped out of their corral.

Then the Major Sheriff said,
As if he was going to cry,
"Cortez, hand over your weapons;
We want to take you alive."

Then said Gregorio Cortez,
And his voice was like a bell,
"You will never get my weapons
Till you put me in a cell."

Then said Gregorio Cortez,
With his pistol in his hand,
"Ah, so many mounted Rangers
Just to take one Mexican!"

* Américo Paredes, *With His Pistol in His Hand* (Austin: University of Texas, 1958).

(5)

Everyday Racism*

The following letter from T. W. G.
Lyons of Brawley, California to
Governor Stephens in 1919 serves
to indicate the complexities of
American racism in practical day-
to-day affairs.

My Dear Governor:

I herewith enclose resolutions adopted by the Magnolia-
Mulberry Farm Center, December 19 in regard to the exclusion of Japanese, Hindus, and Mohammedans.

If something is not done in the way of legislation to bar
these races, it will be only a comparatively short time until
they will have crowded out the white race from the most
fertile parts of California, and I believe that it would be to
the best interest of the State of California if you would
cause an extra session of the State Legislature at the earliest
moment to consider such legislation as is necessary to
eliminate this evil. . . . It has been my experience from
employing all of such laborers that the best possible substi-
tute we could get, and one which would be agreeable to our
American people, is Mexican laborers. In other words, I
believe if we had a war with Mexico, or an intervention
whereby we would establish a permanent government in
that unfortunate country, or annex a portion of it, or all of
it, and turn loose some eight or ten million peon laborers,
who are now virtually starving in that ungoverned country;
I have no enmity or ill will towards these people, even
though we were forced into a war with them, or with the
unstable government which now tries to rule them, and
particularly so when it comes to using those people or getting them into our country for laborers, for this reason: that
you well know that when we took California over from
Mexico, a great many of the Mexican residents of this terri-

* *California and the Oriental: Japanese, Chinese and Hindus. Report
of the State Board of Control of California to Governor Wm. D. Stephens*
(Sacramento: California State Printing Office, 1922).

tory had grants from Mexico, all the way from 1,000 acres of land to 100,000 acres of land, and as you well know, that very little, if any of these lands are held by their original owners. In other words, the Mexicans will never undertake to run our business, or acquire our land and crowd out the white people of this country.

Furthermore, if you look at them in the right light, they are to a certain extent, natives of this land, being a mixture of Indian and Spanish blood. It is true that an ordinary Mexican will not accomplish in a day as much as a Chinese laborer, or as much as a Japanese laborer, but if they are paid according to what they do, they accomplish the same results, as far as labor is concerned, and in this letter I will say that if the white farmers, or white men in the State of California could get an ample supply of Mexican labor, they could do all the truck gardening, raising of sugar beets, cantaloupes, vegetables, and other products which the Japanese and Hindus and Mohammedans are now doing. . . .

I might also state that the Mexicans are employed to do practically all of the railroad section work in southern California, and practically all the common labor in the Imperial Irrigation District.

Now if this Mexican labor could be extended up through the entire state, the white farmers could do the managing and superintending of the farms, as the Japanese and Hindus do now, and we could get along very well without our Japanese and Hindus, and Mohammedans in the agricultural pursuits of the state.

(6)

Deporting Jesús*

> When Mexicans agitated and organized in the mines or in the fields the government often deported them. The Bureau of Immigration frequently worked in concert with mine, railroad and ranch owners to deport "undesirable elements."

* Philip Stevenson, "Deporting Jesús," *The Nation,* July 18, 1936.

On June 29, Jesús was deported as an undesirable alien. Jesús Pallares is a skilled miner and an accomplished musician. He has spent twenty-three of his thirty-nine years in the United States. For nineteen years he worked here, supporting his family. Of the remaining four years, two in childhood were spent in school, the last two on relief. Born in the state of Chihuahua, Mexico, Jesús joined the Madero revolution at the age of fifteen, fought four years, and mustered out in 1915 with part of his lower jaw missing. He entered the United States legally and obtained work as a miner. As miners' standards went, Jesús did well. He was an exceptional worker. There never was a time when he could not get a job. On the whole he got along with his bosses. In 1923, during an unorganized strike at Dawson, New Mexico, when anarchists among the men wanted to blow up the tipple in answer to company violence, Jesús convinced them of the anti-labor effect of such tactics, and prevented catastrophe. Labor's best weapon, he contended, lay in solidarity of organization.

The onset of the depression, 1930, found him working for the Gallup-American Coal Company, a subsidiary of the Guggenheim giant, Kennecott Copper. In 1930 Gallup was unorganized. So when Jesús found himself being paid but irregularly for his prospecting work on a new entry, he kicked—as an individual—and like individual protestors in all depressed coal fields, was promptly fired.

Jobs were scarce now. For the first time Jesús was up against it to support his wife and four children. But after several months of unemployment he obtained work at Madrid, New Mexico. Madrid is typical of thousands of marginal and sub-marginal coal camps. The town is company-owned.

Jesús was elected local union organizer. But the union's demands remained a dead letter. Jesús and his aides decided to ask the aid of the federal government in enforcing Section 7-a. When the company prohibited all union meetings in Madrid, the unionists walked four miles to Cerrillos for meetings, passed resolutions, drew up petitions, framed protests, and sent them to the coal board, to General Johnson, to Senator Cutting, to the state Labor Commissioner. From the coal board came a promise of a hearing—if the miners would withhold their strike and wait. And wait they did—weeks—and sent more telegrams—and waited more weeks. Not until the tail-end of the busy season—February, 1934—did T. S. Hogan, chairman of the Denver District Coal Board, arrive in Madrid for an "impartial" hearing.

Results of the Hogan hearing were zero. Grievances went unredressed. Union meetings continued to be prohibited. A new coal code went into effect, only to be violated even more flagrantly by the company. Plainly, the men must either strike or lie down. They struck—in the slack season. The strike failed. Jesús was marked for riddance.

Under the NRA he could not be fired for union activity. He finished work in his "room" in the mine and was assigned a new location. His eighteen years' experience told him that he could make at best sixty-seven cents a day here—and the mine was then working only one day a week—while his rent alone amounted to $3 per week. Yet the boss refused him any better location. Then a fellow worker offered to share his place with Jesús. It showed a good seam of coal, and both could make a living there. Jesús asked the superintendent's permission to accept this offer.

"No. Take the place assigned you, or none," Huber said.

The alternative was peonage—progressive indebtedness to the company. Jesús refused. His fifth child was expected shortly. His savings went for food. Arrears on his rent to the company piled up. He was told to vacate his house or be evicted. He stayed put. The child arrived. Asked by a fellow miner, "What is it, boy or girl?" Jesús replied:

"I think it's a bolshevik!"

Soon after the birth Jesús was charged with "forcible entry" of his house. The "court" was the company office, the justice of the peace a company employee. Superintendent Huber, furious that Jesús had made a public hearing necessary, clung like Shylock to his pound of flesh. Evicted, blacklisted as a miner, Jesús moved to Santa Fe and for the first time in his life went on relief. The family of seven lived in one room, on two cents per meal per person—the starvation standard still current in New Mexico's relief.

The native New Mexicans, a Spanish-speaking peasant people, had never been successfully organized. Yet they were half the population of the state. If organized in their own interest, instead of the interest of the railroads and mines, they could be a force to help themselves out of their 300-year-old bondage. At least they could end racial discrimination in relief. So in the fall of 1934 Jesús began organizing for the Liga Obrera de Habla Española (Spanish-speaking Workers League) which concerned itself specifically with the problems of the Spanish-American rank and file. In November there had been a few hundred members. By February, 1935, the Liga had grown to some 8,000. The politicos were frightened out of their wits. Jesús was elected organizer for the whole district, serving without pay and hitch-hiking to organize the most remote hamlets on his days off from FERA work.

This time Jesús had won the enmity not merely of one coal company but of the organized rulers of New Mexico. On April 23, 1935, he was arrested while at work on his FERA job and jailed on deportation charges. After three weeks' confinement, a secret hearing was held in an attempt to prove Jesús active in "communistic" organizations. N. D. Collear, federal immigration inspector, acted not only as an initiator, investigator, and prosecutor, but also as judge and jury, and even as court interpreter

To the amazement of Jesús, he found his opening remarks at the Hogan hearing of the year before cited as "evidence" against him. Jesús had said: "We have been most patient. . . . Mr. Hogan, I hope you come here to bring us full justice, if justice exists for the workingman. If you cannot see that we get it, we shall find other ways of getting it for ourselves."

Obviously Jesús referred to the strike which had been

postponed at Hogan's request. At the deportation hearing, it was offered as evidence of "communistic" activity!

Here is an item from the testimony of a Madrid lapdog:

Q. Have you ever heard him make inflammatory speeches about the government?
A. No, not exactly—he urges the Mexicans to fight for their rights.

On such trumpery charges Jesús was held for deportation under $1,000 bond pending a review of the case. The bond was promptly furnished, and Jesús was a "free" man—as free as a labor organizer can be in a vigilante-ridden state—as free as an alien can be who faces deportation and separation from his American-born children.

He continued his task of organizing the Liga Obrera so successfully that the rulers of New Mexico redoubled their efforts to be rid of him. After all, the government's case against Jesús was weak, involving only trade-union activity —a constitutionally guaranteed right. Could he not be provoked into open violence?

As a leader in the Liga Obrera, Jesús often accompanied delegations to the local relief office presenting cases of discrimination or deprivation. Recently, a worker in that office has disclosed in a sworn affidavit the methods employed against Jesús "in an effort to create reasons for his deportation." Says Esther Cohen, formerly of the New Mexico ERA:

Attempts were made by my office to intimidate Pallares by withholding relief and by inventing reasons by which he could be removed from relief jobs which were the only types of employment open to him. He was repeatedly called into my office where threats were made to starve his family in order to involve him in an argument which the relief agency hoped would give rise to violence on his part, which in turn would give sufficient reason for a complaint to the Labor Department. Such violence never took place, even though situations were carefully prepared in advance such as the placing of a hammer on the supervisor's desk within his easy reach. Nevertheless a complaint was made to Washington on the vague and flimsy basis that Pallares was a "troublemaker."

I gave Pallares's case history to Mr. Colyear [N. D. Collear], the immigration officer from Washington, who stated that he found no data therein which would incriminate Pallares to the extent of seriously considering deportation. He wondered if it would be possible to extract some information from Pallares himself by any means available which would further the plan to get him out of the way.

Towards this end Pallares was once again called into the office and this time a stenographer was planted where he could not see her and Colyear was also listening behind the closed door where Pallares could not see him. Again threats were made to "starve out" his ailing pregnant wife and six American born children to whom he was passionately devoted, if he did not admit that he was interested in organizing his friends into an unemployed council. . . .

At the hearing on his case before the Labor Department's Board of Review last spring Jesús was represented by an attorney for the American Committee for the Protection of Foreign Born. Among the papers on file in the case two remarkable documents came to light, the existence of which had hitherto been kept secret.

The first was a letter to Secretary of Labor Perkins from Governor Clyde Tingley of New Mexico, urging that Jesús's deportation be "expedited" on the extraordinary grounds that the Liga Obrera was "the New Mexico branch of the Communist organization." But the Governor, fully aware of how preposterous this charge was, and how unethical his interference in a federal judicial question, had been cautious enough to mark his letter "Personal and Confidential."

The second document was a telegram to the Immigration Bureau in Washington, so *in*cautious as to be worth quoting in full:

Having trouble with Jesús Pallares on strike in this county. I understand he is under bond on account of the strike at Gallup, New Mexico, where the sheriff of that county was killed last spring. He is an alien from Old Mexico. We must act at once to save trouble and maybe lives in this county.

Francisco P. Delgado, Sheriff [of San Miguel County].

In four sentences the telegram managed to utter five deliberate falsehoods or innuendoes. 1. The sheriff's trouble was not with Jesús but with the strikers at the American Metals Company's mine at Terrero, New Mexico, who embarrassed him by their accurate shouts of "Scab!" 2. Jesús was not on strike—did not even live in the sheriff's county. 3. Jesús was under bond for deportation, not for strike activity in Gallup or elsewhere. 4. At the time of the death of Gallup's sheriff, Jesús was living 230 miles away in Santa Fe—was totally unconnected with the event. 5. The deportation of Jesús could not possibly save "trouble and maybe lives" so long as the sheriff insisted on breaking the strike by armed force and violence.

Curiously enough, two truths did creep into the sheriff's wire: first, that Jesús was indubitably "an alien from Old Mexico"; second that "we"—that is, New Mexico officials and the Bureau of Immigration—were acting in concert to railroad Jesús out of the country. And they have had their way. Jesús is deported.

(7)

The Zoot Suit Riots*

When Governor Warren called for an investigation of the causes of the Zoot Suit Riots in Los Angeles in 1943, the Citizens Committee concluded, in a classic understatement, that race prejudice was indeed a factor of such "outbreaks."

REPORT AND RECOMMENDATIONS OF CITIZENS COMMITTEE
Under Governor Warren's call for an investigation for the purpose of curative action, the Citizens Committee has carefully investigated the outbreaks of violence in Los Angeles during the week of June 6, 1943. . . .

* *Governor's Citizens Committee Report on Los Angeles Riots, 1943.*

THE COMMITTEE HAS FOUND. . . .

There are approximately 250,000 persons of Mexican descent in Los Angeles County. Living conditions among the majority of these people are far below the general level of the community. Housing is inadequate; sanitation is bad and is made worse by congestion. Recreational facilities for children are very poor; and there is insufficient supervision of the playgrounds, swimming pools and other youth centers. Such conditions are breeding places for juvenile delinquency. . . .

Mass arrests, dragnet raids, and other wholesale classifications of groups of people are based on false premises and tend merely to aggravate the situation. Any American citizen suspected of crime is entitled to be treated as an indivdiual, to be indicted as such, and to be tried, both at law and in the forum of public opinion, on his merits or errors, regardless of race, color, creed, or the kind of clothes he wears.

Group accusations foster race prejudice; the entire group accused want revenge and vindication. The public is led to believe that every person in the accused group is guilty of crime.

It is significant that most of the persons mistreated during the recent incidents in Los Angeles were either persons of Mexican descent or Negroes. In undertaking to deal with the cause of these outbreaks, the existence of race prejudice cannot be ignored. . . .

(8)

La Raza*

> A good example of the meaning of *La Raza* to many Mexicans comes from a Mexican-American testifying in court about a case concerning restrictive covenants after World War II.

---

* *I. N. Clifton et al. v. Abdon Salazar Puente,* F-44264 73rd Judicial District, Bexar County, Texas.

1. . . . I was born in that country in which the first book published in the North American continent was given to the people, a Prayer Book published in what is now the Republic of Mexico.

2. . . . It was not given to me to be born in the United States of America or any of its territorial possessions, but I am now a fully naturalized citizen of the United States of America where I hope to live a peaceable, lawabiding life with my family and in peace and harmony with my neighbors.

3. . . . my mother was of that blood, Mexican blood, that has given so much to the North American continent, where the first free public school west of the Appalachian Mountains was founded.

4. . . . my father was of that blood, Mexican blood, which largely caused the establishment of the first Republic in Texas, founded in San Antonio, Texas, twenty-three years before the Battle of San Jacinto was fought.

5. . . . my grandfather and my grandmother were of Mexican blood, that blood which has given so much of courtesy, charity, and bravery to the people of North America.

6. . . . I am of the extraction of the people which gave to the people of Texas the four greatest laws it has, the law of community property, the law of the separate property rights of married women, the law of descent and distribution and the homestead law, taken by Stephen F. Austin from a decree of Ferdinand and Isabella, and all of which are radically different and superior to the common law and are just as Mexican as the glorious poinsette. . . . I am of Mexican blood and Mexican descent, of the people that gave to Texas six Congressional Medal of Honor winners in World War II, and it is my earnest prayer to so live as have my people with the desire to do good to every one and to live and act as a first-class gentleman and a loyal and devoted citizen of the United States of America.

Yes, I am also a member of that race, two of whom were the only native-born Texans who signed the Texas Declaration of Independence and who were San Antonio Mexicans.

(9)

American Sportsmanship*

> The following account by a *chicano* questions American sportsmanship.

A professor from outside was hired to teach in a Mexican school. He took an interest and organized the boys for a spelling match. The Mexicans won, to the surprise of all. Then he organized a basketball team, and it won in the city finals. The Anglos said, "Let the Mexicans win something. It is good for them." But when the football season came around and the Mexicans won again, the professor was told that he was hired to teach school. The Anglos didn't intend to have their children whipped by the Mexicans, and the next year this professor wasn't hired again.

(10)

Horatio Alger for Mexican-Americans†

> These grade-school texts are read by Mexican-American children in the Los Angeles School System. Appropriate titles for them might be: "Study Hard and You Will Succeed and Help Your People," and "When It Was Over, Poof, . . . California belonged to the United States."

* Sister Frances Jerome Woods, *Mexican-American Ethnic Leadership in San Antonio, Texas* (Washington, D.C.: Catholic University of America Press, 1949).

† *Angelenos Then and Now* (Los Angeles: Los Angeles City Schools, Division of Instructional Services, 1966).

LEOPOLDO SANCHEZ

Leopoldo's mother and father were born in Mexico, but they met and were married in Los Angeles. They spoke Spanish in their home, and thus Leopoldo could not speak or understand English when he first went to school. . . .

Each day, Leopoldo hurried home from school. He had to have a very good reason if he was late. His parents also expected him to behave in school. They did not have the opportunity to go to school in Mexico, but they knew the value of an education. They were determined to help their children receive a good education. . . .

[After high school,] . . . Leopoldo entered the army. While in the army, he visited many places in our country. When he was discharged, he returned to Los Angeles to attend college. He had learned to study hard and again did good work. . . .

Upon graduation from college, Leopoldo knew what he wanted to do. He wanted to be a lawyer. To earn money for law school, Leopoldo worked as a laborer, unloading box cars for a big factory. This was very hard work, and the pay was very low, yet it was enough to help him through law school.

When he was graduated from law school and began working as an attorney, Leopoldo realized that there were many people who needed his help. As he worked, he decided that he could best serve the people of the community as a judge. He began talking to his friends. He talked to everyone he met. He told them of the importance of this office. Leopoldo also urged the people to register to vote. He told them it was the duty of every citizen to vote in an election. When election day came, he reminded the people to go to the polls and vote. The people elected him judge of the Municipal Court.

Now Leopoldo listens to many cases each week. He makes sure that each person is treated fairly. Because he stayed in school and worked hard for many years, Judge Leopoldo Sanchez is better able to help the people of Los Angeles.

CRISTOBAL AGUILAR

When Cristobal Aguilar was born in Los Angeles, the Spanish period of California's early history had just ended. The land which was to become the state of California was ruled by Mexico.

Cristobal's father was a ranch owner. Because he owned land and was wealthy, he was called *Don* José Aguilar instead of José or Señor Aguilar. His son was called Don Cristobal. . . .

Don Cristobal went to school, but the schools were not always open. Old soldiers were the teachers. Sometimes, they left the school to do other things. Then the schools were closed. Still, Don Cristobal learned to read and write. He was a good student. He studied at home every evening. There were times for fun, too. After the work of the day, everyone gathered for a feast or barbecue. There was much laughter as well as singing and dancing. . . .

As Don Cristobal grew older, many people from the East came to live in California. It was difficult to reach California from the United States. California was also far away from Mexico. Sea voyages were rough and difficult. The road from Mexico was very dangerous. There were many deserts to cross. There were many unfriendly Indians along the way. The road from the United States was dangerous, too, but it was not as difficult as the road from Mexico.

As more people from the United States began to live in California, they began to think it should belong to our country. The settlers wanted their own government. Along the borders between the United States and Mexico, there were many quarrels. There was a war with Mexico. When it was over, California belonged to the United States.

Everyone living in California at that time became a citizen of the United States. Now Don Cristobal was a U.S. citizen. California needed a new government. A good government is important if people are to live together peacefully. In Los Angeles, the *ayuntamiento* of the Mexican fully. In Los Angeles, the *ayuntamiento* of the Mexican government was replaced by a mayor and a city council. A city council is a group of people elected by all the people of a city to work together with the mayor to govern the city. Don Cristobal wanted to help the new government. He wanted Los Angeles to be a great city. He talked to all his friends. A good government is important, he told them. Everyone must work together. At election time, every citizen must vote.

Don Cristobal was elected to the City Council of Los Angeles in 1850. He was the first American of Mexican descent elected to the City Council. Because he was a very good councilman, he was elected to the City Council four different times. . . .

For more than twenty-two years, Don Cristobal Aguilar served the city of Los Angeles as a councilman, mayor, and zanjero. All his life, he worked to make Los Angeles a great city.

(11)

Tijerina and the *Alianza*

The Alianza Federal de Mercedes, organized to reclaim Mexican-American lands stolen by Anglos and the Anglo government, is led by Reies Lopez Tijerina who has dramatized the plight of the northern New Mexico *chicanos*. Tijerina has formed close associations with other colored militant groups, as the Black-Brown Treaty indicates.

ALIANZA STATEMENT*

WE ACCUSE the Legislature of New Mexico of:

1. Progressively destroying Indo-Hispano language, culture, and history in the minds and persons of the Indo-Hispano population of New Mexico.

* *El Grito* (Espanola, New Mexico: January 29, 1968).

2. Lavishly financing a state university system whose major institution (the University of New Mexico) has only 6 percent Indo-Hispano students while at the same time allowing (for lack of small matching sums in state funds) large sums of federal money to go unused in welfare and health benefits that would go to the poor who are disproportionately Indo-Hispano.

3. Putting money for public schools—almost all (about 85 percent) for administrators' and teachers' salaries—ahead of the content of what is taught and the purposes for which the schools are in fact being used.

4. Refusing and failing to enforce the provisions of the Constitution of New Mexico designed to protect and preserve Indo-Hispano language, culture and history. This often results in Indo-Hispano kids hating themselves and their origins.

5. Allowing teachers to be hired into the state's public school system without any regard for the Constitutional requirement that they speak Spanish and without being trained in New Mexico's historical background.

6. Allowing Indo-Hispano kids to be pushed out of the public schools.

7. Favoring the rich (particularly rich Anglos) over the poor (particularly Indo-Hispanos): for example, the legislature is even now intending to raise the sales tax which falls heaviest on the poor to finance greatly increased public school expenditures for an education that is designed to, and has the effect of, destroying the Indo-Hispano culture in all its aspects.

8. Refusing and failing to pass laws to preserve and protect the land—particularly the land grants—of the Indo-Hispano population; instead the legislature has consistently passed legislation to enable rich Anglos to take and/or keep land rightfully that of the Indo-Hispano population.

9. Passing laws to allow the public utilities and services to milk the poor, such as telephones, gas, electricity, banking, insurance, finance companies, buses, and the judicial system.

10. Allowing the system of the common law to grow up in New Mexico that brings with it the necessity for extensive legal services and the principle that the man with the most money wins, rather than encouraging the system of the civil law and attempting to minimize the use of lawyers and the effectiveness of money to decide judicial proceedings.

11. Encouraging and allowing the use of the police power of the state against Indo-Hispanos in a discriminatory manner, resulting in great political crimes going unsolved, such as the death of Eulogio Salazar and Tommy Valles in Albuquerque.

12. Using Indo-Hispanos as front men for the conspiracy set forth above, particularly by promising and giving them money and/or prestige in the Anglo-dominated society and/or power over their fellow Indo-Hispanos.

SANTA FE BERETS' TEN POINT PROGRAM*

Presented to the Legislature of New Mexico on January 21, 1969, and to the people of Santa Fe and New Mexico:

1. We want to see BILINGUAL EDUCATION become a reality soon, a right guaranteed over a hundred years ago in the Treaty of Guadalupe Hidalgo. Education must not continue to be biased against Spanish-speaking people.

The colleges in New Mexico should reflect and teach our Chicano heritage, and not just turn us into brown Anglos. We don't want to be absorbed!

2. We want SCHOOL COMMUNITY CONTROL BOARDS consisting of parents, to make sure that bilingual education and studies of Mexican-American cultural heritage are carried out. The schools and teachers should be responsible to the parents who pay for them, and whose children's lives are being molded by them.

3. The POLICE should be directly responsible to community control boards of local people. They should live in

* *Ibid.*

the neighborhoods they work in. Police are to protect the people, not intimidate them.

4. We think that if eighteen-year-olds are old enough to be drafted, they are old enough to VOTE.

5. People forced to live on WELFARE should get enough to live on and be treated like human beings. We need more jobs in Santa Fe with decent wages.

6. We need medical CLINICS for poor people, where they can get treatment without having to travel long distances. These clinics should have pharmacies to fill prescriptions. If local people were trained to work in these clinics, many jobs could be provided.

7. We need a stronger MINIMUM WAGE LAW. Many of us—especially service workers—must try to live on $1 an hour. But it costs as much to live here as in California or New York, where wages are higher.

8. CORPORATION TAX LAWS should be revised. The big corporations must put back some of the millions they take out of New Mexico every year.

9. We support the demands of those who want to get back some of the LAND GRANTS that were stolen from Chicanos.

10. All POLITICAL PRISONERS should be freed from jail immediately. This means all who have stood up for the rights of Spanish-speaking people.

INTERVIEW WITH REIES TIJERINA BY DELLA ROSSA*

To urban blacks, the police are the symbol of an oppressive white power structure. To the Spanish-Americans of northern New Mexico, that symbol is the U.S. Forest Rangers, because these are the men who stand as armed guards over land which they say has been stolen from them during the last 119 years through legal and financial trickery. . . .

"These U.S. Forest Rangers are drunk with the stupid idea of Anglo superiority," Tijerina said. "They go around with guns on their saddles. They have the idea the whole

* *Los Angeles Free Press* (Los Angeles: Nov. 10–17, 1967).

world is supposed to bend their knees before them. The rangers have burned the homes of people on disputed land. Governor Cargo has testified against this. The rangers have been torturing, oppressing."

Tijerina said that about 500 Alianza members were at the campground last October on land which the Alianza claims actually belongs to them through the land grant of El Pueblo de San Joaquin del Rio Chama. . . .

The biggest confrontation between the Alianza and the Establishment came on June 5 of this year in Tierra Amarilla when they attempted a citizens' arrest of District Attorney Alfonso Sanchez.

On May 14, in a meeting in the Tierra Amarillo courthouse, Tijerina spoke to 500 people about "their rights under the land grants, the progressive destruction of Spanish culture, and their social, economic and political disenfranchisement."

After Tijerina's speech the people of Tierra Amarillo, in the "land grant" county of Rio Arriba, proceeded to elect a new mayor, council and militia chief. This development was too much for the ranchowners and their political representatives who comprise the anglo power structure. Subsequently District Attorney Alfonso Sanchez proceeded to arrest Alianza members. Governor Cargo said of this incident, "Sanchez was guilty of inciting to riot through his provocative arrests of Alianza members."

June 5 was set as the date for the arraignment of those arrested. Alianza members announced that they would go to the courthouse on that date to make a citizens' arrest of District Attorney Sanchez.

Sanchez was not at the courthouse, but as the Alianza approached, police opened fire. Shots were exchanged and two police were injured. For ninety minutes the Alianza controlled Tierra Amarillo, and then they escaped.

The night of June 5 was a night of terror, with National Guard tanks searching the hills for Alianza members. Those found camping in the Tierra Amarillo area were rounded up, including old people and babies, and held in a corral overnight, an action which caused the American Civil Liberties Union to go to the defense of the Alianza.

Tijerina and others were charged with kidnapping and assault. He spent nearly a month in the penitentiary following June 5, winning the support of Spanish-American prisoners and guards, and is now out on bail, with the preliminary hearing on that case set for January 29. This means there will be more confrontations ahead between Tijerina's land grant movement and the New Mexico "white power structure. . . ."

I probed the philosophy and motivation behind Tijerina and the land grant movement when Tijerina was in Los Angeles October 12 to 15. Here is a portion of that interview:

DR: Do most of the people of the Alianza Federal de Mercedes, the Federal Alliance of Land Grants, get their living from the land?

RLT: Yes, most of them, but in a very limited way, often through the grazing of cattle rather than from farming. The grazing lands are controlled by the U.S. Forestry Service and there is a great discrimination against the Spanish-Americans.

The most they get is a permit for eighteen head of cattle, one horse, one milking cow, and from there down, most of them four or six cows.

DR: While at the same time the Anglos get lands for up to 500 cattle?

RLT: Yes, that's the difference and that's what angers the Spanish-Americans. Sometimes one of these Anglo ranchers has a permit for 1,000 cattle in one forest and at the same time another 1,000 head of cattle in another forest.

DR: I have the report that in Rio Arriba County, where the Tierra Amarillo "land grant uprising" took place in June, about half of the 23,000 people who live there are unemployed and on welfare. What are their living conditions?

RLT: The living conditions are pitiful. I don't know how to describe it, but most of them are on welfare and they have lost hope. Most of the children are drop-outs. It wasn't until the Alianza was born that these people started to organize.

DR: Why has the fight been around the old land grants?

RLT: The forefathers of these people have been depending on these land grants for hundreds and hundreds of years. The Spanish Crown vested on these pueblos millions of acres of common lands. Nobody owned these lands (as individuals) but they depended on these lands and shared them.

The fencing of these lands was prohibited by town or pueblo laws. Naturally, when the government confiscated these lands, the people were forced to move to the big cities and their source of living was destroyed and now they are in a very desperate condition.

DR: Why was the Alianza replaced for a time, or paralleled by, the Confederation of Free City States?

RLT: The Alianza is a civil organization. The property we are demanding belongs not to individuals but to the pueblos, or political units, governmental bodies.

DR: What brought about the June action in Tierra Amarilla? Does the land grant movement now feel that court actions and peaceful demonstrations will not win its objectives?

RLT: We are using many methods and tactics, not just court actions. The June action in Tierra Amarilla was not a revolution, as the press claimed, but a citizens' arrest.

DR: What did happen in Tierra Amarilla?

RLT: Well, the truth was that for a whole month we had published through the news media that we were going to have a national conference in Coyote, N.M. We were to have two days of conference and a picnic dinner in the open. Alfonso Sanchez, the Santa Fe district attorney, decided that these people should be arrested and imprisoned and that they were assembling unlawfully.

DR: Do you see your people as colonial subjects? This is the point many of the black militants are bringing up, saying blacks in America are colonial subjects, in that they are confined to a certain area and do not have the rights of citizens.

RLT: We do feel as colonial subjects. We feel we have a master over us, the white supremacist. He is the one who has raped our cities, raped our culture, deprived us of our language. He forces all peoples to speak English only. There are many crimes against us, but the biggest crime is the deprivation of our own language. We feel as subjected and as humiliated as the black man. Like him, we are fighting now for our identity and our self-respect. We are trying to unite not only with the Puerto Ricans and all Latin Americans, but also with the black people here. We want to join forces. We have already written treaties and will present them to our convention in Albuquerque October 21 and 22.

(The Alianza's mutual assistance treaty was signed in Albuquerque by representatives of the Los Angeles Black Congress, "US," Student Nonviolent Coordinating Committee, the Black Student Union, Congress on Racial Equality, and the Black Youth Conference.)

DR: Who do you see as the main enemy?

RLT: The capitalists, the industrialists, the bankers, the political powers. And these powers are incarnate in the white, the Anglo.

DR: Alianza members face charges growing out of both the Carson National Forest incident last year and the Tierra Amarilla confrontation this June. How strong do you think the Alianza is at this time?

RLT: I remember when I came to New Mexico—I remember very well. The members were fearful, frightened. They wouldn't dare raise their heads. When I first went on radio I called the New Mexico judges all kinds of names of contempt. They were devils. Then I challenged them to arrest me for contempt. My people pleaded "Please, Reies, they will kill you!" Now, I attack Senator Montoya and the whole system. For two or three years I was teaching the people, teaching, teaching. I showed them there was nothing to fear. There were dark clouds, but there was nothing there.

After the incident in the park last year they became stronger—after they made citizens' arrests of two forest rangers. Then there was the Tierra Amarilla incident when they decided to arrest District Attorney Sanchez. Now they are like lions and tigers. They don't know what fear is. They are ready to fight. Men, women and children—gladly! They got rid of the fear and terror and that sense of subordination.

DR: Is this the way you see it, that if you have one man with a gun, he's a murderer, but if you have a mass movement with guns, it's democracy?

RLT: Right! The people is the government. Therefore when forty people arrived at Tierra Amarilla courthouse that was government! Of course, the officials refused to see it that way, but that was democracy!

BLACK-BROWN TREATY*

Treaty of Peace, Harmony, and Mutual Assistance Between the Spanish-American Federal Alliance of Free City States, and in the Name of God Almighty

Art. I

Sec. (A): Both peoples (races) will consider this *treaty* as a *solemn* agreement, and subject to the Divine Law of the *God* of *justice*.

Sec. (B): Both peoples solemnly promise, to respect the Faith, the culture, of each other, and every *right* and *liberty* that *God* has given to the *human race*.

Sec. (C): Both peoples do promise not to permit the members of either of said peoples, to make false propaganda of any kind whatsoever against each other, either by *speech* or by *writing*. . . .

Art. II

Sec. (C): Both peoples will strive, without limitations whatsoever, to materialize and make real, the truth of *justice* on earth.

* *Harambee* (Los Angeles: November, 1967).

Art. III

Sec. (C): Both peoples make a *solemn* promise to cure and remedy the historical errors and differences that exist between said peoples.

Art. V

Sec. (A): Let it be known that there will be a Mutual understanding over events, Elections, and Political activities, that will better the National status of the said two peoples.

Sec. (B): Let it be known that both peoples will have a political delegate to represent his interests and relations with the other.

Sec. (C): Both peoples (races) promise to consult and inform one another in each and every National case of importance, that affects each of the two said peoples.

Art. VI

Sec. (A): In case a Nuclear War should erupt upon the earth, the two peoples *solemnly* promise to assist each other.

Sec. (C): This *treaty* will be valid between the two said peoples, as long as the Sun and Moon shall shine.

Art. VII

Sec. (A): The two peoples agree to take the same position as to the *crimes* and *sins* of the government of the United States of America.

Sec. (B): Neither of said both peoples shall intervene in the holy *judgement* of *God* against the United States of America.

(12)

The Story of Tierra Amarilla*

Through the *corridos* history is recorded and passed along. "The Story of Tierra Amarilla" is but one of the versions written and sung about the Alianza's attempt to reclaim the land in northern New Mexico.

* *Corrido* de "Rio Arriba." By a local *mariachi* group. Translated by Saul Landau.

Year of the nineteen-hundred
and sixty-seven
and the news
comes on TV and radio

Beloved New Mexico
County of Rio Arriba
Spanish-Americans
have there risked their lives.

The second of June
I don't want to remember
They arrested the leaders
of the Alianza Federal

They took their documents
Their arms and ammunition
They took them to Santa Fe
and put them in prison

In the town of Canjillon
they held the conference
To ask for their rights
they had to use violence

The fifth of June
about two in the afternoon
Sixteen armed men
took over the jail

People of Tierra Amarilla
did their job,
freed the prisoners,
leaving several wounded

They got in their cars
heading to Canjillon
They reached the Sierra
and they claimed it as theirs

Out came the officers
all like dogs
and they did not give chase
because they were afraid.

Sixteen armed men
would not be cowed
by the State Police
or the National Guard

Spanish-Americans
doesn't your heart tremble
your force will be remembered
in the Sierra of Canjillon

Because they were afraid
to fight them face to face
They return to the town
and arrest the innocent

They made them prisoners
although they'd committed no
    crime
and Tijerina tells them
One day I will take revenge

The poor Alfonso Sanchez
can't find a way out
The injustices he has done,
he will pay for some day

To the governor of the state
I talk with a warning:
If you don't do something
Violence will continue

Who composed this story
has no grace
But he could sing
This *corrido* to his race.

If I'm wrong about anything
you must forgive me
This testimony is left to you
By your paisano Juan Roybal.

(13)

¡Ya Basta!*

Mexican-American college and high school students began to organize themselves around Brown Power and Third World themes by 1967, and to think of themselves as having a revolutionary obligation: revolution, reasoned many of the *chicano* student leaders, was the only way to solve the problems of Mexican-Americans.

MEXICAN AMERICAN STUDENT LEADERSHIP CONFERENCE

"Protest the injustices being committed upon Mexican Americans in the United States."

I. Unjust treatment of Reies Tijerina who was trying to recover lands that have been stolen from Mexican Americans in the Southwest by Anglos.

II. 45% of Mexican Americans eligible for the draft are being drafted, while *only 19%* of Anglos eligible for the draft are drafted!!

III. 20% of casualties in Viet Nam are Mexican American, whose families are still living in poverty and deprivation.

IV. 65% of students in mentally retarded programs in Santa Ana are Mexican Americans due not to actual retardation but to the failure of the Anglo educational system which is not geared to meet the needs of bilingual children of the Mexican-American Culture.

V. Mexican American farm workers and migrant workers in the Southwest are subject to exploitation because they are not covered by Social Security, Unemployment Compensation and other benefits.

* *El Infierno,* San Antonio, Jan. 11, 1967.

  VI. The drop-out rate among Mexican American high school students in the Southwest is 60% which again indicates the failure of the Anglo educational system when dealing with Mexican American students.

 VII. The average educational level of Mexican Americans in the United States is 8.6 years, which is 4 years below the national average.

VIII. Only 2% of Mexican Americans are in college, again way below the national average.

  IX. And finally, discrimination in employment and housing.

TIMES OF STATISTICS AND STUDIES
ARE OVER!!!
THE TIME FOR A REVOLUTIONARY
CHANGE AND ACTION HAS COME!!!

(14)

The Advertisement*

> Steve Gonzales was a graduate student in Anthropology when he published the following satire in a Mexican-American journal, *El Grito*.

The following advertisement originally appeared in the September 6 issue of THE WHITE LIBERAL'S DIGEST, *and the September 9 issue of* THE SOUTHWESTERN JOURNAL OF CULTURAL ENGINEERING. *It is being brought to you as a public service by* EL GRITO:

American Ethnic Supply Company, a Division of I.B.M. (Intergalactic Business Machines, Inc.), is proud to present the latest model in its popular "Other Minorities" line—the all-new Mark IV MEXICAN-AMERICAN!! Superbly crafted and made of only the finest foamium, chromium, and tacomium, the Mark IV has been expertly engineered and

---

* Steven Gonzales, "The Advertisement," *El Grito, A Journal of Contemporary Mexican-American Thought* (Berkeley: Fall, 1967).

computer-programmed to efficiently serve all your Mexican-American needs.

Far ahead of the field with its advanced design, the Mark IV MEXICAN-AMERICAN is the first model to offer you that long-hoped-for engineering breakthrough—Multipox Stereotypification—a literal triumph of American ingenuity and technology! Produced after ten years of intensive Social and Cultural Engineering research by our team of dedicated industrial Anthropologists and Cybernetic Sociologists, the Multipox Stereotypification system allows you by the simple turning of a dial to select the *particular* MEXICAN-AMERICAN you need to suit your particular purpose:

1) a familially faithful and fearfully factional folk-fettered fool

2) a captivating, cactus-crunching, cow-clutching caballero

3) a charp, chick-chasing, chili-chomping cholo

4) a brown-breeding, bean-belching border-bounder

5) a raza-resigned, ritual-racked rude rural relic

6) a peso-poor but proud, priest-pressed primitive

7) a grubby but gracious, grape-grabbing greaser

A second significant design feature of the Mark IV is its Instantaneous Convertibility. With this engineering innovation, you'll never again have to worry about being caught in an embarrassing position with your MEXICAN-AMERICAN; when the need arises for him to disappear, a simple utterance of the verbal command "Civil Rights" will instantaneously convert the MEXICAN-AMERICAN into an inconspicuous muted-brown tea-tray, complete with service for six.

The all-new Mark IV is truly revolutionary in terms of safety design—it is the first 100 percent guaranteed safe MEXICAN-AMERICAN!! If at any time the Mark IV should begin behaving in a contrary, threatening, or subversive manner, a clear enunciation of the verbal command "Traditional Culture" will immediately initiate the self-destruct mechanism, culminating in the Mark IV committing full hari-kari with the blunt end of an original 1914 Edition of

William Madsen's *The Mexican-Americans of South Texas*.
In the event of this, of course, you will be immediately
furnished another MEXICAN-AMERICAN at no cost to you by
the American Ethnic Supply Company.

For complete specifications and a full description of the
many quality features of the Mark IV, send for our free
illustrated brochure, or better yet, visit your local dealer
and try out a MEXICAN-AMERICAN for yourself. Upon purchase of the Mark IV, the American Ethnic Supply Company will furnish, at no extra cost to you, your MEXICAN-
AMERICAN's lifetime supply of American Grease Pellets—
the very latest in easy insertion! And remember, when it
comes to the MEXICAN-AMERICAN—"Only your Supplier
Knows For Sure!"

(15)

I Oppose the War as a Chicano*

> Ernest Vigil, 20, Denver native
> and associate editor of *El Gallo*,
> was the first *chicano* in the South-
> west to refuse induction. The fol-
> lowing is a statement by Vigil ex-
> pressing the reasons for refusing
> induction.

On May 7, 1968, I reported to the New Customs House
in downtown Denver to take an induction physical for the
Armed Forces. I passed the physical examination but refused to go through with the induction ceremony. I was
ordered for immediate induction as a "delinquent"; there is
no reason for my being classified delinquent, and therefore
there is no reason for being called for immediate induction
as such. For refusing to cooperate I face a felony charge
that can bring a minimum of 5 years, $10,000, or both.

I was fully aware of the consequences; I did not do this
for kicks. . . .

The Selective Serve-Us System *is* inadequate and discrim-

* *El Gallo,* Denver, Colorado, May 1, 1968.

inatory and should be opposed until it is changed, so that the Spanish-surnamed, the Black, and the general poor do not have to bear the brunt of this undeclared war. I oppose the war on grounds of personal conscience and I oppose the war as a Mexican-American, a Chicano.

I look at the discrepancy between what our country says and what it does; between what it is and what it should be; and I arrive at the decision that it is beneath my dignity as an intelligent, well-meaning human being to quietly submit or blindly conform to a system that attacks noble meaning (if not meaning altogether) and whose values and practices will not and do not serve the ends of truth, peace, and justice.

Therefore, I hereby submit my draft-card as a gesture of my dissatisfaction and disaffection for the social, governmental, and political system of this nation.

My country is not my God; I will (and must) first serve the dictates of my mind, heart and conscience. There are laws and values that are higher than those of this nation's government and sometimes these come from the conscience of one lone individual; they cannot be legislated by politicians nor enforced by policemen and soldiers.

In this belief I now state that I will not fight the war of a power and system that I feel is unjust, hypocritical, deceitful, inadequate, and detrimental to peaceful, legal social revolution. . . . This forces people to prepare for what has been called "the fire next time." All of this is happening, while America says it will not condone violence as it sits and watches war movies on color T.V.

All this, while America says "I'm sorry" for the death of Dr. King and "We sympathize with the poor." Then during riots they say "Shoot to kill! During demonstrations they say "Arrest those people." All of this in a country that has a gross national product of 800 billion dollars and 20% of its people in poverty. All this, while America says "Might does not make right." Yet look what happens to anyone who gets in the way of the American Establishment. Look at what happens to Tijerina. All this, while Uncle Sam preaches democracy and then supports every dictator in South America with money, equipment and "military advisors."

All this, in a nation that condemns racism and genocide—but what has happened to the first Americans, the Indians? In South America they comprise anywhere from 1/3 to 95% of the total population. In America it is 1/10 of one percent. All this, while America continues to say "Do as I say, not as I do." And when Mexican-Americans are only 3 to 5% of the total population and 19 to 20% of the Vietnam casualties, it is obvious to me, as it should be to everyone, that something is happening that has to be stopped.

I'm specifically making reference to the Selective Service System and the Vietnam war, but my concerns are far greater than this. Every major institution in this nation is directly or indirectly responsible for the great inequities that exist between the elite, white, middle-class power structure and the disenfranchised minority groups whether Mexican-American, Afro-American, American Indian or Puerto Rican.

What we need as much as the changes to be made, is for the people to make the changes. NOW!

(16)

La Raza Quiz*

> *Raza* consciousness is stressed by all militant *chicano* groups and newspapers try to provide young and old readers with a sense that *chicanos* are and have been vital to the history of America. Denver's *chicano* newspaper, *El Gallo*, printed the *Raza* quiz.

1. Sam Houston of Alamo fame was a citizen of what country?
   (1) England   (2) Mexico   (3) U.S.A.

* *"La Raza* Quiz," *El Gallo* (Denver: March, 1968).

2. Who discovered Pike's Peak?
   (1) Jim Bowie (2) Zebulon Pike (3) Juan De Anza

3. Which is the oldest pioneer settlement in Colorado?
   (1) Platteville (2) Walsenburg (3) San Luis

4. Malinche was a
   (1) Spanish Duchess (2) Mexican Virgin (3) Aztec Princess

5. What percentage of Mexicanos are drafted?
   (1) 15% (2) 45% (3) 28%

6. What percentage of the Vietnam casualties are Spanish speaking?
   (1) 8% (2) 3% (3) 20%

7. What percentage of the total American population are the Spanish sur-named
   (1) 20% (2) 8% (3) 3%

8. Anglos constitute _____ percent of the American population?
   (1) 30% (2) 87% (3) 66%

9. What percentage of eligible Anglo draftees are drafted?
   (1) 38% (2) 19% (3) 42%

10. Joaquin Murieta was considered by the Mexican people to be a _____.
    (1) Vicious Bandit (2) Robin Hood
    (3) Murderer (4) Spanish General

11. Emiliano Zapata was a _____.
    (1) Convicted killer (2) South American bandit
    (3) Revolutionary hero (4) Spanish landowner

12. The mining techniques of the Southwest were initiated and developed by the
    (1) Welsh (2) Spaniards (3) English
    (4) French

13. The cattle industry was started and developed by the
    (1) Australians (2) Irish (3) Spaniards
    (4) Mexican Mestizos

14. Henry Thoreau went to jail for refusal to pay taxes because of the "unholy war" against

(1) Spain (2) Vietnam (3) Mexico (4) Cuba

15. Los Niños de Chapultepec were heroes of ——————
——————.

(1) New Mexico (2) Texas (3) Mexico
(4) Spain

ANSWERS:

1. Sam Houston, was a Mexican Citizen. He gave up American citizenship and swore allegiance to Mexico in exchange for a Mexican land grant in Texas.
2. Pike's Peak was first discovered by Spanish Governor Anza 160 years before Pike claimed discovery.
3. San Luis is the oldest settlement in Colorado.
4. Malinche was an Aztec princess who betrayed her people to the Spanish.
5. 45% of eligible Mexican-Americans are drafted.
6. Spanish-speaking people suffer 20% of casualties in Vietnam.
7. The Spanish-speaking people represent 3% of the total American population.
8. Anglos or white people constitute 87% of the total American population.
9. Only 19% of the Anglo youth eligible for the draft are drafted.
10. Robin Hood.
11. Revolutionary hero.
12. Spanish.
13. Spaniards & Mestizos.
14. Mexico.
15. Mexico.

How many did you answer right?

12 to 15	*Chicano on the ball*
9 to 12	*You need a little polish but you know who you are*
7 to 9	*You identify and can be salvaged*
1 to 7	*You're brainwashed, come to the Crusade for Justice; YOU NEED HELP.*

(17)

Chicano Power*

> Mario Compean Mayo, a columnist
> from the Texas *chicano* paper, *El
> Inferno*, tries to persuade his peo-
> ple that even though politics in the
> past meant nothing but swindles,
> *chicanos* must now participate in
> order to control their own com-
> munities.

The United Race is our goal. The United Race is the end
which we seek and the goal which the Mexican-American
people ought to seek. The United Race in everything and
always will be our salvation. When this theme is realized it
will be the day in which the Mexican-American people will
liberate themselves from discrimination, injustice, and the
barbarism to which we have been submitted by the gringo,
the name that we have preferred to call this individual for
more than a hundred years.

Above all, the solution proposed to achieve our goal and
our salvation, that of the United Race, sees political activity
as the most important. The years have gone by with previous solutions failing completely or else they would need a
hundred years to be implemented. We are not disposed to
wait another one hundred years so that formal education
brings us to live a life without hope and without light, a life
in complete darkness. For this reason, today we are raising
the voice in an open call and proclaiming to the Mexican-
American people that the salvation of our people lies in
activism and political participation.

The United Race in politics will be a very potent force
and a respected one when it is realized. In order to accomplish this goal it is necessary first of all to change the attitude that politics is something bad, and at the same time

---

* "Chicano Power," *Inferno* (San Antonio: January 11, 1968).

change the misunderstanding that the very word connotes.

Politics only does harm to those who don't have control of the governmental machinery, local, state, or federal. Those that have control only think to perpetuate their own improvement and they forget they are there in order to serve the people and not for their own interests.

Thus, in order to be able to get control, it will be necessary to destroy the misunderstanding of the word and then to induce the people to participate on all levels of politics. Participation is not enough without seeking the means of control. The United Race as a whole and forever will accomplish this goal if we dedicate ourselves to it.

(18)

Brown Power*

> The following poem and article represent the kind of political and aesthetic expression that is found in some of the *Raza* newspapers and magazines from Texas to California.

brown power!
¿qué?
Together we must . . .
¡Sí!
The problem . . .
¿qué?
It's your Fault . . .
who?
I mean . . .
¿qué?
brown power!
testing, testing, testing
uno, dos, tres . . .

* John J. Martinez, "Brown Power Conference Centennial," *El Grito, A Journal of Contemporary Mexican-American Thought* (Berkeley: Winter, 1968).

THE LAND, OUR HERITAGE*

The gringos control, they rob, and they have Texas by the throat. This machine or Establishment (as they call it) gives life to itself by its very own activity and is a symbol of gringo insanity. This insanity is called schizophrenia. When one invents a lie and then believes in his own lie or wants to make it true, one has schizophrenia.

To be part of this machine, or establishment, one has to be gringo. That's the whole scene. In order to be gringo, one has to adopt their selfish behavior. Also one has to distinguish people by the color of their skin, eyes (they love the color blue); the name (the names Garza, Martinez, or Gutierrez are worthless): and religion. One has to make himself a hypocrite. He has to think that the gringos are God's children. It is also helpful to take advantage of a Mexican or two. If one practices these rules he is a good gringo.

They protect one another. They defend themselves against all that isn't gringo. They cover themselves with the same blanket and they believe themselves very close to the Virgin. After all this, their system is protected. The Establishment continues because they work together. There is unity among gringos.

The gringos think they are the cream of Texas society. They think they are very saintly and responsible for all people. They protect the United States as if it were their wife. All that is gringo is not naturally covered by these things. These individuals are *inferiores* according to the gringo.

Mexicans, they think, don't have anything to contribute but cheap labor. We are much lower than they. They also think that the race in general is criminal, drunk, lazy, ignorant, and irresponsible.

These are pure lies and inventions of the gringo!

This has gone on for many years. The gringo and his

* José Angel Gutierrez, "The Land, Our Heritage," *El Inferno* (San Antonio: January 11, 1968).

Establishment have exploited (robbed, killed), discriminated, and oppressed (kept down) the Mexican people since we were Mexicans from Mexico. All these lies that they tell about us are how they sap the pride of being Mexican and make us search for a means to make ourselves gringos. Mexicans also are and make themselves into gringos. Beneath this hypocrisy and the lies that we have freedom, justice, and democracy, the gringos have brought misery and ruin. What nice democracy, freedom, and justice when one lives on his knees and at the pleasure of the gringo.

Brothers, we needn't make ourselves stupid. This land was Mexican and the gringos robbed us. They have made our grandfathers, fathers, and ourselves dependent on them. They have made our way of life an ugly thing. Now they make us ashamed to bring tortillas to work if there are gringos there. The Spanish that we speak isn't permitted by gringos. Our culture (they don't have any) of many years is now important because one can make money with it. Look at the HemisFair if you don't believe it. After they have done all this to us, and have used us as floor moppers, the gringos say, " 'Los mescans' are inferior to us, they are worthless." They created this lie in order to rise. Today they believe it as if it were true! That's why I say that the gringos are nuts. Just schizophrenics.

The ugliest thing that has happened is that very few of us have the balls to admit that the gringo is using us. We want to make fools of ourselves because the truth hurts us. But we know that when one removes a backbone the pain will be gone. The same is also true with the gringo; if we get him out of here the problem will be gone. If there is unity and spirit the gringo can't take us. As they say to the blacks, "Go back to Africa!" we ought to say to them, "Dogs! Go back to England or wherever you came from. This land belongs to the Mexicans!" Viva La Raza!

(19)
Blame It on the Reds*

On a warm May day in San Francisco's local *barrio,* the Mission District, Vincent Gutierrez had a fight with his wife. He was high, maybe on drink, maybe on drugs—the popular pills known as Reds—and his wife called the police. Vincent, known as "Chente" in the Mission, supposedly ran away and the police supposedly had to subdue him. Before he arrived at San Francisco's Hall of Justice, Vincent "Chente" Gutierrez died. The police admitted hitting "Chente" on the back of the neck, but after an autopsy the coroner claimed he had overdosed on Reds. For most of the people in the *barrio,* "Chente" had been another victim of police racism. Hundreds attended his funeral and the procession followed from St. Peter's Church to Holy Cross Cemetery by car. A *barrio* poet, Roberto Vargas, who had been chairman of a Brown Beret chapter and who was arrested during the San Francisco State College strike for Third World Liberation Front activities, expressed the growing political consciousness of *barrio* youth in his poem "They Blamed It on the Reds."*

I

Thursday . . . crying . . . St. Peter's church . . . organ
Incense . . . lagrimas . . . 10:30 morning . . . sun/hot
Faces . . . old/young . . . Vincent gone
Anger/love . . . Chente gone now
Eunuch chronicles plastered with lies
Reds, Reds melting in American minds

* San Francisco *Good Times,* May 15, 1970.

Brought to you in living color by CBS
Dial soap and the puppet-coroners
of the TV world . . .
("Reds will make you dead" they squeal)
And the priest lites another candle/

II

Tears (saladas) . . . dry lips
Black hearse yawns/swallows
18 years of Chente . . . gone
Not killed in Cambodia . . . but war
(Padre nuestro que esta en los . . .)
Walking now . . . the last 24th st.
Business as usual . . . slower
Hundreds of sisters/brothers
Following behind/in you
Angered in love walking
past walls of cornucopia
Solid-lined by Pig-nalgas
7-up signs gleaming
Sears . . . Bank of America
Old Glory still . . . stop/go
Madre/Hija/Esposa . . . crying
Llantos . . . stop/go
Chente en el medio de mayo
Gone!
And the priest raises the chalice
("This is my body   This is my blood.")

III

South Van Ness red light
In cars now pollution (F–310)
Firestone Rent-a-Limousine stop/go
The mechanical centipede slowed
by Progress   stop/go
                Business as usual
"¡Hijo, hijo . . . te an asesinado!"
I just tapped him across the . . .
It seems an overdose of . . .
business as usual . . . stop/go

IV

Look back
Look back Chente . . . si Puedes
Remember the Roach Pad hunger
Joys . . . highs, sorrows?
Mission sidewalks (BART raped)
Hum goodbye pa siempre carnal
But the genocide trail begins su fin
Trembling with the weight of our guns . . ./
Chente 18 brown and dead
In the land of E Pluribus Unum
Dead in the land of the Apollos 13/
Edsel . . . Titanic . . . U2 and Gary Powers
Mission Hi . . . State College
                and business as usual/

V

Now passing local draft board
Vision of monsoon flies
Bloodsmell cheeks of bronze
Organisms   shell pierced   screams of death
Vietnam! Vietnam!
        Chente dies everywhere
        (Blame the reds!)
Cambodia . . . brown and 18 . . . Laos
    Chente dead in babylon
    (Blame the reds!)
En los barrios de Guatemala
San Francisco o Mississippi
    (Blame the reds!)

VI

Holy Cross . . . silent in wait
Lagrimas de madre soak black lace
    Hijo.   Hijo no te vayas
    Wife wails ripped/soul fright
                alone now . . .
Chente flows into open wound
In earth . . . magic dance of

Mayan ancestors . . . tears
Silent war drums sound
Chente killed by The Guardians
                of Enterprise
Their red white and blue
Phallic symbols thrust deep
        In our throats . . .
Moist dirt falls . . . covers
Ashes to ashes . . . peace brother
Peace . . .   business as usual
        "Blame It on Reds!"

Mayo 15, 1970
Aztlan/Babylon

BIBLIOGRAPHY

The African Repository and Colonial Journal. Washington: Vol. XXII, No. 2. February, 1846.

Aguinaldo, General Emilio, and Albano, Vicente. *A Second Look at America.* New York: Robert Speller & Sons, Publishers, 1957.

Alexander, Arthur C. *Koloa Plantation, 1835–1935.* Honolulu: 1937.

Allen, Gwenfread. *Hawaii's War Years, 1941–45.* Honolulu: University of Hawaii Press, 1950.

American Friends Service Committee. *An Uncommon Controversy.* Published by the National Congress of American Indians, 1967.

Anderson, Robert William. *Party Politics in Puerto Rico.* Stanford: Stanford University Press, 1965.

Anderson, Major William H. *The Philippine Problem.* New York: G. P. Putnam's Sons, 1939.

Andrews, Charles M. *Colonial Period of American History.* New Haven: Yale University Press, 1934.

Annals of The American Academy of Political and Social Science, Vol. XXVIV, No. 2, September, 1909.

Aptheker, Herbert. *Nat Turner's Slave Rebellion: The Environment, The Event, The Effects.* New York: The Humanities Press, 1966.
———. *"One Continual Cry": David Walker's Appeal to the Colored Citizens of the World: Its Setting and Its Meaning.* New York: The Humanities Press, 1965.

Asiatic Exclusion League. *Proceedings of the Asiatic Exclusion League.* San Francisco, January, 1909.

Bailey, Thomas A., ed. *The American Spirit—United States History as Seen by Contemporaries.* Boston: D. C. Heath & Co., 1963 & 1968.

Ball, Charles. *Fifty Years in Chains.* New York: H. Dayton, Publisher, 1859.

Bancroft, Frederic. *Slave Trading in the Old South.* New York: Frederick Ungar Publishing Co., 1959.

Bardolph, Richard. *The Negro Vanguard.* New York: Vintage Books, 1961.

Barth, Gunther. *Bitter Strength.* Cambridge, Mass.: Harvard University Press, 1964.

Beard, Charles A. *An Economic Interpretation of the Constitution of the United States.* New York: Macmillan Co., 1956.

Beatty, Willard W. *Education for Cultural Change.* Chilocco, Okla.: U.S. Department of the Interior, Bureau of Indian Affairs, 1953.

Beckett, Y. B. *Baca's Battle.* Houston: Stagecoach Press, 1962.

Bell, Irvin Wiley. "Out of the Mouths of Ex-Slaves." *Journal of Negro History,* Vol. XX, July, 1935.

Bennett, Lerone. *Before the Mayflower: A History of the Negro in America, 1619–1964.* Revised. Baltimore: Penguin Books, 1966.

Bishop, Rev. Artemas. "An Inquiry Into the Causes of Decrease in the Population of the Sandwich Islands." *The Hawaiian Spectator,* January, 1838.

Boddy, E. Manchester. *Japanese in America.* Los Angeles: published by author, 1921.

Bosworth, Allan R. *America's Concentration Camps.* New York: W. W. Norton and Co., 1967.

Brainerd, Cephas, and Warner, Eveline, eds. *New England Society Orations,* Vol. II, New York: The Century Co., 1901.

Brameld, Theodore. *The Remaking of a Culture.* New York: Harper & Bros., 1959.

Breitman, George, ed. *Malcolm X Speaks:* Selected Writings and Statements. New York: Grove Press, 1965.

Brown, Henry Box. *The Narrative of Henry Box Brown: Written by a Statement of Facts Made by Himself.* Boston: Brown & Stearns Publishers, 1849.

Brown, Wenzell. *Dynamite On Our Doorstep.* New York: Greenberg Publishers, 1945.

Bruce, John E. "Concentration of Energy." In the *Arthur B. Spingarn Collection of Negro Literature* at Howard University. Washington, D.C.

Bulosan, Carlos. *Sound Of Falling Light: Letters In Exile.* Edited by Dolores S. Feria. Quezon City, The Philippines: 1960.

Burma, John A. *Spanish Speaking Groups in the United States.* Chapel Hill: Duke University Press, 1954.

Calderon, Enrique. *El Dolor de un Pueblo Esclavo.* New York: Azteca Press, 1950.

California Citizens Committee on Civil Disturbances in Los Angeles. *Report and Recommendations,* June 12, 1943.

California, Department of Industrial Relations, San Francisco. *Facts About Filipino Immigration into California,* April, 1930.

California, State Board of Health, Sacramento. *First Biennial Report,* 1870–71.

California Historical Society. *Neville Scrapbook,* Vol. 7, July, 1877.

Cash, W. J. *The Mind of the South.* Garden City, New York: Doubleday & Co., Inc., 1941.

Catterall, Mrs. Helen H., ed. *Judicial Cases Concerning Slavery and the American Negro.* Washington, D.C.: The Carnegie Institution of Washington, 1937.

Cayton, Horace. *Long Old Road.* New York: Trident Press, 1965.

Chai, Ch'u, and Chai, Winberg. *The Changing Society of China.* New York: Mentor Books, 1962.

Chief Flying Hawk. As told to M. I. McCreight (Tchanta Tanka). In *Chief Flying Hawk's Tales.* New York: Alliance Press, 1936.

Chinn, Thomas W., ed. *A History of the Chinese in California: A*

Syllabus. San Francisco: Chinese Historical Society of America, 1969.

Chui, Ping. *Chinese Labor in California.* Madison, Wis.: State Historical Society of Wisconsin, University of Wisconsin Press, 1963.

Clark, Victor S. et al. *Puerto Rico and Its Problems.* Washington, D.C.: The Brookings Institution, 1930.

Cochran, Thomas. *The Puerto Rican Businessman.* Philadelphia: The University of Pennsylvania Press, 1959.

Cohen, Felix. *The Handbook of Federal Indian Law.* Washington, D.C.: U.S. Government Printing Office, 1942.

Collier, John. *On the Gleaming Way.* Denver: Sage Books, Inc., 1962.

Commager, Henry Steele, ed. *Documents of American History.* New York: Appleton-Century-Crofts, Inc., 1958.

Communist Party of Puerto Rico. *The Case of Puerto Rico: Memorandum to the United Nations.* New York: New Century Publishers, 1953.

Conroy, Hilary. *The Japanese Frontier in Hawaii, 1868–1898.* Berkeley: The University of California Press, 1953.

Cook, James, and King, James. *A Voyage to the Pacific Ocean,* Vol. II. London: G. Nichol and T. Cadell Publishers, 1785.

Coolidge, Mary Roberts. *Chinese Immigration.* New York: Henry Holt & Co., 1909.

Corpuz, Onofre D. *The Philippines.* Englewood Cliffs, N.J.: Prentice-Hall Co., 1966.

Corretjer, Juan Antonio. *La Lucha por la Independencia de Puerto Rico.* San Juan, P. R.: Publicaciones de Union del Pueblo pro Constituyente, 1949.

Crichton, Kyle S. *Law and Order, Ltd.* Santa Fe, N.M.: New Mexican Publishing Co., 1928.

Cronon, Edmund David. *Black Moses.* Madison, Wisc.: University of Wisconsin Press, 1955.

Cross, Ira B. *A History of the Labor Movement in California.* Berkeley: University of California Press, 1935.

Cruse, Harold. *Crisis of the Negro Intellectual.* New York: W. R. Morrow & Co., 1967.

Culin, Stewart. "Chinese Secret Societies in the United States." *Journal of American Folklore,* July, 1890.

Cunningham, J. C. *The Truth About Murieta.* Los Angeles: Wetzel Publishing Co., 1938.

Current, Richard N., ed. *Reconstruction.* Englewood Cliffs, N.J.: Prentice-Hall Publishing Co., 1965.

Curtin, Philip D. *Africa Remembered: Narratives by West Africans from the Era of the Slave Trade.* Madison, Wisc.: University of Wisconsin Press, 1967.

Davis, David Brion. *The Problem of Slavery in Western Culture.* Ithaca, N.Y.: Cornell University Press, 1966.

Daws, Gavan. *The Shoal of Time.* New York: Macmillan Co., 1968.

Day, A. Grove, and Stroven, Carl, eds. *A Hawaiian Reader.* New York: Popular Library, 1961.

deBar, Gabriella. *José Vasconcelos and His World.* New York: Las Americas Publishing Co., 1966.

Delany, Martin R. *The Condition, Elevation, Emigration, and Destiny of the Colored Race.* Philadelphia: published by the author, 1852.

Diffie, Bailey W., and Whitfield, Justine. *Puerto Rico: A Broken Pledge.* New York: The Vanguard Press, 1931.

Dillon, Richard H. *The Hatchet Men.* New York: Coward McCann Publishing Co., 1962.

Dobie, Charles Caldwell. *San Francisco's Chinatown.* New York: D. Appleton-Century Co., 1936.

Dobie, J. Frank. *The Flavor of Texas.* Dallas: Dealey & Lowe Publishing Co., 1936.

Documents on the Constitutional History of Puerto Rico. Washington, D.C.: Office of the Commonwealth of Puerto Rico, 1948.

Donnan, Elizabeth. *Documents Illustrative of the History of the Slave Trade to America.* Washington, D.C.: The Carnegie Institution of Washington, 1935.

Downey, Fairfax. *Indian Wars of the United States Army, 1776–1865.* Garden City, N.Y.: Doubleday & Co., 1963.

Du Bois, William Edward Burghardt. *Black Reconstruction in America: An Essay Toward a History of the Part which Black Folk Played in the Attempt to Reconstruct Democracy in America, 1860–1880.* Cleveland, Ohio: World Publishing Co., 1964.
Dusk of Dawn. New York: Schocken Books, 1963.
The Souls of Black Folk. Chicago: A. C. McClurg & Co., 1909.

El Grito: A Journal of Contemporary Mexican-American Thought. Berkeley: Quinto Sol Publications, Inc.

Elkins, Stanley. *Slavery: A Problem in American Institutional and Intellectual Life.* New York: Grosset & Dunlap, 1959.

Evans, Maurice. *Black and White in the Southern States.* London: Longmans, Green & Co., 1915.

Farb, Peter. *Man's Rise to Civilization.* New York: E. P. Dutton & Co., 1968.

Felt, Joseph B. *History of Ipswich, Essex and Hamilton.* Cambridge, Mass.: Charles Folsom Co., 1834.

Fergusson, Erna. *Our Southwest.* New York: Alfred Knopf, 1940.

Fiedler, Leslie. *The Return of the Vanishing American.* New York: Stein & Day, 1968.

Filipino Students Magazine, April, 1905.

Fisk University Social Science Institute. "Orientals and Their Cultural Adjustments." Nashville, Tennessee: 1946.

Fiske, John. *The Beginnings of New England.* Boston: Houghton Mifflin Co., 1889.

Fitzhugh, George. *Cannibals All! or Slaves Without Masters.* Cambridge, Mass.: Belknap Press of Harvard University, 1960.

Fleagle, Fred K. *Social Problems in Puerto Rico.* New York: D. C. Heath & Co., 1917.

Fogel, Walter. "Job Gains of Mexican-American Men." *The Monthly Labor Review,* October, 1968.

Foner, Philip D. *History of the Labor Movement in the United States,* Vol. III. New York: International Publishers, 1955.

Forbes, W. Cameron. *The Philippine Islands.* Cambridge, Mass.: Harvard University Press, 1945.

Fortune. "The Negro and the City." January, 1968.

Frank, Waldo. "Puerto Rico and Psychosis," *The Nation,* March 13, 1954.

Franklin, John Hope, and Starr, Isidore, eds. *The Negro in 20th Century America.* New York: Vintage Books, Inc., 1967.

Fuchs, Lawrence H. *Hawaii Pono: A Social History.* New York: Harcourt, Brace & World, Inc., 1961.

Garvey, Marcus. *Marcus Garvey: Philosophy and Opinions.* New York: Universal Publishing Co., 1925.

Gates, W. Almont. *Oriental Immigration on the Pacific Coast.* Bound in *Pamphlets on Japanese Exclusion.* Berkeley: Phelan Collection of the University of California.

Genovese, Eugene. *The Political Economy of Slavery.* New York: Pantheon Books, 1965.

"The Legacy of Slavery and the Roots of Black Nationalism." *Studies on the Left,* Vol. 6, No. 6, 1966.

Giddings, Joshua. *The Exiles of Florida.* Gainesville, Fla.: University of Florida Press, 1964.

Glick, Clarence. *The Chinese Migrant in Hawaii.* Ann Arbor, Mich.: University Microfilms, Inc.

Golden, Harry. *Forgotten Pioneer.* Cleveland: World Publishing Co., 1963.

Goldfinch, Charles W. *Juan Cortina, 1824–1892: A Re-Appraisal.* Brownsville, Texas: Bishop's Print Shop, 1950.

Goldman, Eric. *Rendezvous with Destiny.* New York: Vintage Press, 1958.

Gong, Eng Ying, and Grant, Bruce. *Tong War!* New York: Nicholas L. Brown Publishing Co., 1930.

Gonzalez, Nancie L. "The Spanish-Americans of New Mexico, a Distinctive Heritage." In *Mexican-American Study Project, Advance Report,* No. 9. Los Angeles: University of California, 1967.

Goveia, Elsa V. *Slave Society in the British Leeward Islands at the End of the 18th Century.* New Haven: Yale University Press, 1965.

Grant, Joanne. *Black Protest: Documents, History and Analysis from 1619 to the Present.* New York: Premier Fawcett, Fawcett World Library, 1968.

Greenway, John. "Will the Indians Get Whitey?" *National Review,* March 11, 1969.

Greenwood, Robert. *The California Outlaw.* Los Gatos, Calif.: The Talisman Press, 1960.

Griffith, Beatrice, *American Me.* New York: Houghton Mifflin Co., 1948.

Griswold, A. Whitney. *Far Eastern Policy of the United States.* New York: Harcourt, Brace & Co., 1938.

Gruening, Ernest. *Mexico and Its Heritage.* New York: The Century Co., 1928.

Gulick, Rev. and Mrs. Orramel Hinckley. *Pilgrims of Hawaii.* New York and Chicago: Fleming H. Revell Co., 1918.

Guzman, Ralph. *The Function of Ideology in the Process of Political Socialization: An Example in Terms of the Mexican-American People Living in the Southwest.* Unpublished manuscript, August, 1966.

Hackett, Charles William. *Revolt of the Pueblo Indians of New Mexico and Oterman's Attempted Reconquest, 1680–82.* Translation of original documents by Clair Shelby. Albuquerque, N.M.: University of New Mexico Press, 1942.

Hagan, William T. *Indian Police and Judges.* New Haven: Yale University Press, 1966.

Hanson, Earl Parker. *Puerto Rico: Land of Wonders.* New York: Alfred A. Knopf, 1960.

Hapgood, Hutchins. *A Victorian in the Modern World.* New York: Harcourt, Brace, 1939.

Harada, Tasaku, ed. *The Japanese Problem in California.* Printed for private circulation. San Francisco.

Harap, Louis, and Reddick, L. D. *Should Negroes and Jews Unite?* Negro Publication Society of America, 1943.

Heller, Celia S. *Mexican-American Youth.* New York: Random House, 1967.

Higham, John. *Strangers in the Land; Patterns of American Nativism, 1860–1925.* New York: Atheneum, 1963.

Hofstadter, Richard. *The American Political Tradition.* New York: Alfred A. Knopf, 1948.

Holt, John Dominis. *On Being Hawaiian.* Honolulu: Star Publishing Co., 1964.

Hoy, William. *The Chinese Six Companies.* San Francisco: Chinese Consolidated Benevolent Association, 1942.

Hughes, Langston, and Meltzer, Milton. *A Pictorial History of the Negro in America.* New York: Crown Publishing Co., 1956.

Hughes, Louis. *Thirty Years a Slave: Autobiography of Louis Hughes.* Milwaukee: South Side Printing Co., 1897.

Ichihashi, Yamato. *Japanese in the United States.* Stanford: Stanford University Press, 1932.

Iyenago, T., and Sato, Kenoske. *Japan and the California Problem.* New York: G. P. Putnam's Sons, 1921.

Jackson, Helen Hunt. *A Century of Dishonor*. Reprint. Minneapolis: Ross and Haines, Inc., 1964.

Jane, Cecil, trans. *Journal of Christopher Columbus*. New York: Clarkson N. Potter Publishing Co., 1960.

Japanese Relocation Papers. Bancroft Library, University of California, Berkeley.

Jay, William. *Causes and Consequences of the Mexican War*. Boston: Benjamin G. Mussey & Co., 1849.

Jenkins, William Sumner. *Proslavery Thought in the Old South*. Chapel Hill: University of North Carolina Press, 1935.

Jennings, John E. *Our American Tropics*. New York: Thomas Y. Crowell Co., 1962.

Johnson, Herbert B., D. D. *Discrimination Against Japanese in California: A Review of the Real Situation*. Berkeley: Press of the Courier Publishing Co., 1907.

Johnson, James Weldon. *Along This Way*. New York: Viking Press, 1933.

Black Manhattan. New York: Arno Press, 1968.

Jordan, Winthrop D. *White over Black*. Chapel Hill: University of North Carolina Press, 1968.

Josephy, Alvin M., Jr. *The Indian Heritage of America*. New York: Alfred A. Knopf, 1968.

The Nez Percé Indians and the Opening of the Northwest. New Haven: Yale University Press, 1955.

Kalaw, Maximo M. *The Case for the Filipinos*. New York: The Century Co., 1916.

Kamakau, S. M. *The Ruling Chiefs of Hawaii*. Honolulu: Kamehameha Schools Press, 1961.

Kardiner, Abram, and Ovesey, Lionel. *The Mark of Oppression: Explorations in the Personality of the American Negro*. Cleveland: World Publishing Co., 1962.

Katz, Shlomo, ed. *Negro and Jew, An Encounter in America*. New York: Macmillan Co., 1966.

Kawakami, K. K. *The Real Japanese Question*. New York: Macmillan Co., 1921.

Kelly, Marion. "Changes in Land Tenure in Hawaii." Unpublished M.A. thesis, University of Hawaii, Honolulu: 1956.

Korngold, Ralph. *Two Friends of Man*. Boston: Little Brown & Co., 1950.

Kraditor, Aileen S. *Means and Ends in American Abolitionism: Garrison and His Critics on Strategy and Tactics, 1834–50*. New York: Pantheon Books, 1967.

Kung, Shien-Woo. *Chinese in American Life*. Seattle: University of Washington Press, 1962.

Kuykendall, Ralph S. *The Hawaiian Kingdom, 1778–1854*. Honolulu: University of Hawaii, 1947.

Lam, Margaret M. "Racial Myth and Family Tradition-Worship

Among the Part-Hawaiians." *Social Forces,* Vol. 14, No. 3, March, 1936.

Lasker, Bruno. *Filipino Immigration.* Chicago: University of Chicago Press, 1931.

Lee, Calvin. *Chinatown U.S.A.* Garden City, N.Y.: Doubleday & Co., 1965.

Lee, Rose Hum. *Chinese in the U.S.A.* Hong Kong: Hong Kong University Press, 1960.

Leiris, Michael. *Race and Culture.* Paris: UNESCO, 1958.

Lewis, Gordon. *Puerto Rico: Freedom and Power in the Caribbean.* New York: M. R. Press, 1963.

Lewis, Oscar. "The Culture of Poverty." *Scientific American,* Vol. 215, No. 4, October, 1966.

———. "Culture of Poverty or Poverty of Culture." *Monthly Review,* Vol. 19, No. 4, September, 1967.

———. *La Vida: A Puerto Rican Family in the Culture of Poverty—San Juan and New York.* New York: Random House, 1965.

Lewis, Tracy Hammond. *Along the Rio Grande.* New York: Lewis Publishing Co., 1916.

Liebow, Elliot. *Tally's Corner: A Study of Negro Street-Corner Men.* Boston: Little, Brown & Co., 1967.

Life of Joaquin Murieta, The Brigand Chief of California. San Francisco: Butler & Co., 1859.

Life of Kinzaburo Makino. Edited by the Compilation Committee for the Publication of Kinzaburo Makino's Biography. Printed in Japan: 1965.

Liliuokalani, Queen. *Hawaii Story by Hawaii's Queen.* Rutland, Vt. and Tokyo, Japan: Charles E. Tuttle Co., 1964.

Lincoln, C. Eric. *The Black Muslims in America.* Boston: Beacon Press, 1961.

Lind, Andrew W. *Modern Hawaii.* Honolulu: University of Hawaii Press, 1967.

Lloyd, B. E. *Lights and Shades in San Francisco.* San Francisco: A. L. Bancroft and Co., 1876.

Locke, Mary. *Antislavery in America.* Chapel Hill: University of North Carolina Press, 1961.

Los Angeles City Schools, Division of Instructional Services. *Angelenos Then and Now.* Publication No. EC—226, 1966.

Lyman, Stanford Morris. *The Structure of Chinese Society in 19th Century America.* Unpublished Ph.D. thesis, University of California, Berkeley: 1961.

McCague, James. *The Second Rebellion: The New York City Draft Riots of 1863.* New York: Dial Press, 1968.

McKee, Ruth E. *California and Her Less Favored Minorities.* Washington: War Relocation Authority, April, 1944.

McKenzie, R. D. *Oriental Exclusion.* Chicago: University of Chicago Press, 1928.

McReynolds, Edwin C. *The Seminoles.* Norman, Okla.: University of Oklahoma Press, 1957.

McWilliams, Carey. *Prejudice: Japanese-Americans, Symbol of Racial Intolerance.* Boston: Little, Brown & Co., 1944.

North from Mexico. Philadelphia: L. B. Lippincott Co., 1949.

Malcolm X Speaks: Selected Writings and Statements. Edited and with prefatory notes by George Breitman. New York: Grove Press, 1965.

Malo, David. *Letters.* In the Archives of the State of Hawaii, Honolulu.

"On the Decrease of Population in the Hawaiian Islands." Translated by L. Andrews. Honolulu: The Hawaiian Spectator, Vol. II, No. 2, April, 1839.

Malone, Dumas, and Rauch, Basil. *Empire for Liberty.* New York: Appleton-Century-Crofts, 1960.

Mannix, Daniel P. *Black Cargoes.* New York: Viking Press, 1962.

Mears, E. G. *Resident Orientals on the American Pacific Coast: Their Legal and Economic Status.* Chicago: University of Chicago Press, 1928.

Meier, August. *Negro Thought in America, 1880–1915: Racial Ideologies in the Age of Booker T. Washington.* Ann Arbor: University of Michigan Press, 1966.

Merriam, George S. *The Negro and the Nation.* New York: Henry Holt & Co., 1906.

Miller, Stuart Creighton. *The Unwelcome Immigrant: The American Image of the Chinese, 1785–1882.* Berkeley and Los Angeles: University of California Press, 1969.

Millis, H. A. *Japanese Problem in the United States.* New York: Macmillan Company, 1915.

Mills, C. Wright; Senior, Clarence; and Goldsen, Rose Kohn. *The Puerto Rican Journey.* Reissue. New York: Russell and Russell, 1967.

Miyamoto, Kazuo. *Hawaii, End of the Rainbow.* Bridgeway Press, 1964.

Moorehead, Alan. *The Fatal Impact: An Account of the Invasion of the South Pacific, 1767–1840.* New York: Harper & Row, 1966.

Morley, Charles, trans. "Sienkiewicz on Chinese in California." *California Historical Society Quarterly,* Vol. 34, 1955.

Morison, Samuel Eliot. *Oxford History of the American People.* New York: Oxford University Press, 1965.

Murphy, Thomas D. *Ambassadors in Arms.* Honolulu: University of Hawaii Press, 1954.

Myrdal, Gunnar. *An American Dilemma: The Negro Problem and Modern Democracy.* New York and London: Harper & Bros., 1944.

Nichi Bei Times, San Francisco.

Nichols, Charles H. "Slave Narratives." *Negro History Bulletin,* March, 1952.

Nolen, Claude H. *Negro's Image in the South.* Lexington, Ky.: University of Kentucky Press, 1967.

O'Gorman, Edmundo. *The Invention of America.* Bloomington, Ind.: Indiana University Press, 1961.

Okubo, Mine, *Citizen* 13660. New York: AMS Press, Inc., 1966.

Okumura, Takie, and Okumura, Umetaro. "Hawaii's American-Japanese Problem, Report of the Campaign, 1921–1927." [no citation of publisher or date.]

Olmsted, Frederick Law. *The Cotton Kingdom: A Traveller's Observations on Cotton and Slavery in the American Slave States.* New York: Alfred A. Knopf, 1953.

A Journey in the Seaboard Slave States. New York: Dix & Edwards, 1856.

Osofsky, Gilbert. *The Burden of Race: A Documentary History of Negro-White Relations in America.* New York: Harper & Row, 1967.

Ozawa, Takao v. United States, 260 U.S. 178 (1922).

Paredes, Américo. *With His Pistol in His Hand.* Austin: University of Texas Press, 1958.

Parton, James. *The Life of Andrew Jackson.* New York: Mason Bros., 1860.

People v. *George W. Hall,* 4 Cal. 399 (1854).

Petersen, William. "Success Story, Japanese-American Style." *The New York Times Magazine,* January 9, 1966.

Petrullo, Vincenzo. *Puerto Rican Paradox.* Philadelphia: University of Pennsylvania Press, 1947.

Phillips, Ulrich B. *American Negro Slavery.* Baton Rouge: Louisiana State University Press, 1918.

Pier, Arthur S. *American Apostles to the Philippines.* Boston: The Beacon Press, 1950.

Pitt, Leonard. *The Decline of the Californios.* Berkeley: University of California Press, 1966.

Polanco, Vicente Géigel. *El Despertar de un Pueblo.* San Juan, Puerto Rico: Biblioteca de Autores Puertorriqueños, 1942.

Porter, Dorothy B. "Sarah Parker Remond, Abolitionist and Physician." *Journal of Negro History,* Vol. XX, No. 3, July, 1935.

Pratt, Julius W. *Expansionists* of 1898. Baltimore: The Johns Hopkins Press, 1936.

Quarles, Benjamin. *The Negro in the Civil War.* Boston: Little, Brown & Co., 1953.

The Negro in the American Revolution. Chapel Hill: University of North Carolina Press, 1961.

Negro in the Making of America. New York: Macmillian Co., 1964.

Rand, Christopher. *The Puerto Ricans.* New York: Oxford University Press, 1958.

Reid, Whitelaw. *Problems of Expansion.* New York: The Century Co., 1900.

Richardson, Lewis C. *Puerto Rico: Caribbean Crossroads.* New York: U.S. Camera Publishing Corp., 1947.

Robinson, Alfred. *Life in California During a Residence of Several Years in that Territory.* San Francisco: W. Doxey Co., 1891.

Rogers, Joel Augustus. *Sex and Race.* New York: Rogers Pub. Co., 1941–44.

Romanell, Patrick. *Making of the Mexican Mind.* Lincoln: University of Nebraska Press, 1952.

Roosevelt, Theodore. *Presidential Messages and State Papers.* New York: Review of Reviews Company, 1910.

Ross, Arthur M., and Hill, Herbert, eds. *Employment, Race and Poverty.* Harcourt, Brace & World, 1967.

Rowan, Helen. "A Minority Nobody Knows." *The Atlantic Monthly,* June, 1967.

Royce, Josiah. *California, A Study of American Character.* New York: Alfred A. Knopf & Co., 1948.

Samora, Julian. *La Raza: Forgotten Americans.* Notre Dame, Ind.: University of Notre Dame Press, 1966.

Saxton, Alexander Plaisted. *The Indispensable Enemy: a Study of the Anti-Chinese Movement in California.* Unpublished Ph.D. thesis, University of California, Berkeley: 1967.

Sayre, J. G. "More Chinese Atrocities." *The Nation,* August 10, 1927.

Scheer, Robert, ed. *Eldridge Cleaver: Post-Prison Writings and Speeches.* New York: Random House, 1969.

Schlesinger, Arthur M. *The Rise of Modern America.* New York: Macmillan Co., 1951.
The Age of Jackson. Boston: Little, Brown & Co., 1945.

Senior, Clarence. *The Puerto Ricans: Strangers—Then Neighbors.* Chicago: Quadrangle Books, Inc., 1961.

Seward, George F. *Chinese Immigration in Its Social and Economic Aspects.* New York: Charles Scribner's Sons, 1881.

Sexton, Patricia Cayo. *Spanish Harlem.* New York: Harper & Row, 1965.

Simpson, G. E., and Yinger, J. M. *Racial and Cutural Minorities.* New York: Harper & Row, 1953.

Smith, Bradford. *Americans from Japan.* Philadelphia & New York: J. B. Lippincott, 1948.

Smith, Robert F. *The United States and Cuba.* New York: Bookman Associates, 1960.

Smith, William Henry. *A Political History of Slavery.* New York: G. P. Putnam's Sons, 1903.

Smyth, Albert Henry, ed. *The Works of Benjamin Franklin.* New York: Macmillan Co., 1905.

Smyth, George B. "Causes of anti-Foreign Feeling in China." *The Crisis in China.* New York: The North American Review, 1900.

Social Process in Hawaii. Published jointly by the Romanzo Adams Social Research Laboratory and the Sociology Club of Hawaii. Honolulu.

Soyeda, J., and Kamiya, T. *A Survey of the Japanese Question in California.* San Francisco: 1913.

Sparks, Jared, ed. *The Works of Benjamin Franklin.* Boston: Hilliard, Gray & Co., 1836.

Spears, John Randolph. *The American Slave Trade.* New York: Charles Scribner's Sons, 1900.

Stampp, Kenneth M. *The Peculiar Institution: Slavery in the Antebellum South.* New York: Vintage Books, 1956.

———. *The Causes of the Civil War.* Edited by Kenneth M. Stampp. Englewood, N.J.: Prentice-Hall, Inc., 1959.

———. *The Era of Reconstruction, 1865–1877.* New York: Alfred A. Knopf Co., 1965.

Steiner, Stan. *The New Indians.* New York: Harper & Row, 1968.

Storey, Moorfield, and Lichauco, Marcial P. *The Conquest of the Philippines by the United States, 1898–1925.* New York: G. P. Putnam's Sons, 1926.

Sullivan, Josephine. A *History of C. Brewer & Co., Ltd.: One Hundred Years in the Hawaiian Islands, 1826–1926.* Boston: 1926.

Sung, B. L. *The Mountain of Gold: The Story of the Chinese in America.* New York: The Macmillan Co., 1967.

Sun Yat-sen et al., eds. *Sources of Chinese Tradition.* New York: Columbia University Press, 1960.

Sydnor, Charles S. *Slavery in Mississippi.* Gloucester, Mass.: P. Smith, 1965.

Taylor, George E. *The Philippines and the United States: Problems of Partnership.* Published for the Council on Foreign Relations. New York: Frederick A. Praeger Co., 1964.

Tebbel, John, and Jennison, Keith. *The American Indian Wars.* New York: Harper & Row, 1960.

ten Broek, Jacobus; Barnhart, Edward N.; and Matson, Floyd. *Prejudice, War and the Constitution.* Berkeley and Los Angeles: University of California Press, 1954.

Thomas, Dorothy Swaine; Kikuchi, Charles; and Sakoda, James. *The Salvage.* Berkeley and Los Angeles: University of California Press, 1952.

Thomas, Dorothy Swaine, and Nishimoto, Richard S. *The Spoilage.* Berkeley and Los Angeles: University of California Press, 1946.

Thomas, Piri. *Down These Mean Streets.* New York: Alfred A. Knopf, 1967.

Trumbull, Henry. *History of the Indian Wars.* Boston: George Clark Co., 1841.

Tuck, Ruth. *Not With the Fist.* New York: Harcourt, Brace, 1946.

Tugwell, Rexford Guy. *The Stricken Land: The Story of Puerto Rico.* Garden City, N.Y.: Doubleday & Co., Inc., 1947.

United States Army, Western Defense Command and Fourth Army. *Final Report: Japanese Evacuation from the West Coast.* Washington, D.C.: Government Printing Office, 1943.

U.S., Congress. *American State Papers.* Class V, Vol. VI. Washington. Gales and Seaton, 1832–61.

U.S., Congress. *Hearings of the Select Committee Investigating National Defense Migration.* San Francisco, Feb. 21–22, 1942. 77th Cong., 2nd sess., part 29.

U.S., Congress, House. *Hearings before Subcommittee no. 5 of the Committee on the Judiciary.* 83rd Cong., 2nd sess., 1954.

U.S., Congress, House. *House Executive Documents.* 48th Cong., 1st sess., 1883–84, Vol. II.

U.S., Congress, House. *Depredations on the Frontiers of Texas: House Executive Documents.* 42nd Cong., 3rd sess., 1872–73, Vol. VII.

U.S., Congress, House. *Difficulties on Southwestern Frontier: House Executive Documents.* 36th Cong., 1st sess., 1859–60, Vol. VIII, No. 52.

U.S., Congress, House. *Troubles on Texas Frontier: House Executive Documents.* 36th Cong., 1st sess., 1859–60, Vol. XII, No. 81.

U.S., Congress, House. *Texas Frontier Troubles: House of Representatives Reports.* 44th Cong., 1st sess., 1876–77, Vol. II, No. 343.

U.S., Congress, Senate. *Report of the Joint Special Committee to Investigate Chinese Immigration: Senate Document No. 689.* 44th Cong., 2nd sess., February 27, 1877.

U.S., Congress. *Senate Report No. 1664.* 89th Cong., 2nd sess.

U.S., Department of the Interior, Annual Reports of the Commissioner of Indian Affairs.

United States Federal Writers Project. "Unionization of Filipinos in California Agriculture." Bancroft Library, University of California, Berkeley.

Vasconcelos, José. *Aspects of Mexican Civilization.* Chicago: University of Chicago Press, 1926.

——— *Mexican Ulysses.* Translated and abridged by W. R. Crawford. Bloomington, Ind.: Indiana University Press, 1963.

Vivas, José Luis. *Historia de Puerto Rico.* New York: Las Americas Publishing Co., 1960.

Vogel, Virgil J. *The Indian in American History.* Chicago: Integrated Education Associates, 1968.

Walker, David. *David Walker's Appeal to the Colored Citizens of the World, 1829–30.* Published for the American Institute for Marxist Studies. New York: Humanities Press, 1965.

Waskow, Arthur I. *From Race Riot to Sit-in.* Garden City, N.Y.: Doubleday & Co., 1966.

Webb, Walter Prescott. *The Texas Rangers.* Boston: Houghton Mifflin & Co., 1935.

Weinberg, Alfred Katz. *Manifest Destiny: A Study of Nationalist Expansion in American History*. Baltimore: Johns Hopkins Press, 1935.

Wheeler, Col. Homer W. *Buffalo Days*. New York & Chicago: A. L. Burt, Publishers, 1923.

White, Mary Frances. "Wewoka and the Seminoles." *Journal of the Daughters of the American Revolution,* February, 1967.

White, Owen P. *Them Was the Days*. New York: Minton, Blach & Co., 1925.

White, Trumbull. *Puerto Rico and Its People*. New York: Frederick A. Stokes Co., 1938.

Whitfield, Theodore M. *Slavery Agitation in Virginia*. Baltimore: Johns Hopkins Press, 1930.

Williams, Eric. *Capitalism and Slavery*. London: Andre Deutsch Co., 1914.

Williams, Robert F. *Negroes with Guns*. Marc Schleifer, ed. New York: Marzani and Munsell, 1962.

Williams, William A. *The Contours of American History*. New York: World Publishing Co., 1961.

Wish, Harvey. *Slavery in the South*. New York: Farrar, Straus, 1964.

Witherbee, Sidney A., compiler and ed. *Spanish-American War Songs*. Detroit: Sidney A. Witherbee, pub., 1889.

Wolff, Leon. *Little Brown Brother*. Garden City, N.Y.: Doubleday and Co., Inc., 1961.

Woodman, Lyman L. *Cortina, Rogue of the Rio Grande*. San Antonio: The Naylor Co., 1950.

Woodson, Carter G. *History of the Negro Church*. Washington, D.C.: The Associated Publishers, 1945.

Woodson, Carter G. *The Negro in Our History*. Washington, D.C.: Associated Publishers, 1966.

Woodward, C. Vann. *Origins of the New South*. Baton Rouge: Louisiana State University Press, 1951.

Young, John P. "The Support of the Anti-Oriental Movement," *Annals of the Academy of Political and Social Science*. Vol. XXIV, No. 2, Sept., 1909.

Zilversmit, Arthur. *The First Emancipation*. Chicago: University of Chicago Press, 1967.

INDEX

VINTAGE POLITICAL SCIENCE
AND SOCIAL CRITICISM

VINTAGE HISTORY—AMERICAN

A free catalogue of VINTAGE BOOKS *will be sent at your request. Write to* Vintage Books, 457 Madison Avenue, New York, New York 10022.

VINTAGE HISTORY—WORLD

VINTAGE WORKS OF SCIENCE
AND PSYCHOLOGY

A free catalogue of VINTAGE BOOKS *will be sent at your request. Write to* Vintage Books, 457 Madison Avenue, New York, New York 10022.

VINTAGE FICTION, POETRY, AND PLAYS

A free catalogue of VINTAGE BOOKS *will be sent at your request. Write to* Vintage Books, 457 Madison Avenue, New York, New York 10022.

VINTAGE HISTORY AND CRITICISM OF
LITERATURE, MUSIC, AND ART

A free catalogue of VINTAGE BOOKS *will be sent at your request. Write to* Vintage Books, 457 Madison Avenue, New York, New York 10022.